By COLIN M. TURNBULL

The Human Cycle
The Mountain People
Tibet (*with Thubten Jigme Norbu*)
The Lonely African
The Forest People

THE HUMAN

A TOUCHSTONE BOOK
Published by Simon & Schuster, Inc.
New York

CYCLE

COLIN M. TURNBULL

Copyright © 1983 by Colin M. Turnbull
All rights reserved
including the right of reproduction
in whole or in part in any form
First Touchstone Edition, 1984
Published by Simon & Schuster, Inc.
Simon & Schuster Building
Rockefeller Center
1230 Avenue of the Americas
New York, New York 10020
TOUCHSTONE and colophon are registered trademarks of Simon & Schuster, Inc.

Designed by Edith Fowler

Manufactured in the United States of America

10 9 8 7 6 5 4 3 2 1

10 9 8 7 6 5 4   Pbk.

Library of Congress Cataloging in Publication Data
Turnbull, Colin M. date.
    The human cycle.
    1. Turnbull, Colin M. 2. Anthropologists—
Great Britain—Biography. I. Title.
GN21.T85A33   1983   306'.092'4 [B]   82-19473
ISBN 0-671-22620-7
ISBN 0-671-50599-8 Pbk.

For Arnold L. van Gennep,
whose admirable work on rites of passage
has helped so many of us

CONTENTS

THE
HUMAN CYCLE

INTRODUCTION

THE HUMAN CYCLE

ALL AROUND US, at every moment in our lives, reaching out and touching us, there is a world of excitement and fascination. Its riches are denied to none, for beauty and wonder lie at every stage of the life cycle, from childhood to old age, transforming poverty into wealth, squalor into magnificence, tedium into sport, fear into recognition, hatred and bigotry into understanding. Access to this world does not require any great feat of intellect, nor does it demand a lifetime dedicated to the quest. All that is needed is a mind and a soul, the soul being that which opens the mind, breathing life into it, making it infinitely curious. The senses that are common to all of us, regardless of who or what we are, provide us with all the tools we need. The anthropologist is no more and no less blessed than any other in this respect; if he is blessed at all it is perhaps only with a particularly intense curiosity about humanity and its many manifestations, a curiosity that never lets him rest, for each fresh discovery merely reveals more that is unknown.

In a sense, all of us who are consciously aware of and involved with the total world around us, however small and parochial that world might seem, are anthropologists in the making. Nowhere is the world richer, more exciting, or more beautiful than it is in our own lives, and the pursuit of the exotic in no way contradicts the essential truth that beauty is an internal quality rather than an external reality. Just as when a tourist travels thousands of miles to spend only a week or two on some tropical island he is really seeking a beauty that is inherent in the life that he lives at home, so when the anthropologist studies the exotic ways of other peoples in other cultures, he is really learning the truth about himself.

This does not make the pleasure and excitement of immersing ourselves in the exotic any less real or worthwhile; it merely suggests that the value may be even greater than we suppose, for we are likely to discover more about ourselves than about others, and in so doing discover unknown riches in our own lives. We anthropologists are frequently described as romantics because of a tendency to stress the good qualities to be found in other cultures, but this tendency may well reflect our recognition of some new potential for good discovered in our *own* society. This is rather what I hope will happen in the following pages as we follow the life cycle as it is lived in different cultures, seeming to praise them for what they do, for their humanity and their social consciousness, while decrying our own lack of humanity and our social irresponsibility. Like the tourist, we shall make a journey in the hopes of coming back enriched, rejuvenated. And, also like the tourist, we may well come back with new ideas, even with a new vision, that may help bring that same richness to the lives of others. For such purposes there is not much point setting forth in search of an ugliness we know we can find anywhere, nor in bringing it back with us when we do find it.

One advantage of taking the life cycle as a topic is that it is something we all go through, though in very different ways. Moreover, it touches us directly as individuals, so each of us can bring to the discussion his or her own unique experience of being born and growing up to be whatever we are. This is as good a way as any of learning about our own society, by looking at our own individual lives, for in large measure we have become what society has ordained that we shall become by the way it controls or neglects each stage of life. This does not deny that there is a certain extent to which individuals, in all cultures, are free to develop as they wish, but that freedom itself is in large measure culturally determined, for we are born dependent. Independence and freedom are qualities that we have to learn, and one of the major differences that we will find between our way of doing things and the ways that others do the same things is that whereas we carefully teach the values of freedom and independence, other cultures equally carefully teach the merits of bondage and dependence and seem to emerge just as successfully.

Such teaching takes place, consciously and unconsciously, virtually from the day we are born. The degree to which the teaching of social values (such as those of freedom, independence, bondage, and dependence) is formal and conscious, or informal and unconscious, varies from each society to the next. What may be appropriate (and therefore "good") for one society may well be inappropriate (and therefore "bad") in another. This is as true of behavior as it is of values. But in all cultures the teaching takes a different form at each stage of life, for each stage of life has its own special potential both for the individual and for society. This is in part determined by human biology, our capacities for expression and action varying from moment to moment as we progress through the life cycle; that much we all share in common. And indeed, despite the outward appearance of almost irreconcilable difference between the way we and others do the same things, there is often much more similarity than might first have been supposed.

This compels us to ask whether or not, then, there are any universal truths, any universal values that must be maintained for all men at all times. We are not about to attempt to establish any such universals here, but the question should make us think twice when dealing with apparent differences in values and concepts, and it should make us all the more careful to define the terms we use, particularly when applying them to different cultures. Thus by comparison with small-scale, tribal societies we in Western society seem to pay little heed to what the word "society" really means, in the way that we teach and train individuals passing through the various stages of the life cycle; by comparison, indeed, we do almost nothing to inculcate the value of social consciousness, let alone social responsibility. Yet few people in our society would question their own social consciousness or their own sense of responsibility to others. The reason for this apparent contradiction may simply be that in the two contexts, the word "soci-

ety" and the whole concept of social responsibility, or sociality, have entirely different meanings. It may be that there is
no universal phenomenon of sociality. But whatever the case,
the truth is that in other cultures the concept is much more
clearly defined, much more widely understood, and given
much more prominence in every stage of the life cycle and the
educational system than in our own. We may not want or
need our children and adolescents to grow into the same kind
of social consciousness as do the hunters of the Ituri Forest in
the heart of Africa, or tribal farmers in the same part of the
world, or as do the religious devotees in so many parts of Asia.
But by making the contrast between what *they* do and what
we do, we at least become aware of things we normally take
for granted, and while there is no shame in being critically
aware, willful ignorance *is* culpable.

That is one objective of the contrasts we shall be making between the ways different peoples handle the various stages of
the life cycle. It is not with the thought that we should try to
imitate their way of doing things, or persuade them to imitate
ours, but rather that we should become more aware of just
what we *are* doing, and of its many unforeseen consequences.
As well as making a contrast, we shall also be making a comparison, and that is something slightly different and even
more informative. For instance, in discussing adolescence I
describe the "uniform" of initiates in an African circumcision
school. The uniform is, to begin with, total nudity, which is
gradually covered by paint at one stage, then by vines, then
by raffia skirts, then by more paint, and so forth. It is a clear,
precise, and predictable sequence of events. I have seen hundreds of these initiations now, and every time it is the same.
The uniform is highly symbolic, each element clearly emphasizing a very specific social value, something that society
wants the young boys to learn and assimilate and carry with
them into adulthood. I compare this (and other aspects of
adolescence) with my own personal experience of the school
I attended during my adolescence, and of the equally dramatic
uniform (top hat and tails) that we were required to wear.
But whereas the boys in that African society knew as well as
the teachers the significance of their uniform, so far as I know
none of the boys that I went to school with were aware of

anything more than the fact that their uniform defined them
as belonging to a certain social and economic segment of the
population, associating them with a certain historic tradition.
I doubt if any of the teachers gave it any more thought than
that either; if they did they never told us. And whereas the
young African adolescents were gradually led from the exo-
teric significance of their clothing to its esoteric symbolism so
that every day a new lesson was learned about their changing
role in life, for us the top hat and tails remained forever whatever they meant to us at the outset . . . *at the conscious level*.
However, the value of comparison, as distinct from contrast,
is that goaded by the shrewdness with which the African
teachers in that initiation school taught the boys how to become men, how to manifest the social consciousness and accept
the responsibilities that would be expected of them as adults,
I was persuaded to look more closely at what went on at *my*
initiation. And while I saw that indeed there was an enormous
difference in the extent to which my teachers did *not* use and
manipulate the usage of our uniform to teach us social values
like our fellow adolescents in Africa, from our uniform and
from the ways in which *we* found we could manipulate it we
too learned a lot about ourselves and the society in which we
lived. And much of what we learned in this way undermined
what we *were* formally taught about social values.

Throughout I shall be referring to my own personal experience of the various stages of life in what for some will be a
culture just as exotic as that of central Africa. Much of that
experience in itself is trivial, and to others may seem absurd.
In itself, so it is, but the point of including it is to show how
much we can learn about ourselves and our own societies from
a minute examination of precisely that which, by being so
familiar to us, too often escapes our scrutiny. Had the teachers
at Westminster School paid the same critical attention to their
own past, perhaps they would have dealt with the adolescence
of those in their charge with a little more wisdom or social
consciousness. This study of the life cycle is a game in which
we can all participate equally, each individual bringing his
own personal experience into the arena for contrast and comparison. If there *are* any universal truths, then perhaps they
may emerge, but at the very least we will have learned a lot

about ourselves, our societies, and how we have come to be what we are. Perhaps even more important, we might also learn about the many other things that we might have become under different circumstances, or could still become if we so wished; for no stage of the life cycle is devoid of the potential for becoming something else.

It is this constant and dynamic interaction between self-awareness and awareness of others that removes us from the realm of dry, lifeless, ivory-tower academia. It is that interplay between each of us as an individual and the whole world around us that will be explored in this book.

Perhaps one of the most important things about the anthropological perspective is that we see society as an integrated whole, not as the sum total of a number of distinct parts. However, a necessary technique for analytical purposes is to make certain broad divisions, areas of social organization, so that we can better see how they interweave and interconnect. Four very broad such areas are the areas of domestic life, economic life, political life, and religious life. Within these we do not merely observe what people *do*, though that (the ethnographic description) is an essential beginning, but again we seek to understand the concepts, to look for the regularities and relationships that can be seen throughout all spheres of social organization. When it comes to religious life, our work is perhaps the hardest. While it is easy enough to observe ritual behavior (though not always to observe *all* ritual behavior; much is concealed from us whether we know it or not), it is not possible to observe religious belief. The two are very different things, the one every bit as important as the other.

To understand religious belief we have to have very special linguistic skills, but all the intellectual skill in the world is not enough. We also have to *feel* and ultimately, ourselves, believe. This of course is anathema to those who think of themselves as "scientists" in the most restrictive sense of that word as used by many "social scientists" some of whom say quite openly, that if you cannot count it, it cannot be worth anything! Now one can count the number of times a ritual is performed, measure the frequency of manifestation of its component parts, but how can one begin to measure the *intensity* with which man believes? Yet it is that intensity, just as much as what he believes in, that affects our social behavior and organization. However much or little we have learned about religious behavior and belief, we can be sure that it is one of the most powerful integrative forces in any viable society, and indeed this may be its most important function. Through religious concepts life becomes a consistent and relatively predictable whole.

In the history of mankind the amount of time civilization has existed is minute or microscopic, depending on how we define our terms. But supposing we say that civilization began ten thousand years ago and that "man" began one million years ago, then civilization has only existed for one percent of man's time on earth. If we push man's beginnings back to two million years ago, then the amount of time civilization has existed dwindles to one half of one percent. However, that is being ultraconservative, for few of us, if compelled to live as man did even a mere ten thousand years ago, would recognize anything of what today we understand by the term "civilization." Civilization is very much an immature and ongoing experiment, the success of which is by no means yet proven.

There are many who say that for the primitive, life was and is, in Hobbesian terms, nasty, brutish, and short. On the whole, anthropologists have found otherwise, and over the years have accumulated an enormous mass of data to support their view. This evidence is based on years of living within such societies, suffering the same deprivations, including sickness and, sometimes, premature death. If we measure a culture's worth by the longevity of its population, the sophistication of its technology, the material comforts it offers, then many primitive cultures have little to offer us, that is true. But our study of the life cycle will show that in terms of a conscious dedication to human relationships that are both affective and effective, the primitive is ahead of us all the way. He is working at it at every stage of life, from infancy to death, while playing just as much as while praying; whether at work or at home his life is governed by his conscious quest for social order. Each individual learns this social consciousness as he grows up, and the lesson is constantly reinforced until the day he dies, and because of that social consciousness each individual is a person of worth and value and importance to society, also from the day of birth to the day of death. It all begins in childhood.

PART ONE

CHILDHOOD

THE ART OF BECOMING

I N ALL CULTURES, at all times known to us, the children are
a source of wonderment for they are the supreme example of
the human potential for creation. They are themselves filled
with wonder during their first years, as the strange world
around them slowly reveals itself. Their wonderment is one of
the major tools that will shape their destiny, for in looking at
the world around them they have to discover not just what
things *are*, what they can do to or with them, and what things
can do to or with them, but what things *mean* for children. A
sense of mystery·transforms mere curiosity into wonder, suggesting to children that everything and everyone has a special
meaning for them as individuals. In discovering what that
special meaning is, children slowly become conscious beings
that not only receive, but impart meaning to others. In part,
at least, the art of becoming is the art of learning who and
what you are by learning to give and receive of yourself and
for yourself. In their ability to wonder and to question the
meaning of all they see and touch and hear and smell, children
discover, and become themselves, constantly growing, constantly becoming something else. At first the family hearth is
as much a mystery as the wider world; later in childhood that
wider world is as filled with mystery as is the universe beyond. Perhaps in our culture we romanticize childhood as we
do because the child serves as an omnipresent reminder of a

wonder and mystery with which we tend to lose touch as we grow older. In other cultures, however much the child may be a source of wonder, people do not idolize the condition of childhood. On the contrary, they recognize it as a time of ignorance and pain, a time of deep emotional hurt just as much as a time of joy. If they do not look back to childhood with nostalgia, perhaps it is because, for them, the world has remained a place of wonder, and the older they get the greater the wonder.

In some of these cultures people also differ from us by not differentiating children according to gender; until puberty they are (with reason) considered neuter, and consequently are treated with scrupulous equality. Some people do not even consider children fully "human," in the sense that they have not yet developed their full human potential. In referring to children in such cultures it is not only permissible but correct and proper to refer to a child as "it," a usage that bothers some of us. But then, in Africa the Mbuti say we expect too much of our children in some respects, and do not demand enough of them in others. Here is a difference in approach to childhood that surely we can learn from, so in what follows I retain, as far as is possible, the Mbuti usage of not differentiating children according to gender.

Most of us tend to think of our coming into being as coinciding with the miracle of birth. There are people, however, who see their beginning as taking place at least nine months earlier than that, even thinking of themselves in the most individual and material sense. In recounting their life history they do not start with "When I was born . . . ," but rather with "When I was conceived . . ." Others see their true beginnings, the first assemblage of those forces that ultimately lead to their being what they are, as predating the act of conception by eons and reaching back into antiquity. Among those who hold this view are some of the foremost scientists in the world, thinking in terms of biological evolution, and remote, nonliterate tribal philosophers, thinking in terms of spiritual descent from the first ancestors, the continuity of one single life force.

While not for a moment denying or minimizing the importance of biological and spiritual considerations, as a social anthropologist I am more concerned with how and where we became social, as distinct from individual, creatures and with the learned aspect of socialization. The crux of this aspect lies in the relationship the individual develops with the world around him. It is a total relationship. We divide it into artificial segments and talk of man's relationship with the human or animal worlds, with the natural and the mechanical or technological worlds, and in many other ways. But for true socialization to be learned, the individual has to gain confidence in his relationship with all the various segments of his experience and perceive the world as a single totality instead of as the mere sum total of separate relationships.

It is in childhood that we develop such ability as we later possess to deal with the world we live in and the social horizons and concepts that will influence, if not determine, our human relationships throughout life. Though it may not always be thus, the prime arena for this process of becoming has long been the family which, in this context, is more than the mere biological unit of procreation. In some societies it is the nucleus of parents and their offspring. Then, as in our society, remoter kin such as aunts, uncles, and first cousins may be of minimal significance in the process of socialization. In other societies the word may connote the extended family, which would include more distant relatives, not only in a theoretical sense, but in the very practical matters of residence, economic cooperation, political responsibility, and religious belief and practice. Families may trace descent through the male line, the female line, or both. The form and structure of the family in any given society usually varies with the social context precisely because it serves that particular context and assumes the form best suited to the needs of that society. The role of the family in our own society may still be detected in the use of kinship terminology, especially as applied to religious practitioners, where the terms "father," "brother," "sister," and "mother" are commonly used to connote membership in a spiritual family. The same terms may equally well be used to connote political allegiance to a political party, a nation, or a "family of nations." In our society we generally only use those terms that indicate equality, such as "brother" and "sister"; but in other societies other terms are used, following the model of family authority, to indicate dominance, superordination or subordination; in this way a head of state (just as for Roman Catholics the head of the Church) may be called father or mother, and his or her subjects referred to as "children." In rural areas it is still the practice often to bring nonkin into a closer relationship, for economic or other reasons, by using kinship terms; "cousin" is most often used in this respect. In the sixties the black American manifested a new sense of unity, based on identity and equality, by consistent usage of the terms "brother" and "sister," a usage that continues today with even wider scope.

Two major concerns of all human societies are conflict and aggression. One of the prime functions of social organization is to provide the means of resolving conflict when it occurs or of avoiding it altogether. Childhood is the period for training in this area. In some societies the training is more consciously directed than in others and it may be formal or informal, schools and games being well-known examples of each. So while learning positive attitudes toward human relationships through the model established by family, children are also learning how to deal with the negative aspect: they are, or should be, learning how to cope with their own potential for aggression and violence. Although the extent to which the human being is biologically programmed to be either a social or an aggressive, predatory animal may be questionable, there can surely be no question as to the human *potential* for both sociality and aggressivity. Our physiological capability for violence is not unimpressive, but our mental capacity is staggering, for it not only enables us to devise and fabricate weapons, it also enables us consciously to plan and chart our course of aggression and to execute it with all the malice of forethought. And that, perhaps, is the most dangerous and destructive form of violence.

However, if humans have a seemingly limitless capacity for violence, for aggression, they have an equally great potential for nonviolence and nonaggressivity. A notable feature of many small-scale societies is the great amount of concern shown, in a wide diversity of institutionalized forms, for the reduction of man's violent potential to a remarkable minimum. It is not that primitive people were or are any more moral than ourselves, or necessarily more pragmatic; if they see the wisdom of minimizing violence and aggressivity, of reducing hostility to a level far below their mental and technological potential, it is perhaps simply because that best answers their overall needs for survival. So our own maximal development of the aggressive potential may answer our needs, if not our tastes.

The art of becoming as practiced by the Mbuti hunter-gatherers still living in the Ituri Forest of northeastern Zaïre may seem utterly unrelated to our modern industrial world. Nevertheless, those who are conceived and born there have to grow up, if they survive, into responsible adulthood and learn how to relate to each other and to their neighbors in such a way as to maximize their potential for humanity, as they understand it, and minimize their potential for inhumanity. These terms would translate to them best as nonviolence and violence, respectively. In looking at the way childhood is lived out in that equatorial forest, we see something of what we *could* be, though not necessarily as we *should* be. What is right and possible for the Mbuti is not necessarily what is right or possible for us, but it may well remind us of a possibility (for nonviolence, for instance) with which we have almost lost touch, except as an unreachable ideal. If we wish to reduce violence we have to assess very carefully its full implications in our society and recognize that the "limited violence," such as that which we legalize in the name of peace, or of law and order, is a relative concept. It may well be that the limits have, for us, merely expanded, necessarily, to encompass the open violence on the streets and in our homes that we all abhor. It may be part of the cost we have to pay for our particular chosen form of life style. To a large extent it *is* a matter of choice and the Mbuti afford us a look at one option, though one that is more open to them than to us, because of the context in which they live. Theirs is a much more isolated world, for one thing: there is much less intercultural mobility and a much higher level of predictability.

As idyllic as their life may seem in many respects, a number of factors contribute to give the Mbuti context an explosive potential that makes their nonaggressive and nonviolent life style all the more noteworthy. One of the major areas of potential conflict is, in a sense, external to the "real" world by which they regulate their daily lives. It is the profane world of the African cultivators from different tribes who now encircle the forest—the Mbuti's sacred domain—in small, isolated villages. The cultivators depend for their survival upon cutting down the forest for their ever-shifting plantations, whereas the Mbuti depend for *their* survival upon retaining the forest intact and uncut. It is a classic confrontation of opposites that finds nonhostile resolution not in compromise, not in any coming together or modification of opposed values and beliefs, but rather in the conscious *accentuation of the difference*. Each group has retained both its own life style and its own beliefs and values, however seemingly antithetical. They have achieved this by agreeing to a territorial separation, the Mbuti remaining in the center of the vast forest, continuing to hunt and gather as they have for thousands of years, the cultivators stringing themselves out around the periphery, never spreading toward the middle. But while the cultivators see the potential conflict primarily in economic terms, for the Mbuti it is more of a spiritual issue. For them the forest is sacred, it is the very source of their existence, of all goodness. It is to preserve that sanctity, as much as to preserve their economy, that they go to the lengths they do to dissuade the villagers from entering their world. Yet this very insistence that the forest is sacred also creates a potential for conflict in the inner, ideal world of the Mbuti, for as hunters and gatherers they can only survive by the supreme desecration of taking forest life. It is this inherent conflict that leads them to be the conservationists they are, minimizing their killing of game to meet their barest and most immediate needs, so as to minimize their sin.

The Mbuti concept of the forest permeates their whole life. During my first visit, I discovered that young or old, male or female, whenever on their way through the forest (except during a hunt, obviously), the Mbuti talk, shout, whisper, and sing to the forest (*ndura*), addressing it as mother or father or both, referring to its goodness and its ability to "cure," or "make good" . . . it is the same word. Whether to address the forest as mother or father or both is an individual choice, depending, the Mbuti say, on how they feel at the moment. In the Mbuti system of kinship terminology, the only terms that distinguish between male and female are at the parental level, and there is one significant point in the life of a young child when he or she accepts the father as "a kind of mother." So even when addressing the forest as "father," and that is less often, the Mbuti are really saying "a kind of mother," and that gives us a very strong clue as to what is going on in their minds, for it defines a specific relationship.

In explaining why they address the forest this way, the Mbuti say: "Like our father and mother the forest gives us food, shelter, clothing, warmth, and affection." The word that I translate as "affection" is *kondi*, which may equally be used to mean love and need, between which the Mbuti seldom differentiate when discussing human relationships. At this point we get even closer to the way Mbuti think. The imagery is reiterated by every Mbuti practically every day of his life, and many times in each day. It is no empty formality, no mere courtesy; it is something done with joy and meaning. Sometimes there is conscious intent, to make sure that "the forest" is alert and watchful, to ensure protection. Perhaps more frequently it is without conscious intent, being rather a spontaneous expression of emotion. What is that emotion? And how can we avoid merely reading into the situation our own emotion?

It is clear that on occasion the emotion is one of sexual love, for the sexual nature of the relationship between an Mbuti man or woman, boy or girl, and the forest is sometimes demonstrated overtly enough by an erotic gesture of the body, in imitation of the act of copulation. Playful youths may even specify verbally that they want to copulate with the forest, and if this wish is accompanied by well-executed body movements, it is sure to give rise to mirth among the youth's companions. But as a motive, that hardly obtains when a youth behaves like this in privacy and solitude, as I have often seen done. Then, at least, it is done for something other than the approval and laughter of others; it is more in the nature of a spiritual, if sexual, communion with the forest. To move closer to the heart of the matter, we have to ignore such questions as to how, since all Mbuti refer to the forest as "mother" or "father," an Mbuti girl can in this way wish to copulate with her "father," or a boy with his "mother." These are questions that the Mbuti find infinitely tedious because they miss the whole point. Sex in itself and sexuality are not the heart of the matter, as the Mbuti see their world. And since it is their world I prefer to rely on their categories.

On other occasions the emotion is sometimes more one for which I can only use the word "adoration." I use the word without shame, rather with the joy felt by Teleãbo Kengé when he slipped into the *bopi* (the children's playground) one moonlit night. He was adorned with a forest flower in his hair and with forest leaves in his belt of vines and his loin cloth of forest bark. Alone with *his* inner world he danced and sang in evident ecstasy. And in answer to my question, he said, *"me bi nduṛa, me bi na songé."*—"I am dancing with the forest, dancing with the moon." It is reasonable to assume that the Mbuti child, growing up, sees all this and much more and is transformed accordingly.

The Mbuti conceive of their universe as a sphere. We are normally always in the center of this sphere. When we move in time and space the sphere moves with us, so we remain in the center, which provides security. If our movement in time or space is too violent or too sudden, we can reach the edge of the sphere before the center has time to catch up. When this happens, a person becomes *wazi-wazi*, or disoriented and unpredictable. If the violence of the movement is too blatant, we risk piercing through the safe and known boundaries of our sphere into the other world. If you do that, you may let something else in to replace you. At this point, the Mbuti start discussing the reflective qualities of water. They ask, what is the image that you can see, that looks like you and does everything you do, and which you can even touch and *feel* if you place your foot ever so carefully onto the surface of the water so that the other foot comes up to touch yours? And what happens if you place your foot *in* the water? The other foot comes up and disappears into your leg. The deeper you submerge yourself, the more that image-self enters your body, passing through you into the world you are leaving behind. And if you completely submerge yourself, say, to cross underwater to the other side of a river, on emerging the reverse process takes place. Then which is the real self and which the real world? This is something like what happens, they say, when you pierce through the safe and known boundaries of your sphere. The word they use for sphere is one of their words for womb. They are not thinking of a womb in a literal sense, of course, and this was made plain by trying alternative words on me; "stomach" for instance. An alternative word, more to their satisfatcion than stomach, was *endu*, which is the spheri-cal-like dwelling of sticks and leaves in which they live, which they build out of forest materials for shelter and protection, for warmth and comfort. From this womb, then, within our own conceptual sphere, let us move to another womb, that of a pregnant mother.

The act of intercourse between an Mbuti husband and wife is filled with joy, and it is sacred because it is a creative act that results in life (the Mbuti say that extramarital sex, how-ever pleasurable, is in no way the same thing, and is neither sacred nor creative). Intercourse may continue after the first indisputable signs of pregnancy, but that is a matter of in-dividual choice. Among Mbuti couples I know well, it has been the woman that makes the decision, according to what-ever makes her and the child within her "feel good." As the pregnancy progresses, the mother-to-be pursues her normal everyday life without much change right up to the moment of delivery, but she increasingly avoids activities or situations that might tax her physically or emotionally. She adorns her body with leaves and flowers, perhaps in readiness, like Kengé, for *her* dance of adoration. It is clearly a form of consecration. In the last few months she takes to going off on her own, to her favorite spot in the forest, and singing to the child in her womb.

The lullaby that she sings is special in several ways. It is the only form of song that can be sung as a solo and it is composed by the mother for that particular child within her womb. It is sung for no other, it is sung by no other. The young mother sings it quietly, reassuringly, rocking herself, sometimes with her hands on her belly, or gently splashing her hands or feet in the water of her favorite stream or river, or rustling them through leaves, or warming herself at a fire. In a similar way she talks to the child, according it the intelligence, though not the knowledge, of an adult. There is no baby talk. What she says to the child is clear, informative, reassuring, and comforting. She tells it of the forest world into which it will soon emerge, repeating simple phrases such as those perhaps already "heard" by the unborn baby while its mother was off on the hunt: "the forest is good, the forest is kind; mother forest, father forest."

Some mothers describe the place where the child will be born, the other children it will meet and play with, grow up with; and tell the womb-child that if he is a boy, somewhere there is an unborn girl baby that one day he will marry. Both the physical and the social world may be described to children in this way. And once the children are born and begin to learn to speak they hear these stories over and over again and it all becomes so familiar that it is as if they were conscious of being conceived at that place and at that time of day, and of all that went on around them as they were being carried through the forest in their mothers' wombs. Mbuti see their life as beginning the moment they were wanted, for that is when they were conceived, and from these stories told them throughout childhood all Mbuti have a detailed, though not necessarily exact or verifiable, knowledge of their earliest beginnings.

In one sense it is not of the slightest importance that the unborn child can hardly be expected to understand what is being said to it. Nor does it matter whether or not the emotional content of what the mother is thinking and doing and saying and singing is in any way transferred to the unborn baby's consciousness. It is enough that the mother, at least, is reinforcing *her* own concept of the world and is readying *her*self for the creative act about to unfold, giving *her*self confidence that the forest will be as good and as kind to her child as it has been to her; providing food, shelter, clothing, warmth, and affection. That confidence alone would be an auspicious beginning to any life.

A few days before her time is due, the mother may restrict her activities and perhaps refrain from going off on the hunt each morning, though it is common enough for a girl to give birth while actually on the hunt, merely staying back either by herself or with a friend and rejoining the hunt an hour or two later. Always, a few days before, while on one of her solitary trysts with the forest, perhaps singing to her child more as a lover, she selects a vine that will yield her favorite bark. She cuts it, brings it to the camp, and with a hammer made from the tusk of an elephant she beats out a soft piece of bark cloth, sweet-smelling and clean and light in color, like those called *lé 'engbé* or *esélé*. The smell should be pleasing to the infant, the color light, perhaps to reflect more light inside the dim interior of the hut in which the infant will spend most of its first three days or perhaps, as most mothers say, because a light-colored bark cloth shows the baby off to better advantage. But above all the smell must be sweet; and the texture should be smooth enough to be comfortable, but rough enough to assure the infant that it is enveloped in the all-protective womb of the forest. Some Mbuti assert that the first Mbuti was indeed born out of a tree, so what could be more reassuring to the child than the smell and the texture of a tree? Once the cloth is made, the mother may decorate it with free-flowing designs painted with a twig dipped in the dark juice of *kangé*, the gardenia fruit.

The infant was conceived in love and joy, and that is how it is born, equally wanted and welcome whether it is a girl child or a boy child. If the mother is by herself, she may sit on her haunches, or on a log. If she feels there may be any difficulty at all, she may place herself with her feet against a tree. Some say they put a vine around a tree and hold onto that. Others say that if they felt there would be any difficulty, they would have a friend sit opposite them, feet to feet, "like trees in the forest." However, even minor difficulty in delivery seems to be rare. The infant emerges easily, helped only by the mother's hands or those of a friend, and is immediately placed to the mother's breast as she lies down. The umbilical cord is cut in anything from a few minutes to as much as an hour or more later. At that time or soon after, the father and close friends may be invited to see the child, who by then is happily suckling. Women say this is a decision made by the mother *and* the child. When I have been present in the camp at the time of a birth, the newborn infant has sometimes given two or three tiny bleats, as though aggravated at having been made to do something it really did not want to do. But then it has better things to do than cry, such as explore its mother's body, feel her warmth, try the new and satisfying experience of drinking its mother's milk, all the while being reassured by the familiar sounds of her voice, singing the newborn's own special lullaby, rocking in a familiar rhythm.

Usually about three days after birth, another important educational event takes place in that young life. The child, who has been in constant contact only with the mother, is presented to the camp. The mother emerges from her *endu* (leaf hut) and hands the child, wrapped in sweet-smelling *lé 'engbé,* to a few of her assembled family and close friends, not just to look at, but to hold close to their bodies. The infant learns that there is a plurality of warm bodies, similar in warmth (which is comforting) but dissimilar in smells and rhythmic movements and sounds. If it is disconcerted enough to cry in protest, its mother immediately takes it back and puts it to her breast. Thus an initial model of predictability and security is reinforced.

After introducing the child to the hunting camp, the mother takes it back to her home. Inside the hut the light is always subdued, though mothers often sit close to doorways in those first three days, as if to accustom their newborn to the light of day. The light in the camp is quiet and cool, the trees meeting high overhead, making yet another kind of sphere that in time proves to be just as protective and satisfying as all other spheres. Shortly after presentation to the camp, usually, the child is given a first name decided on by family and friends together, often after some favored form of forest life, animal or vegetable. From the moment of naming onward, the child is treated as a full person with individual rights. Its mother now seldom talks to it in the same way she did during pregnancy, and the child seems to learn to speak more by listening to her talk with other adults than by direct instruction. As before, no baby talk is employed.

As the newborn passes from infancy through childhood into youth, he explores progressively the four major areas in which conflict is most likely to occur in his life: territory, family relationships, differences in age, and differences in gender. These areas are explored in approximately that order, and by the time a Mbuti boy reaches youth his total experience has equipped him to enter a stressful situation with confidence, supported by a whole repertoire of specific conflict-resolving skills and techniques well learned and practiced throughout childhood. If he feels a degree of uncertainty, he feels none of the fear and perceives nothing of the threat that would lead ultimately and exclusively to a violent solution to conflict. His education is not rigidly programmed by adults. To some extent he is educated in all four areas at the same time. I believe the same to be true for the Mbuti girl, but at the levels of youth and adulthood my own male gender gave me greater access to Mbuti males, so it is safer for me to speak primarily from that point of view.

Infancy is by no means a time of total protection but rather one of controlled experimentation and perpetual learning. It is the time for exploring territory. Now that it has left the very clearly defined territory of the womb, the newborn utilizes every sense available to it to explore the new territory that is its mother's body. There is not an inch of that new world that the infant has not explored within the first few weeks of life. And while exploring the relatively familiar confines of his mother's body in total security, it is constantly being introduced to other sensations that will also be associated with total security in the future. At birth, for instance, the newborn is bathed in water, not from a forest stream, but from one of several enormous vines which, when cut, give forth a sweet-tasting water that, sacred as is everything of the forest, must surely be close to the very essence of the forest. The mother herself usually prefers this water for bathing and drinking during the first week following childbirth. The child is enveloped in bark cloth. Little circlets of vine are placed around its neck, wrists, and ankles; little pieces of special wood are threaded onto some of these circlets. The child explores all these things even before it can crawl. It smells, feels, tastes, listens to, and squints at them, just as it smells, feels, tastes, listens to, and squints at its mother. It finds that she has similar vines around her neck, wrists, and ankles, similar pieces of forest wood, and is perfumed by that same scent of the water of forest vines.

Once the child can crawl it is time to be born again into yet another world, that of the *endu*, the dwelling made of forest sticks and leaves. The floor of the *endu* will be explored just as thoroughly as was the mother's body. A thorn brought in when the father returned from the hunt, a biting ant, or the sharp edge of a leaf or sliver of bamboo may cause the child trouble; but rather than prevent it from discovering these things, the mother will either leave it to discover them alone or help it discover their harmful potential and the fact that harm can be avoided or readily alleviated. The child may already be trying to explore vertically, pulling itself upward on the stick frame of the *endu*. Again, the mother is more likely to encourage such exploration than not; she certainly would not prevent it. If the child falls, however, or in any other way comes to minor harm in its exploration of space, she quickly comforts it before turning it loose to try again. In a matter of weeks the *endu* has been fully explored in all but its upper reaches, and the young child is ready for yet another rebirth, this time into the sphere of the *apa*, or camp.

The Mbuti make the point that the *endu*, like the womb, is spherical, and so is the *apa*. Most campsites are natural clearings, roughly circular, but with the branches of trees all meeting high overhead, creating yet another spherical world, enclosing, including, and for the Mbuti, comforting and familiar. The clearing might be as much as fifty yards across, or only ten or twenty, but it always has this feel of being a throbbing, vital world within a world that is probably within yet other worlds. It is like a huge *endu*. The patterns formed by the trees and leafy canopy of the *apa* are less regular and, unlike those of the *endu*, they are constantly shifting and changing. The same all-pervasive smell of a wood log fire is in both spheres, but in the *apa* it is the smell of many fires (the plurality of models again) in many directions, all to be explored with confidence. After all, smelling so much like the fire in the thoroughly safe and proven *endu*, the other *endu* hearths could not be anything but safe also.

The dwellings, or *endu*, in this roughly circular camp are at the edge of the circle facing inward. Thus, each *endu* has another opposite to it. Groups of *endu* may be opposite other groups of *endu*. The child learns that to be opposite may be the same thing as to be opposed. It will already have noticed the distinction between the various *endu* territories that make up the overall, inclusive territory of the *apa*, and now it begins to note that *endu* tend sometimes to group themselves within the camp in opposition to other groups. The child, perhaps, will have sensed the opposition also, because of its increasingly sensitive awareness of emotional relationships within the camp, and be aware that oppositions and potential conflict exist between individual *endu* as well as between groups. By noting these oppositions it is possible to predict with remarkable certainty the lines along which any camp will split or come together when the time comes, once a month, to abandon an old camp and build a new one. Just noting the direction in which people face their huts when the camp is first built already provides this kind of information, and is a clear example of how opposition can work without hostility, for to face your *endu* directly across the camp at another *endu* is either to offer or to demand special friendship and trust. Like looking another directly in the eyes, as children learn to do in the *bopi*, it opens up just the kind of intimate relationship from which conflict can spring.

As the child crawls all over the camp exploring every nook and cranny, it learns vital lessons that have to do with both territory and kinship. The further it strays from its own family hearth the more dangerous and more exciting its wanderings are likely to be. If it keeps to the territory defined by sounds, smells, taste, touch, and appearance associated with its own *endu*, it will be comforted quickly if trouble arises. If it wanders into another similar, but subtly different, territory and runs into trouble, the child can still expect to be comforted but by a different kind of mother, with a different smell and taste and touch and sound and appearance. It could be an old man or a young girl. This enlarges the child's concept and experience of motherhood and its sense of security. Now it obviously has a plurality of mothers and safe territories, but they are not quite as predictable as its original womb/mother, and if it wanders into a territory where there are no mothers at all and gets into trouble, something quite new is likely to happen. Even its own womb/mother is likely to come over, and after pulling it out of the hot ashes into which it has crawled, instead of putting the infant to her breast, feeding it and comforting it with its own familiar lullaby, she is likely to slap it, carry it back by an arm or leg to its own safe territory, and dump it with unaccustomed roughness onto the ground. The child, who up to this point has had independence of action while exploring successive worlds, now learns that there are restrictions on its movement. Certain territories are safer than others, certain territories must not be violated (it will be slapped or shouted at, for instance, if it crawls into another *endu*). Each child finds that while other motherlike people are likely to provide it with what it needs, just as its own mother does, they and its own mother are beginning to make certain demands on it. For the moment these demands are associated with its own good, for at this stage the Mbuti only discipline a child for endangering itself, such as by crawling into a fire. Only when it learns to walk, in another few months, and can walk well enough to join others of the same age and create with them its own territory (the *bopi*, or playground), is any child likely to be disciplined for merely "being a nuisance."

Sometime in its second year, the child receives a first lesson in classificatory kinship. The adult male who has been sharing the familiar leaf bed with its mother, and whose body smell, sound, taste, appearance, and rhythm it knows almost as well, and which has been found to be every bit as secure and safe, begins to fondle the child as its mother does. He takes it to his breast and holds it there. With everything else so familiar, the child explores for milk, but instead of milk is given its first solid food. Here is another kind of mother indeed. This person offers everything the mother has always given; however, the food he offers comes not from the breast but from his own mouth or his fingers. The child thus learns to distinguish between *ema* and *eba*, mother and father. At the same time it learns to equate them. The relationship with each one is based on the same trust and dependency and increasing obligation, for it discovers that the *eba* is yet another person who will slap it if it gets into unnecessary trouble. But the lesson in kinship, or family, has been unmistakable. "Kinship" now has nothing to do with shared smells or sounds, with human biology; it has to do with the larger territory, the *apa*, as distinct from the smaller, rather safer but more confining sphere, the *endu*. Anyone appearing to the child's now clear vision as being like its mother or father in general size or shape (or whatever sensory images it uses) expects to be addressed in exactly the same way, as *ema* or *eba*, and the child can expect much the same treatment from any of them. The child can expect this new kind of solid food it is learning to eat, whenever it wants; it can expect comfort and affection; it can also expect discipline if it infringes on the few simple rules of the game.

Every child learns that other kinds of people, clearly distinct to its senses, must be called *tata* (grandparent) regardless of sex or biological relationship. It can make certain demands on them but seldom need expect discipline of the same kind now expected from its parents. On the contrary, *tata* are people to whom the child can go for comfort when comfort is denied by its plurality of *ema/eba*. Another distinct group it comes to recognize is less easy to define. In some ways they behave like *ema/eba*, in some ways like *tata*; they are closer to the child's own age and they call it, and each other, *apua'i* (sibling). By the age of two, when it has learned these terms and many others, and can already talk with ease and walk and run, the young Mbuti is beginning to associate more with the children of other *endu*, some of which *apua'i* will eventually take it to yet another territory, the *bopi*. Those older Mbuti who call it *miki* (child) seldom come to the *bopi*. Now the child is being introduced to that all-important (for the Mbuti, at least) principle of social organization, age. In the same way that it has been made aware of differences between different territories and different families, it now has to deal with the fact that there are four distinct age levels: children, youths, adults, and elders. All seem to have their appropriate territories and appropriate activities and relate to each other in an ordered way.

It is in the *bopi* (the children's playground) that the child, from between the ages of two or three and eight or nine, begins to face the problems of conflict, aggressivity, and violence. On leaving the *endu*, the child transfers its trust and confidence to this new sphere and does not find it misplaced. Children of the same age provide the same sense of security that it has felt in all its other spheres. When it returns to the *apa* the old security is still there, and its *endu* and mother spheres are equally intact. The child can take them for granted; it senses no conflict in loyalty or trust.

Bopi activities are primarily physical, but they begin to

provide a sense of direction for emotional outlet that will come into use in a more rational manner when the child leaves the *bopi* and becomes a youth. *Bopi* activities are pastimes rather than games because they are not competitive. The only competition encouraged by Mbuti pastimes is an inner competition between each individual and its abilities. To succeed, children must conquer their disabilities as best they can; at the same time they must restrain any excess of ability. To be better or worse than anyone else is to fail. If an individual child's ability in one direction is limited, perhaps through some physical handicap, then some ability possessed in abundance may be developed above the norm in compensation. In a word, the goal is equality through noncompetitiveness.

Two pastimes illustrate the kind of education that takes place in the *bopi*. The youngest children begin to explore hanging vines. They pull themselves upward, developing their young muscles while getting to know the vines. They climb and they swing and soon they learn skipping and hoop-jumping, which, like climbing and swinging, can be done in a variety of ways and can be done alone or with others. This ultimately leads to the most difficult of all these vine pastimes, which the children will be able to indulge in only when they are youths when it is mainly a male activity. An enormous vine is strung from high up between two trees with a clear space between them. Swinging from an axis perhaps thirty feet above ground, but with the loop a bare two feet from the earth, one youth sits in the swing and swings himself higher and higher. Then the others join in. As their companion starts his backward arc one runs after him, grabs one side of the vine swing, and, when it soars upward, leaps with it, and does a somersault over the head of his companion, who jumps to the ground, allowing the other to take his place. It requires perfect coordination, as well as considerable strength and agility. There are variations that at first may look like competitiveness. but that in fact demand just the opposite. The "jumper" may swing himself right over the head of the youth sitting in the swing and land on the ground in front of him as the swing descends. If the "sitter" does not sense what is happening and also jumps, expecting the other to take his place, there is a moan from the spectators; both have failed, the perfection of the ballet has been spoiled. Alternatively, the "sitter" may decide to remain sitting and the "jumper" has to make the extra effort demanded to complete the swing over his head and land safely. There can be no question of the one trying to outdo the other, for the fun is in developing daring maneuvers spontaneously and executing them together.

Similarly, climbing leads gently and steadily from individual development to social development. The children are all adept at tree-climbing by the age of four or five, limited only by their physical size and the size of the trunk and the limbs of the tree. At first they climb alone, exploring every branch, testing every way of getting from one branch to another, one tree to another. The idea is never just to get to the top, it is to know more about the tree. The younger are constantly stopping, riveted with fascination at a tiny detail of the bark they had not seen or felt or smelled before, or to examine the movement of ants up and down the tree, or to taste some sap oozing from its side. Put your own ear to a tree one day, as they told me to do, and see if, like an Mbuti child, you can hear it sing with happiness or cry with sorrow.

A little later, the Mbuti children develop tree-climbing into a pastime that like the vine swing, has serious educational import at a social rather than a personal level. A group of anything up to about ten children in the *bopi* climb a young sapling. When they reach the top, the sapling bends down until they are all within a few feet of the ground. At that point they all jump together with precision. If one lingers, either because of fear, or more likely out of bravado, it is not something it will do again. The child is flung upward as the sapling springs back, and it may well fall and be injured. Even if it survives with nothing worse than a minor bruise, it receives no credit for "bravery," because again it has spoiled the joint effort to "dance" (which is *their* term: *bina*) life's ballet of perfect cooperation and coordination. These are precisely the qualities demanded in adult life for the hunt. And in the same way that the sapling will not bend to the ground unless the majority of older children in the *bopi* climb it together, so the hunt will be unsuccessful if the majority of hunters in the *apa* do not participate.

Little that the children do in the *bopi* is not full of value in later adult life. While they are learning the fun and beauty of working and playing *with* not *against* others, they are in a positive way learning by prescription rather than proscription, by being told what they should do rather than what they should not do. There is the essence of cooperative, communal life, of which competition is the antithesis. With cooperativeness in action comes community of spirit, and with community of spirit the foundation for truly social behavior is secured; social order becomes possible without law, as we know it, and without the threat of physical coercion, and without anything even approaching a penal system.

But now how do children learn, as they must, to deal with the negative side, the inevitable exception that they themselves will often enough make in their lives in pursuit of their own individual good, without due regard for the good of others? They do not know it, but they have already learned the two most important techniques used by adult Mbuti in averting and resolving conflicts, if they cannot be averted, without violence or hostility. They began to learn one such technique as soon as they learned to crawl and tested out the relative safety of different territories. Even while exploring their mothers' bodies they learned that some places are safer than others, some more comfortable, some more rewarding. Within the *endu* the same lesson was expanded. When born yet again into the *apa* world it was made very clear that if children got into trouble in one territory, they could get out of it by moving to another. Then they found that what so demonstrably applied to geographical territories, *'ndu* (mother/womb), *endu*, *apa* and *bopi*, also applied to kinship territories. If in trouble with *ema* or *eba* any child could seek refuge with any *tata*, who were a very different kind of family. From this it became self-evident that the same technique of avoidance by relocation applied to the age categories already learned. By simple movement, either within any one of these categories or between them, refuge could always be found. Those basic womblike qualities of protection, comfort, and the satisfaction of all needs, including affection, are always to be found somewhere. So in a very real sense the Mbuti child *is* always in the middle of its sphere/womb, for its sustenance moves wherever it moves, provided only that it does not move too fast.

In later life children will find that mobility is one of their prime techniques for avoiding or for resolving a dispute, for once they move elsewhere their spheres move with them and the dispute is discarded. But what if neither opponent chooses to move, what technique is available then? It too has been learned in infancy. That first chortle of joy given by the newborn infant when it realizes that its new world is, after all, just as secure as the old one, is perhaps its first lesson in conflict resolution. Chortles quickly become laughter, and this laughter becomes the Mbuti's prime weapon against conflict, aggression, and violence. Having learned to laugh with joy at birth the Mbuti child learns to use both the joy and the laughter in more of its *bopi* pastimes, pastimes that are lessons in nonviolent conflict resolution.

The child, united with other children by the bond of age, retains all its trust and confidence in kinship and territorial bondings; they have been well explored and tested, and while there is more to learn, those bondings can safely be taken for granted and invoked at will, perhaps even for refuge from fellow age-mates. Meanwhile, in the seclusion of the *bopi*, children explore this new form of age bonding and explore the shared experience of all these other categories and their infinitely complex interrelationships. The category of sex is already beginning to come into play as they grow slightly older and are more in the company of youths in the main camp. So when is a mother a woman and a father a mother? And what does it mean when someone that you address as *ema*, or mother, is addressed by another as *miki*, or child? And why sometimes are personal names used, not these so widely inclusive terms that seem to link every person in the camp to everyone else? And how do you reconcile actions that are appropriate to territorial behavior with those appropriate to kinship or age behavior: which has priority of loyalty?

Here is a whole new realm for exploration, and the appropriate tool, the mind, is ready to undertake the task by about the age of eight or nine. At first the exploration is through imitation. What has largely been unconscious imitation now becomes conscious, and in the *bopi* children explore every possibility. They do not confine themselves dutifully to building miniature *endu* and to "playing house"; nor does imitation of adult activities, such as the hunt or the gathering of nuts and roots and berries, or the making of bark cloth, or even copulation, interest them for long. These are mere techniques, the basics of which are quickly learned and the refinements of which can be mastered only as the body grows in size and strength. More fascinating, as pastimes, are imitations of how the wide diversity of territorial, kinship, age, and sex roles are played. Each child explores through imitation each role it has become aware of: young or old, male or female, good-tempered or bad, happy or sad. Together the children explore situations involving all of these. Little wonder that the *bopi* is full of such loud shrieks of laughter that sometimes an irate adult will come in, shouting and stamping, his or her afternoon nap disturbed. He may try to catch a child to slap it, fail, and resort to even louder shouting and noise-making. Of course once the adult leaves, every last child rushes to the center of the *bopi*, and soon there is a whole swarm of miniature irate adults shouting and yelling at each other, trying to catch and slap each other. And if the adult is stupid enough to stay too long, and sees himself being ridiculed in this way, what happens? Physically he is no match for this bunch of young demons, so either he has to retreat and be subjected to even more ridicule when the children return to the *apa*, where they will reenact the whole scene so that other adults can join in the ridicule of their fellow, or else, if he has sense, he will join in with the children and share their joy and laughter in his own self-ridicule.

But not for a moment do the children think that they have the right to disturb someone else's sleep, anymore than that person has the right to disturb their play. No matter how the adult behaves, whether he joins in the fun or stalks off back to his *endu* in a huff, once he has gone the children will quickly quiet down. They have had yet another lesson in the value of *ekimi*, calm or quiet, over *akami*, disturbance or noise. These are the two words heard most frequently when Mbuti are using speech rather than ridicule in an attempt to resolve a dispute. So the older children in the *bopi*, when tired of physical pastimes, have many verbal pastimes. These often involve jokes, ways of exploring alternative modes of behavior, discovering those that are proper and work and those that are improper and do not work. But they also increasingly involve the rational and verbal use of concepts such as *ekimi* and *akami* in the settlement of play-conflict situations. It may start through the imitation of a real dispute the children witnessed in the main camp, perhaps the night before. They all take roles and imitate the adults. It is almost a form of judgment, for if the adults talked their way out of a dispute the children, having performed their imitation once, are likely to drop it. If the children detect any room for improvement, however, they will explore that. If the adult argument was inept and everyone went to sleep in a bad temper that night, then the children try to show that they can do better. If they find they cannot, then they revert to ridicule which they play out until they are all rolling on the ground in near-hysterics. That happens to be the way many of the most potentially violent and dangerous disputes are settled in adult life. It is difficult to be dangerous or violent if you are laughing so hard you cannot stand. Laughter, jokes, and ridicule are vital elements in Mbuti life, and together they constitute a major factor in developing the affective characteristics of the adults and in minimizing the disaffective.

The child's first nickname, which is acquired in the *bopi*, is likely to contain an element of playful ridicule. It may be the very opposite of what a child would think appropriate for itself. A boy or girl who shows a tendency to be proud of physical strength may be nicknamed "the weak one"; the child who seemingly has everything going for him is likely to be called "the poor one." Or the nickname may suggest a hidden quality. Many of the animal nicknames are of this nature, indicating that the child has the hidden quality of trickiness, slowness, noisiness, grace, wisdom, and so forth. There is much experimentation before a child is finally fitted with an appropriate nickname by other children, who will watch carefully to see how the youngster reacts, those very reactions perhaps leading to more experimentation and ridicule. In this way nicknaming itself is an educational pastime, teaching the child much about the virtue of nonaggressivity, for there is no victimization or hostility; it is all done with laughter, all the children laughing as much at the name-caller's inventiveness or ineptness, as at the child being named.

If any child teases another to the point of bringing it to tears (a more likely reaction at this age for the Mbuti than anger) a new pastime will be improvised that demands that the tearful child play the role of a joyful hero or heroine. The offending name-caller will be absolutely excluded from this pastime. This lesson in the power of ostracism may be the name-caller's first taste of an adult Mbuti sanction one step more powerful than ridicule. The offender must then learn the path of re-entry into the society from which he has just excluded himself, waiting a judicious time until the others have become so engrossed in their new pastime, or the succeeding one, that what happened before has become irrelevant. After all, it belongs to another time/sphere, and is no longer here and now. Then without much, if any, effort he finds himself reincorporated. All that is required is that the offender forget the incident just as the others have done and move with them, a little more slowly, into the new center of life. The cruelty that can arise so easily from ridicule is absent, for cruelty exists in the mental attitude of the performer, not in the act of ridicule itself. At this stage the children are far too occupied with appropriate use of action and speech to be bothered with concepts such as cruelty, or indeed kindness, for that matter. But in the search for the *e*ffective modes of behavior and language, they discover, naturally, that what is most effective also generally happens to be *a*ffective.

The Mbuti child has observed that certain groups are separated according to age, and that each age group has certain activities proper to itself. Indeed, even as children in the *bopi*, it is for them to light the hunting fire, perhaps with some of the younger youths, as a ritual gesture of placation (the explanation of which, among the children, is still another lesson in the value of nonaggressivity). This even gives them a measure of social control as an age group, for if they choose not to light the hunting fire, the adults cannot go hunting. That means they go hungry, whereas the children are free to eat readily available foods forbidden to adults, so they do not go hungry. They do not exploit the power unjustly, however, for they have already learned in the process of growing up that the initial dependence upon a series of mothers has developed into a relationship of interdependence of groups which they have learned to define clearly by the principles of kinship, territory, and age. Now they learn about sexual differentiation.

Already in the *bopi* they will be aware of the nature of sexual relationships between boys and girls and will have imitated and ridiculed an extraordinary number of variations on this theme, working their way through every kind of inter-human relationship (including, for this purpose, villagers as humans), and will have made good headway into the variations involving animals, animals and humans, birds and humans, birds and animals, showing minimal interest in the vegetable world. It would be easy, but wrong, to pass this off as good, bawdy fun. Of course it is that, and the children's considerable ability and expertise in this area are much in demand, not only for entertainment of youths and adults in the main camp, but also, on rather rare but important occasions, in the jural process. This happens when an offender who has chosen to remain isolated in his own sphere must be subjected to a form of ridicule that will either bring him back into the all-embracing sphere of the *apa* or drive him off to join another. It is usually the job of youths to take such jural action, but in the same way that children are recognized as having spirit power (as with the hunting fire), so their ridicule is considered the most powerful of all, perhaps even having the possible effect of transference, or what is often called "sympathetic magic." For the Mbuti that is a matter of discussion and disagreement, however, and there is certainly no *intent* that the sexual inadequacy or impotence being mimed by the children be conveyed in a physical sense to the offender.

Sex and sexual relationships are important to the Mbuti both as a potential source of aggressivity and as a principle of social organization, so it is fitting that their own naming system and kinship terminology teach them at an early age that gender is relatively unimportant. A boy and a girl may well go by the same name. When that happens, they are taught that, indeed, they share a certain identity and are under special obligations to each other, for those obligations hold regardless of the apparently contradictory obligations to the well-established spheres of territory, kinship, and age. But the system of "kinship" terminology is in fact generational, having little to do with descent and biological family. As such, it makes clear that no distinctions of gender are relevant or appropriate when referring to children, siblings, or grandparents, but are indeed relevant and mandatory at the parental level. As soon as it learns the terminology, the child thus learns that gender is important to adults and to the husband/ wife relationships, thus to the *apa* and *endu*, but not the *bopi*. It is then distinguishing between gender and sex, and will soon learn that one of the major sources of *akami* (noise or dispute) in the *apa* is indeed sex, and that most *akami* is associated with adulthood.

A rich symbolism constantlly reminds the Mbuti child of the supreme value of all, *ndura*, or "forestness." The prime symbols are the natural elements: fire, earth, water, and air. The womb, which the Mbuti liken to fire, is seen in this light, not only because it is warm, but because it has the power of transformation. Just as fire transforms inedible food into edible food, so does the womb/fire transform spiritual life into physical life. This symbol is present every day of their lives in the hearths of all the *endu*, the hearth of the *bopi* and the *apa*. And periodically there is the all-encompassing hearth of the *kumamolimo*. Earth is similarly omnipresent, as is water, in their everyday life. They see earth being rubbed into the sacred *molimo* trumpet when they peek through the leaf walls of their *endu*. They see earth used to quench the last embers of the *molimo* fire as their older brothers carry the trumpet back to the forest, after it has restored *ekimi*. At birth their bodies fresh from their first womb are consecrated with water from forest vines; they learn what water can tell them of the "other world" when they catch their reflection in a quiet stream or gently touch their "other" foot at its surface. And again they will soon see, if they have not already, youths washing the *molimo* trumpet with water and giving it water to drink just as they give it fire to eat. Air they know as the breath of life; they recognize its curative power when used to create song or to invoke the presence of the elephant or leopard through the trumpet. They cannot move, eat, or breathe without being conscious of one or all of these symbols, and all are treated with respect, consciously recognized as integral parts of the ultimate giver of life, the forest.

In their progress from one womb into yet another, the children have already touched the essence of the even greater sphere that is *ndura*. After all, they are not merely expected to light a fire before the hunters set out. Nor are they aware only that for some obscure reason the fire has to be lit by them *because* they are children, at the foot of a certain kind of tree, on the trail or in the direction that the hunters will take, so that they must pass it. They know it must be kindled in a special way, using special leaves, so that smoke will be given off. The smoke drifts up through the leafy canopy, disappearing into the depths of the forest. It also swathes the hunters as they pass by. If it is rising too abruptly to cross the path, the hunters casually reach out their hands as they pass, and bring the smoke to them as though washing themselves with it. Mothers with infants at their breasts anoint their suckling babies as well as themselves. It may be done quietly, or the words, Mother Forest, Father Forest, may be sung or shouted with joy. There is plainly more here than smoke, more than the fire that makes the smoke, and more than the wood that makes the fire. There is the forest that is the source of all these things.

That is how Mbuti elaborate when discussing among themselves or with an inquiring youth the stories the oldest Mbuti tell the youngest Mbuti. For the elders, like the children, if not absolutely pure are among the purest. Purity is a position proper, they say, to the other world, but held to its greatest extent possible among mortals by those closest to death, the infants and the aged. Through these stories the children in the *bopi* will have come to realize that all living things, even trees, seem to die. But whereas you can see a firm, green shoot coming out of the body of a dead, fallen tree, who has seen a child born from an old dead woman or a calf from a dead elephant? Mbuti tell the story of the origin of death in a number of ways, all centering on the concept of what we might call original sin. But the story most often told to the children and among children is of how Mbuti were immortal until one killed his brother antelope. Since then, Mbuti too have been condemned to die, just as they brought death to the antelope. And they will continue to die until they can learn not to kill.

As they grow from the age of four to eight or thereabouts (for age to the Mbuti is a matter of personality, skill, and size, among other things, not of mere years) Mbuti children join in the *bopi* pastimes with increasingly active intelligence. Their power of reason develops. They have been with their mothers since infancy, both on the hunt and while they have been off with other women, gathering. Even when being carried it was on the hip, not on the back, so every child had ready access to the breast and a full view of the adult world ahead of it, as seen by its mother. It has begun to make rational judgments about that world and its mother's manner of dealing with it. For both girl and boy children it is the same. Both have learned more than the rudiments of adult economic activity, and they have become increasingly aware that certain activities lie more within the sphere of men and others within the sphere of women, though none are totally exclusive.

During the second four years children add intellectual exploration to physical exploration. They begin to indulge in storytelling, perhaps in imitation of a great storyteller among the adults. But the stories are their own. They draw from their own experience, merely following the model rather than the words of the adult storyteller, who draws on the day's activities, comparing them with other days, other peoples, other activities; comparing the human world with the animal world, the forest with the nonforest, and occasionally passing indirect judgments in terms of *ekimi* and *akami*. The bulk of the children's attention is focused on *bopi* activities, therefore confined primarily to their own age group, which indeed is to become one of their major spheres throughout life. But they also investigate the world of youths, adults, and elders, pooling their observations and ideas with other children of their own age. But still without any distinction according to gender.

Through increasing association with youths, children acquire a different perspective on sexual activity, which boys explore with the girls in the *bopi*. A boy does not exclude other boys, nor does his girl friend exclude other girls: whatever awareness there is of this new emotion is shared, as everything should be, between age-mates regardless of gender. They explore each other's bodies without discrimination and will even imitate the act of copulation with equal lack of discrimination, in the form of dance.

Around the age of eight or nine, perhaps as late as eleven, boy children enter the villagers' *nkumbi* initiation rite. A mere three months later they emerge as adults in village eyes, but as youths in Mbuti eyes. The Mbuti, who have no formal initiation of boys, find it useful to enter the village ritual for a number of complex reasons. For the village farmers the *nkumbi* ritual is of paramount importance in bringing about effective relationships between potentially hostile groups. Within the forest world of the Mbuti it is merely an easy way of marking a boy's rather uncertain transition from childhood to youth. While it has much to teach the village boys, with its explicit sex instruction and moral teaching and by the consecration of the individual to the way of the ancestors and to village society at large, it has nothing to teach the Mbuti about forest life. He has already learned most of what he needs to know, and what remains to be learned by the Mbuti boy he will learn, with his age-mates, in youth, the next stage of life facing him.

In that stage, while all youths explore their new-found sexual potential, however, they also further develop and refine their powers of reason, which they use to temper their sexual activity. During youth, also, the Mbuti become more fully aware of that all-embracing and all-nourishing sphere, *ndura*, or "forestness." Until perhaps in later youth a male kills his first animal on the hunt, he retains a lingering trace of the purity of childhood, so that while his powers of reason place him with the rest of his fellow youths, male and female, in the role of judge, he is also sometimes called on to act in a ritual role, to purify rather than judge or punish. Everything combines to make youth a time of power, but it is political rather than spiritual power that youth wields.

Youths, insofar as they are less pure or more contaminated, are such, *not* because of their increasingly physical concern with sex, but because of their increasing proximity to the daily act of sacrilege, the hunt. If anything their sexual activity would be a purifying element, for it is related to giving rather than taking life. I mentioned that in the *bopi* there was no sexual discrimination in the sharing of love among the children to their fullest capacity. That capacity was limited by their general immaturity: what is remarkable is that the same lack of discrimination persists during youth. Yet not once did I come across a case of homosexual intercourse, although the existence of names for both male and female homosexuality suggests that it may exist. I came across one case of bestiality (a male youth and a female goat) which was openly acknowledged and respected to the extent that neither the boy nor the goat suffered any disability except that they were confined to the village. The grounds for their exclusion from the forest were not uncleanliness or impurity; there was no taint of immorality, merely the practical observation that the boy's "wife" did not know how to hunt and would quickly die if she came with him back to the forest. The boy, torn between two loyalties, finally chose the forest; he pensioned his goat-wife off by presenting her to a villager whom he knew would cherish her and keep her well and alive, since the villager thought he was acquiring enormous control over the forest, the goat being well impregnated with the sperm of the forest people. That boy then married an Mbuti girl with no difficulty; he was back in the center of the forest sphere and the goat was no longer part of the "here and now." I mention the incident because it shows a great deal about the Mbuti concept of love, even when carried into the physical act of sex. Even when so carried, the two things, sex and love, remain distinct. It might well be for similarly pragmatic reasons that there is no recorded instance of male or female homosexuality; one's "wife" or "husband" simply would not know how to gather or hunt.

Homosexuality is not the point, however, any more than is bestiality. The point is that even when boys and girls discover the ecstasy of sex, and for whatever reasons confine it to a heterosexual relationship, they continue to love each other regardless of shared gender and even carry *something* of the physical act into their relationship, as though almost regretful of being separated from age-mates of their own gender by this new phenomenon. I cannot speak for the girls, though I have seen and heard enough similar behavior among them to convince me there is not likely to be much difference, but the male youths delight in bodily contact throughout youth. It becomes interspersed with more formal spacing as serious heterosexual courtship begins, but it continues even into early married life. Male youths tend to sleep together, either in the open around a fire, or in a hut built by one of them and used by all. They sleep in a glorious bundle of young life, full of warmth and full of love. There is little sexual fondling, and what there is is done more in the form of a joke than to give any sexual pleasure. However, there is no doubt that the close hugging is for more than mere warmth, necessary though that is on any night in the rain forest. And there is no doubt that a measure of physical sexual relief, or satisfaction, is achieved in this way, with or without ejaculation. An occasional muttered comment about ejaculation may be made by an individual to himself, much as I might mutter if my shoelace broke while I was walking along a crowded street. Messy or bothersome to the individual, it is of little significance to anyone else. What *is* significant is that the growing separation of the sexes for the physical act of copulation, augmented by the growing division of the sexes by allocation of labor, is being countered, in a very real sense, and love is being shared to the point that even if homosexual intercourse did take place I doubt that it would add anything to the intensity of the relationship, except possibly for that one brief moment. The sacrifice of the pleasure of that moment, somehow, seems to make the relationship all the stronger.

By the time they enter adolescence and youth (between the ages of eight and eleven), Mbuti children have learned the major values that militate against aggressivity and violence and help forge them into full social being. They carry these values with them throughout life, they do *not* put away such childish things. The value of security they learn, I believe, in the womb of birth, and this value is reinforced as they move from womb to womb during the life cycle. It is perhaps primarily a territorial value at first, and is then broadened to encompass all areas of life. Dependence is learned at the mother's breast, and we have seen how this value also is systematically enlarged until children regard the entire hunting band as their "family." The principle at work here is clearly kinship. Interdependence follows naturally as children begin to interact in a more systematic and controlled way with others, perceiving the mutual interdependence of kin, of those within their own age group and within other age groups, and finally the economic, political, and spiritual interdependence between all four age groups. Coordination and cooperation begin as they learn to coordinate their own movements with those of the mother's body and become increasingly sophisticated in their various pastimes, their dancing, their attempts to imitate adult activities, and in their gradual imitation of and participation in the highly complex system of Mbuti song. And of course the values of *ekimi* and *akami* are similarly learned, surely and painlessly, not by indoctrination, but by observation of the positive consequences of the one and the negative consequences of the other.

At first this is all felt rather than reasoned, but on entry into youth the intellect integrates the observable order of things into an integrated, rational, logical whole. During youth the Mbuti become aware of the meaning of gender and sex. They are already familiar with both, but now more and more they accompany their respective parents, male youths helping their fathers on the hunt, female youths helping their mothers. This way they begin to sense man's greater proximity to *akami* as the taker of life, and woman's greater proximity to *ekimi* as the giver of life. This gradually leads them to an awareness of the distance that is growing between them, as *apua'i* of different gender, just as physiological differentiation is beginning to lead them to a fuller awareness of both sex and gender. As youths they play a prominent part in various ritualizations of these differences. One is the tug-of-war between men and women which neither side must win. To achieve this goal, if the men are winning, one will pull his bark cloth up tight, in the manner of women, and cross over to the women's side and pull with them, shouting encouragement in a high falsetto. Women similarly reverse roles, and in so doing they take pains to ridicule their stereotype of the opposite sex. Ultimately all are laughing so hard at each other's antics that they all let go of the vine they are tugging and collapse on the ground in hysterics. During the honey season there is a honey-bee dance, with males playing their real-life role as honey hunters, and women playing the role of the bees, the givers of honey. Here the bee/women are clearly on the winning side, and the dance ritualizes the potential of conflict between men and women.

There are two prime festivals of youth, the *molimo madé* and the *elima*. The *molimo madé* is the sacred trumpet in its manifestation as elephant, the destroyer of the forest. It is associated with *akami*, and it is effectively the exclusive prerogative of the male youths to invoke the *molimo madé* whenever adults or others, but usually adults, bring *akami* into the camp. Bad hunting, illicit flirtations, and marital squabbles are the most usual causes, and it is the youths who determine for all, in this way, just how *akami* is defined at that moment, what is "right" and what it "wrong." The *molimo madé* is thus the manifestation of male youths' all-important jural role in Mbuti society. They invoke the trumpet consciously, by choice, when they and they alone see fit. Children, adults, and elders can do nothing but submit to its rampage as it wreaks destruction in the camp.

By contrast the *elima* is effectively in the hands of the girls; it is a festival of *ekimi*, and it is brought on, not by choice, but by the first appearance of menstrual blood in one or more of the female youths. This is an event that is met with supreme joy, for it means that the girl now has the potential of becoming a woman, which for them means becoming a mother. Like the *molimo madé*, the *elima* festival incorporates all the prime symbols in ritual usage. It is also a form of ritualization of conflict, but between the sexes rather than between different age groups. The boys have to be beaten by the girls before they can enter the *elima* house, and even then they still have to fight their way through a barricade of well-armed and determined adult women. It then develops into a festival of courtship, often resulting in betrothal and, perhaps a few years later, in marriage. Upon marriage both boy and girl leave youth and become adults.

Adulthood is seen as a time of *akami*, of dispute and anxiety, but mostly so for the men. It is here that conflict between the sexes is most likely to flare up, and while ridicule, ostracism, or simple relocation to another camp/sphere are usually more than adequate as conflict resolution mechanisms, the adults are not content to leave it at that. *Their* periodic festival is *ekokoméa*, a transvestite dance performed whenever the mood seizes them, sometimes just for fun but more often when conflict is in the offing. All the men dress as women, and all the women as men, and both ridicule the opposite sex mercilessly. No holds are barred, and Mbuti imagination seems unlimited. Once again, however, while both male and female pride suffer a little, no hurt is intended and no offense taken, but the lesson is learned. This festival, like the tug-of-war, comes to an end when laughter makes it impossible to continue, and participants and spectators alike, young and old, male and female, roll on the ground clutching their sides with laughter, beating themselves to help catch breath for more laughter, tears rolling down their cheeks. But earth, fire, and water play no part, and the breath of life is used only to voice raucous and bawdy song. Adulthood is the most secular time of life, the furthest removed from Spirit. It is a time of work. Even during the *molimo mangbo*, the greatest festival of all, it is the "work" of adults, males mostly, to sing the *molimo* songs every night, from dusk to dawn, for a month or more; and then go off and do a day's hunting. Even then their song alone is impotent. It must be transformed by the youths who alone can handle the sacred trumpet, and who echo the song through the trumpet and deep into the forest. For women, adulthood is not quite as difficult as for men, though they too are tainted by *akami*. The saving grace is that at the beginning of adulthood both are still close to their youth, and for the first few years sometimes revert to youthful company and even youthful roles. At the other end they are growing closer to elderhood, which leads directly into the ultimate *ekimi* of death.

If the final years are golden in any society, it most surely is so with the Mbuti. This is not just because old age affords relief from the *akami* of adulthood, but rather because of the active and vital role the elders play in this tightly integrated society. When a woman is beyond childbearing, a man beyond the adult male work of hunting, in other words when they are both in a sense sexless, as the terminology (*tata*) implies, they become elders. Removed from all major sources of conflict, the elders act as mediators and arbiters. They guard the camp when the hunt is away and spend much of their time playing with children, passing on their wisdom through such play as well as in their role of storytellers. It is truly a joining of the sacred, those coming from the *ekimi* of the other world and those returning to it. Given the logical progression of the life cycle, it is no wonder that the Mbuti do not fear death, for how can that final or, rather, ultimate stage be anything but even more complete, full, and rich? And how fitting that the songs of the *molimo mangbo*, celebrating death, should be songs of joy.

With the Mbuti we see the concept of family as a constantly expanding universe, beginning with the nuclear family and ultimately embracing the whole forest, the entire extent of their experience at any moment. In my case the concept of family was something very different, and although it did indeed also act as a model and was an important part of my training for adult life, it was not only far less functional in this respect, in some ways it was positively dysfunctional. For one thing, World War II and subsequent developments changed the social context so dramatically that the adult life for which I was being trained was no longer possible by the time I was ready for it. The system was too rigid and inflexible and did not allow for such changes. By the time I reached adulthood my childhood was a kind of isolated museum piece; but whereas I can walk out of a museum and leave the fascinating antiquities and exotica behind me, I can never walk away from my childhood. It will be with me, influencing everything I do, until the day I die. At best I can only try to modify its influence.

The first point of departure from the Mbuti is that I know nothing about how or where I was conceived. However, in discussions with my parents a half century later, I did learn two significant things. One was that they were ignorant of any form of contraception and assumed that sexual intercourse would inevitably result in childbirth. In fact, my mother was quite upset when in the course of our discussions she learned that the two of them could have enjoyed a full sexual relationship without having a correspondingly enormous family. She even had a hazy notion that twins were the result of an act of sexual intercourse during pregnancy. However incomprehensible this kind of ignorance of the facts of life may seem in today's enlightened, pill-filled world, at the age of fifty I suddenly realized that I had been intended, I had been wanted, just as every Mbuti child is intended and wanted. I would like to think that for my parents the quality of those two acts of intercourse, filled with the intent and longing of which my brother and I were the results, made up for what they lost in quantity.

As a child, of course, I was unaware of all of this, at least in rational terms. But then, childhood is a time for feeling, for learning about life through the senses rather than reason, and I always *knew* I was wanted and always would be wanted, however much other childhood experiences seemed to indicate that I was little more than a nuisance. The most serious defect in my birth was a seemingly trivial detail, but it involved the important principle of territoriality and was to assume major proportions. Even in our Western industrial world, territoriality is a potent social force and one we all too often fail to recognize.

It emerged from those rather tardy dialogues with my mother that I *should* have been born in Scotland. There had already been severe criticism because my brother had been born in England, where my father had moved, finding it easier to make money there than in Scotland. With me, my parents intended to rectify the error and so mollify the powerful Scottish relatives. Unfortunately, my mother miscalculated and I emerged in Harrow, a genteel but very English place just outside London. As any anthropologist could have predicted, this had serious political consequences and was a major and enduring source of conflict within my family. It was also evidence of the importance, at least in those days and to my family, of the principle of territoriality. My mother was Irish and Episcopalian. Neither of these facts sat well with my father's Scottish Presbyterian kin. Even though my brother and I were both born in England, an even worse fate than being born in Ireland, at least we were both baptized as Presbyterian; but had my mother made it across the border it would almost certainly have led to a much more harmonious relationship between the families. As it was, from the earliest days that I can remember to the day that I took my mother's body back from Virginia to Scotland, to bury her beside my father in the family grave looking across the Clyde to Ben Lomond, there was constant and often bitter conflict. And I was caught in the middle.

Whereas the Mbuti can talk confidently of their life even in the womb and recite events that took place during those nine months as though they had witnessed them, my actual recollections go back no further than to when I was three years old. Even then they do not involve my mother or my father or my brother or our home. I have a hazy but fond recollection of a West Indian nanny. My mother was not allowed to nurse me because of some alleged health hazard, and I have *no* recollections of her at this time. I do not remember the first nanny/nurse into whose arms I was thrust, because she was fired during my first year for keeping me quiet by feeding me with milk well dosed with forbidden sugar. The West Indian nanny I remember so well solved the problem of keeping me quiet by feeding me with teaspoons of some liquor. I also vaguely remember suckling at her huge breasts, or at least being held close to them and feeling happy in their warmth, a closeness that I cannot for the life of me recall having had with my mother until I was five or six years old, although I probably did. Then, when I cried, my mother would pick me up and, it seemed, try to smother me in her embrace. I felt much safer with my nanny. But *that* nanny was also fired, a terrible day I remember well, because my mother, on one of her periodic personal house inspections, discovered an excessive quantity of empty bottles under nanny's bed.

I remember quite a succession of nannies, mostly French or German, in those early days. The last two were distinctively German. Irene Fritzel, a true blonde Aryan, regaled my tender ears with exciting stories of how men gave women babies by urinating in their mouths. She had many such stories, which I remember much more vividly than my mother's occasional bedtime stories, and I treasured them all as a confidence from the adult world from which I was otherwise so securely isolated and of which I was so plainly ignorant. Unfortunately, Irene was a Nazi and did not last longer than two years. I protested her departure loudly and recounted some of the stories she had told me as evidence of what a good nanny she was.

My father, who up to this point had been a shadowy figure, was a powerful man who powerfully expressed his opinions. He had fought in the First World War, in the Royal Artillery, and was slow to forget the horrors he had seen. Irene was to go, not because of her storytelling, nor even because she was a Nazi, but because she was German. He preferred the French nannies. But I evidently insisted on another German nanny; I had begun to learn the language and loved its sound. The last French nanny I had was far too flighty for my taste, and I found French a nasty little language that made me purse my mouth. With German I could be gutteral and spit, both of which I thought were very adult characteristics. My mother took my side, so at the very moment that my father became a reality I was separated from him and made to realize that *ema* and *eba* were two very different people indeed, and that my bread was very definitely buttered on one side and not the other. I began to take my father's differences with my mother as a kind of weakness, and he begins to fade from my memory again.

So my last nanny came to me, a lovely German woman from Wipperfurth, Helen Feldman. She was a Roman Catholic, which intrigued me; I had never heard of them and promptly wanted to become one, Helen was so perfect. She told me no "stork" stories, but she did introduce me to that remarkable storybook character, Peter Strubel, a monstrous boy who delighted in tormenting animals and humans alike. She also introduced me by mail to her younger brother Hans, who was an active member of the Hitler Youth. He used to send me swastika armbands and other paraphernalia that I learned were better kept well concealed. What a way to lose one's innocence. But then came the Munich crisis and Hans sent Helen a letter ordering her to come home at once. My tears were of no avail. Helen left; I lost the last of a succession of mothers and began, at the age of twelve, to know the mother who so undiplomatically gave birth to me in England. Only then did I really begin to know my parents and to exchange the fullness of love with them, to feel secure with them, trusting and understanding. But by then it was beginning to be more of a reasoned relationship than a felt one and it was filled with resentment at the lack of proximity. The *feeling* of love did not develop and begin to truly flourish for another quarter of a century. Reason stood between us. Just at the time when Mbuti boys become youths and live in their communal *endu*, not separated from their plurality (ever-growing) of mothers and fathers because that felt trust and love was already invincibly established through feeling, just at the time that they begin to rationalize this physical separation without in any way weakening the all-important bond of deep affection, my affective life was snatched away from me and I began to be aware of and resent being bound tighter and tighter to the proverbial feminine apron strings. Two more of the principles of social organization, kinship and sex/gender, were already working in very different ways, systematically and according to a clearly established social structure.

My mother ran our household with magnificent efficiency, and that became for me part of the model of motherhood. My father, while always gentle and kind, was equally always distant. He was much closer to my brother, whom I remember mainly because I always wanted to get to know him but never really did. Like my father, he was difficult to find. We had separate nurseries for one thing, and he was very protective of his and did not often admit me unless he wanted to use me for some subversive purpose. We didn't even share the same nannies; he was four years older and had effectively disposed of his to their mutual satisfaction. So in our own home we were separated by both territory and kinship as well as age. Our nurseries became our fortresses. Even when on holiday in Scotland, staying in hotels or rented houses, we never shared the same bedroom. Only once did we do so because of some construction or redecorating going on at home. I was about six years old, he was ten. It was a large room and had two beds, but after "lights out" the opportunity to meet my brother was so irresistible that I leaped into bed with him. So that we would not be overheard we got well under the covers and were having a wonderful conversation when my mother discovered us. Both she and my father reacted in what was to me a totally incomprehensible and violent way, each taking sides as to who was to blame (for wanting to get to know his brother). He

and I never shared the same room again. The barrier established by the geography of our home was confirmed by the
disparity in our ages, our exclusive parental affiliations, and
my ambivalence and ignorance about sexuality.

My fondest and most vivid recollection of my solitary sibling is of when he shot at me with a small-caliber rifle when
I was about nine years old, hitting me on the little finger of
the right hand. I was flattered by the attention this brought me
and cherished the wound for quite a time. On another occasion
he invited me to his nursery and asked me to give a message
to one of the Irish maids, a parlor maid named Bridgit, summoning *her* to his nursery. She stayed there for some time. I
repeated the negotiations on several occasions, wondering why
my mediation was needed, but happy to be of use. But one
day, when I was in the morning room where my mother was
sewing, Bridgit came storming in, her red hair awry, looking
definitely disturbed. She said something about the messages
and referred to Ian as "a daft thing" and burst into tears. My
mother was understandably interested, and with a naivety that
was to become persistent, I told her all and that was the end
of Bridgit. I never liked her much anyway, and she is probably
responsible for my continued distrust of redheads.

I preferred Nellie the cook, also Irish, who used to allow
me into the kitchen when I got bored with my nursery or my
nanny. That was permissible, but the scullery was a forbidden
place and I was roundly spanked for playing there one day
with the gardener, who used to eat his meals there except for
the rare occasions on which Nellie would invite *him* into the
kitchen. Territory, age, and sex all seemed to be linked in a
conspiracy to make life difficult. But it was systematic, and it
was all linked to status, if only I had been aware of it, through
the terms of address that were mandatory. Even though the
servants were for me my real "family," I was never allowed
to address the gardener by name. Indeed, I never knew his
name until I was an adult; I doubt if I ever heard it because we
all simply called him "Gardener." When we had a chauffeur
he was addressed as "Mr. Arnold." Flighty young Bridgit
(and other young parlor maids) I was to address by first name,
a condescension indicative of their inferiority. The cook was
to be addressed, like the gardener, as "Cook," except for Nellie,

whom, because of the length of time she had been with the family, I could call "Nellie" unless guests were present. But she was eventually "retired" and packed off back to Ireland because she, like so many others, took to the bottle. To one and all, even to my parents and brother when they were referring to me while speaking to the servants, I was "Master Colin" until my twenty-first birthday, when for some reason I became "*Mister* Colin." My social horizons, far from drawing us all together, as with the Mbuti, seemed to be splitting us apart at every level.

So much for the immediate *endu* of my childhood, but what of other human relationships? The only relatives of my father ever to visit and actually stay in the house were his two sisters, both spinsters, and they always visited separately except for one truly awful Christmas when they both came. It was the only occasion when I saw my mother roundly defeated in her own home. She was reduced to tears and left for Canada shortly afterward and stayed away for three months, with the aunts taking it in turns to "manage" the household. The other Scottish relatives never visited except for cranky old Cousin Wallace who always stayed in a nearby hotel at Father's expense and lived it up that way about once every two years. He was enormously wealthy and totally stingy. When on holiday in Scotland, if my father was with us, we used to visit the rest of the family, but only for brief teatime visits. Even then their hostility toward my mother was unconcealed and we certainly never stayed with them.

My mother's Irish relatives also used to visit from a distance, so to speak, like Cousin Wallace, staying in hotels. But I noticed that *they* always paid their own way. I can only remember my Irish grandmother actually staying in the house, and one cousin from the part of her family that had emigrated to Canada. With particular affection, in retrospect, on the Irish side of my family I remember an uncle of my mother. He was a great musician and a fine organist from near Dublin. His wife Nancy always wore large straw hats, and unaccountably thoroughly enjoyed our childish pranks, even when my brother set fire to one of those amazing creations while she was wearing it. It was my first real recognition of two important anthropological institutions known formally as "the joking relationship" and "alternate generation affection." I realized I felt much closer to the really old folks, including Nellie, and could be much more open and free and happy with them, which realization served to put my parents at an even greater distance, as troublesome disciplinarians. From then onward I gravitated immediately to that distant generation whenever opportunity arose. I wish I could, like any Mbuti, have known them better and seen more of them; I would have been a lot wiser a lot sooner. The exclusive structure of our household and "family" life effectively curtailed such opportunities, and my social horizons remained limited to areas where the chance to explore people was minimal. In my nursery I could only explore *things*, using my imagination as best I could to turn them into people.

My Great-uncle Willie was the last of that generation to survive on my father's side of the family, still living on what was left of the family land in the Rule Valley in Scotland. Visits there were rare but very special. He would take me down by the Rule Water and make me feel that I belonged to a *place*, a totally new experience for me. It became my *endu*, *bopi*, *apa*, and *ndura* without my knowing it. And despite the friction between my Scottish family and my mother, they always made me feel that I also belonged to a family in the widest, fullest, and richest sense. The Irish kin were fun, but somehow in those days I did not consider them as kin, perhaps because I was not taken to Ireland until much later. Slowly but surely I became "Scottish" despite continued residence in England, and although I never really lived there, except for extended vacations, Scotland still exerts a powerful hold over me. For me, at least, all of this is a dynamic example of how either proximity or territoriality can supersede even kinship, and of how kinship can become dysfunctional when one side of a family competes against the other. I was clearly becoming a pawn in a power struggle between the Scots and the Irish, and perhaps that, rather than money, was the reason that my parents continued to live in England.

If my family horizons were limited and hardly satisfying, my relations with nonkin were equally unsatisfying, though informative. I had "friends" at school, of course, but those I was allowed to bring home, or whose homes I was permitted to visit, were carefully screened and selected and not always to my liking. The operative word was "proper." In particular I remember a boy from Chile, who in school was the best of friends, a real kindred spirit. We talked about good things, we liked to work together, and even though only ten or eleven years old we used to discuss our work earnestly. We also discussed art and religion. But evidently Chile was not a "proper" place to come from. Also, he had jet black hair cut in a fringe, his eyes were slightly slanted, and his skin was an olive color. So that was the end of that as far as ever visiting each other's homes went. Our friendship became clandestine; I don't think it ever soured, however. Out of mutual respect, and perhaps even affection, we returned to our separate little desks, separate corners of the schoolyard, and we each felt foreign, as indeed we were.

Not far away, at the same time, lived a wealthy Hindu family; the father ran some kind of business in England. The mother and my mother worked as volunteers in the same hospital, as wealthy people were wont to do, regardless of qualifications. The boy had private tutors (I can see why now) but I was allowed to visit him when Mrs. Gupta held a meeting of the volunteers at her home and my mother would bring me along. But she stopped bringing me as soon as I started asking for the Indian boy to come and visit *us*. The inference, of course, is that my parents were racists. At one time I thought they were, and in a restricted sense I suppose they were, but not with the usual connotations. The Mbuti taught me otherwise: practically never do they invite villagers into their forest home, *not* because the villagers are inferior, dirty, or whatever else racists think about anyone who is not like them, but because the relationship would be one of *akami*. Perhaps I would have understood better and been less harsh in the things I thought about my parents, if I had translated "improper" as "*akami*," and had realized that it was the relationship that gave rise to concern, not the country or origin and certainly not the quality of the human being I had chosen as a friend. But that can be a dangerous rationalization.

I discovered that I had a lot of proper acquaintances and very few friends. Tradesmen and delivery boys belonged to an exciting world quite unknown to me, but to them I always remained "Master Colin," so I gradually accepted that distance as natural, proper, and inevitable. My best contact with the outside world was when gypsies came and camped in the fields nearby, and with other gypsies sold flowers and vegetables in the small town where my mother used to take me on her shopping expeditions. But the stories they told of the outside world were quite unbelievable; there seemed to be no restraints, nothing was improper, and they had a wonderful indifference to all authority. Naturally, I was ordered to stay away from them and warned that they kidnapped little boys. I immediately asked them to kidnap me, but they refused; not, I imagine, because I was improper, but because they knew of the *akami* that would follow.

A lot can be learned from the games and pastimes that children indulge in. For instance, I cannot for the life of me remember ever voluntarily playing any competitive games. As much as I wanted to know a wider world, I dreaded children's parties where such games were absolutely compulsory. In light of the uncertainty and unpredictability and confusion of the isolated world I *did* know, it is not really surprising that my pastimes were remarkably suicidal. If there was a cliff to climb I would at least make the attempt, but never, that I can remember, with the thought of getting to the top. Several times I had to be rescued from some dangerous perch from which I could go neither up nor down; heights terrified me if I could see in either direction. Trees, of course, were made for climbing, as there was no sensation of height when surrounded by thick foliage. I used to love it when two trees were close enough near the top for me to jump from one to the other in the bland rather than blind conviction that the lower branches would break my fall. I really should have been born an Mbuti. Rooftops were irresistible, only dangerous when you got too close to the edge and could see down. Ruined castles and deserted homes were best explored alone; acquaintances spoiled the fun by making them all too proper. There were only two friends with whom I could share my play life, and they were both what were called "tomgirls." They shrank from nothing until one of them asked me if I knew what boys did to girls in deserted homes, and all I could think of was urinating. I was then made aware that urinating, or whatever boys *did* do to girls, was improper.

What I was learning from this childhood experience is plain enough in some respects. If I was looking for security, territory was of paramount importance. At home my nursery was the safest place, for even my mother did not visit there all that often. My bedroom was next, but much more subject to maternal invasion. Nellie's kitchen ranked third. The parts of the house where my parents, brother, or servants lived were all barred to me. Outside the home the Rule Valley took first place, and I frequently went there in my imagination. Trees and deserted homes came next, then probably the cliffs and rooftops. No wonder one of my childhood fantasies was to become a reclusive monk. The isolation was remarkable, and school only helped to reinforce it while beginning to train my awakening intellect to accept such isolation. First there was a Montessori school where I learned French poetry and French songs, how to play with strange objects, none of which I had in my nursery, and where I also learned that it was easier to mug girls than boys and that some manifestation of physical violence was an absolute requisite for survival. I myself was beaten in my first week or two for inquiring why a certain mistress painted her fingernails red. I was removed from school when not too long afterward I got my revenge by running very fast toward her and butting her in the stomach with my head. I can remember the blank expression on her face, and the satisfaction I felt.

When I was about eight I was sent to my first prep school, where I was introduced to Latin, mathematics, more French, a few other academic subjects, but most of all to still more violence. My brother was already quite senior in the school when I arrived as a "new boy." In the very first week I was grabbed by other senior boys and brought into their classroom where my hand was held in the sunlight while my brother (I *think* against his inclination, basically he too was nonviolent) held a magnifying glass over it until my skin began to smoke. It was the same hand whose little finger he later wounded with his rifle. I do not think I learned anything useful in that school except how to lie with only moderate success, how to cheat, and how to have zero confidence in adults and peers alike. It was another good lesson in the value of isolation, and my own personal survival became very important to me. Being a boys' school it provided no opportunity for getting to know any girls, who remained muggable objects in my estimation, except for my two tomgirl acquaintances.

After a number of rather violent encounters there, I was removed and placed in a much better school. By then I must have been ten or eleven, and I began to learn and study with enthusiasm. Extracurricular activities still included those abominable dancing lessons that began at Montessori, and my training for a future life as a gentleman was furthered by other lessons in etiquette. At least there was also some academic substance, but little encouragement was given to *imaginative* thought. There was an epidemic of diphtheria and one of the most popular teachers, Mr. Perry, died. It was my first brush with death and I was curious to know more. So were others, but we were all assembled and told that this was what would happen if we played around drains and sewers. I wondered at this, as I had never seen Mr. Perry playing around drains and sewers, but I was merely told, when I voiced my suspicion that something was being concealed from us, that he had "gone away" (as though he had been dismissed for improper behavior) and "would not be back." We were all permitted, however, to wear black armbands for one week to celebrate the event. I got the distinct impression that if I did what I was told without thinking, I would live, and if I didn't, I wouldn't. There were no options. But it *was* systematic; the isolation was now becoming, at an appropriate age, not only geographical, familial, economic, social, and physical, it was also becoming intellectual.

Violence at this school was more carefully directed into contact sports, such as football, boxing, and cricket, the last of which for me very much a contact sport since I was frequently hit by that singularly hard leather ball while doing my best to avoid it. My dislike of contact sports was intense. Since there were no girls to mug and I was prudent enough not to attack other boys, for lack of opportunity, perhaps, I became increasingly nonviolent. That was frowned upon. I was so bad at cricket that no team wanted me on its side, so I opted to swim as my compulsory summer sport, but refused to compete. One happy winter I was hit in the eye by a football aimed directly at me by a master from South Africa who, like my parents, thought that my friendship with the boy from Chile was improper. I was stunned, so did not cry and was acclaimed as being brave. I was awarded the school colors and exempted from playing football again. This isolated me still further from the other boys who both ranked themselves and were ranked by the school according to their competitive spirit rather than their academic prowess. My Chilean friend and I clung to the notion that we could win respect by doing well at our studies, and so we both passed our exams with ease but failed totally at winning respect.

Some of the masters, two in particular, were zealous young missionaries who ran holiday camps for Christian boys. Thanks to them I now began to encounter, unknowingly, the ultimate isolation—spiritual. No mention was ever made of any religion other than Christianity, and it was assumed that we were all Episcopalian—but I had been baptized Presbyterian. Since the only thing that made church bearable to me was the occasionally splendid music, I began to study the organ. I used to practice in the church when it was empty of all humanity, and in a bumbling amateur way I attempted to find some spirit in that cold, stark, joyless building. At least I believed in what I was doing, but when I tried to discuss this in a class on religious studies, I was told that just "going" to church was religion enough for me, that I was far too young to think about things like "spirit." An Mbuti boy of my age would already have invoked the Supreme Spirit as a child at the hunting fire, and would now be singing his heart and soul out to the forest, singing into the *molimo* trumpet, restoring *ekimi* and banishing all adult-induced *akami*. I was not growing up very fast, by comparison.

If nobody seemed anxious to teach me about that unknown, mysterious, and wonderful entity I now call Spirit, at least from my succession of nannies and from the Irish household staff I amassed quite a wealth of folklore involving sylvan sprites, leprechauns, pixies, demons, banshees, headless ghosts, and even ancestral spirits, most of whom, I was told, had been massacred by the English. My Great-uncle Willie encouraged me in my struggling belief in Spirit, but more by taking me on walks than by talking. My father, who practically never talked to me, began to do the same thing. But it was when Great-uncle Willie, his eyebrows blowing in the breeze, walked me through the ancestral Rule Valley that I felt strangely at home in a place where I had never lived. He would just sit down and look at the Rule Water and listen to it, and I would do the same and know that with all our massacred ancestors we both belonged to that place and that it filled us with a strange kind of power. It was something like the feeling I got when playing the organ in an empty church. But at school my claim that this surely had something to do with "religion" was held up as an example of the irreligious. And when in an effort to discover just what was so "religious" about church-going, I tried to reconcile what the Presbyterian minister said about hell fire with what the Episcopalian vicar said about charity and forgiveness, and both with what was daily practiced at schoool, I met with active hostility.

The most encouragement I was given to grow and become, other than from those walks through the Scottish countryside, was from a wild old friend of my father, Arthur Poyser. He was organist at Perth Cathedral, and he often brought a fine boy's choir to our house to sing while he accompanied them. He was constantly telling ghost stories about the cathedrals in which he had played, and he too had a penchant for playing all alone, preferably in the middle of the night. That warmed me to him. But most of all, he was utterly irreligious as that had been defined for me. He was constantly embroiled in battle with clerics of every denomination, his whole life was music and music was the only thing that made him enter a church. He filled his churches with Spirit, and he encouraged me to try to do the same. But it was a secret we never divulged. His was the only assurance I had, in my childhood, that church had anything to do with religion, and that religion had anything to do with living.

In comparing the Mbuti childhood with my own a whole host of differences emerge, many of them owing mainly to the obvious difference in the entire context. More significant are some of the similarities that exist despite the context, but which somehow lead in different directions. The most striking difference is in the end product, the child on the verge of adolescence. Mbuti children become something quite different from what I became. All their potentialities have been explored and developed to the limit; not just their bodies, but their senses of sight, smell, touch, and hearing have all been nurtured as instruments of learning and communication. My physical development was measured by the number of inches I grew each year, the number of pounds I weighed, and my shoe size. Qualitatively, my physical growth was measured by brute strength in the gym, aggressivity on the sports field, and violence in the boxing ring. Had an Mbuti written my report card it might have said "Colin is not much good at making other boys' noses bleed, but he has a great gift for telling blindfolded whether the person next to him is a Chilean boy or a South African man by their respective body odors." And they did smell differently. And that report card would probably also have added that I made up for my refusal to accept the dogma delivered to us in religious studies by my ability to detect the presence of Spirit, even in a church filled with smelly people, in the quality of the music. I like to think it might also have said that my resistance to nonrational authority was tempered by my ability to sense order and propriety when I touched the trunk of a sturdy oak tree; and that my parents need not despair of my lack of appreciation of home and family because I could see them all as mine when I looked into my reflection in that shimmering stream that ran through the Rule Valley. What a school that would have been, to have written a report like *that*. But those other physical senses were not what was considered under the rubric of "physical development," and while that section of my real-life report card grudgingly admitted that I had grown nearly two inches, this indication of success was offset by lengthy criticism of my failure to do well in competitive sports, hints that I was a coward and afraid to use my body, and by what was meant to be a mortifying indictment: "Colin cannot stand up in the boxing ring and take his punishment like a man. He must learn to assert himself." What a dismal failure my body was in my world; yet had I been an Mbuti, at least I would have gotten an "A" for effort.

The section dealing with my academic prowess was enlightening. Almost invariably it simply read: "He works well." Then followed the part that dealt with "general behavior," in which I was sharply criticized for being far too inquisitive, assuming that I knew better than my teachers, not choosing my friends wisely, not having any team spirit, and a regrettable tendency to "keep to himself." Here the headmaster invariably, with a deep sigh I am sure, put a heavy ink mark in the box that described my overall performance as "disappointing."

Now that report card tells us pretty clearly what was expected of a child at that school. A body that could be "built" and trained for "punishment," capable of physical violence against other bodies; a mind that was initially totally empty, but capable of uncritically absorbing the prescribed dosage of facts and dogmas and that would not do those facts and dogmas the dangerous impertinence of thinking about them; a team spirit that meant trying to beat everyone else down, either alone or in temporary alliance with others. Are those admirable qualities for any child in *any* society? Are they so very different from the qualities taught in schools today? Are they not amply manifest in the toys we buy our children at Christmas (a veritable arsenal of sophisticated weaponry is what fills the store windows and many a Christmas "stocking")? And look carefully at the many ways in which competition, rather than cooperation, is encouraged. Even the team spirit, still so loudly touted, is merely a more efficient way, through limited cooperation, to "beat" a greater number of people more efficiently. And it is a rare teacher who encourages a child to think and explore and discover for himself. Mostly teachers are far too harassed by the pupils themselves, their parents, and the school boards to do much more than protect themselves and instill the basic minimum of such facts as are permitted by a restricted curriculum. The largely economic and partly political reasons for this state of affairs, however valid, do not make that state of affairs any less dangerous.

By contrast with the Mbuti system I think we can see where the dangers lie. Again, look at the end product. The Mbuti are a people who are inherently no better or worse than any other people, subject to all the same human temptations and failings, but who even under extreme provocation are nonviolent; who even in times of deprivation share what there is without hesitation, as though there were no alternative; and who even in times of confrontation seek and find nonviolent solutions; who are able to maintain a remarkably high level of social order *without* law. Are any of those qualities, all of them learned in Mbuti childhood, unacceptable to us? That is, would they be functional or dysfunctional in our society? Are they really incompatible with our context, with the complex technological and scientific world to which we have to introduce our children? I don't see how. On the contrary, it seems that none of the Mbuti values learned in childhood would be of anything but benefit in any society where the social good is considered at least as desirable as the individual good. And even considering the skills the Mbuti learn, such as how to use the senses of smell and touch and sight and sound, their application would be different in our society, but does that make them any the less worth developing? We just take our senses for granted and leave them where they are; we do not allow them to "become," anymore than we allow the child to "become"; we impose limitations rather than encourage total growth. Mbuti children grow both outward by exploration and discovery of the total world around them, including humanity, and inward by using all their senses to learn who and what they are and where their abilities can lead them as individuals. Their physical, intellectual, social, and spiritual growth are not segmented into different compartments; they are constantly interacting until they become an indivisible whole.

We can also see where danger in our society may lie by comparing one of the most significant similarities, the function of the family as a model for adult interpersonal relationships. I too learned about family loyalty, about the importance of age as a bonding mechanism, of territory in defining human relationships, and the utility of sex/gender as a device for the division of labor. But the kind of caring for one another that I learned in childhood was based both on a possessiveness that divided the family and an insistence that the child, unable to care for itself, had to have goodness, or what was deemed good for the child, imposed on the helpless creature. Almost throughout, the family model taught division rather than unity, competition rather than cooperation, and even hostility rather than the fullness and acceptance of love. Even the love that for so long I only dimly recognized was imposed and demanded rather than felt and feelingly reciprocated. Therein lies the enormous importance of the intense, continuous, and consistent physical proximity between the Mbuti mother and her child during those first three critical years of its life, during which the two share one mutual existence, fully reciprocating everything they have to give each other.

Now *there* is a model that will lead to the child's becoming a truly social being throughout his life, a model of mutuality. And as the model was enlarged, the same theme was repeated in just about everything the child did and experienced, including all activities and all human relationships, as the model steadily expanded. The Mbuti child was offered no challenges that it could not meet, but at the same time was offered new challenges to meet its growing abilities. The model I was given to follow, however different in detail, is not all that different from models found in most other Western cultures, but almost totally different from that of the Mbuti. It is a model that establishes division rather than unity, segmentation rather than integration, competition rather than cooperation. The focus is upon a number of discreet, separated individuals rather than on a single corporate group. The cooperation that emerges later in life—and in our modern society cooperation is every bit as necessary as it is in all societies—is mechanical, rather than organic, because it was learned by imposition rather than felt through reciprocation.

I think we see the consequences of this when we recognize what the plain facts tell us, that unlike the Mbuti we continue in adult life to have to be coerced to behave in a social manner. Order has to be imposed or enforced by violence or threat of violence, it lacks that inner drive that makes such external compulsion unnecessary or minimal. And there, finally, we come back to Spirit, which for the Mbuti is where life begins and where it ends. For them, at least, it is that awareness of Spirit that enables them to accept differences of manner, custom, speech, behavior, even of belief, while still feeling an underlying unity. It is awareness of Spirit that enables them to avoid the conflict and hostility that arise so easily from such differences, not by sweeping them under the carpet or by eternal compromise, but by systematic opposition and ritualization.

By Spirit I do not mean God, though if there is a God it may well be Spirit. I mean that essence of life which cannot be learned except through direct awareness, which is total, not merely rational. The awareness can be helped along by a system of natural symbols, such as that employed by the Mbuti, who live in a natural world. Earth, water, air, and fire; the forest itself. Through these symbols the Mbuti are constantly reminded of Spirit, for wherever they are, whatever they are doing, those symbols surround them and even permeate their whole being. In the more artificial world we have built for ourselves we are not so fortunate; such effective symbols are harder to come by, particularly if we have never learned to employ our whole being as a tool of awareness. But that does not mean that Spirit is inaccessible to us. I am sure that many like myself groped their way through childhood aware that there was something lacking and found their own Great-uncle Willie, their own Rule Water, their own Arthur Poyser, and their own counterpart of what music was for me. All I am saying is that our form of social organization merely allows it to happen as an accident, if at all, whereas that of the Mbuti writes it into the charter from the outset, at conception.

It is there, waiting for all of us in childhood, whether we live in the Ituri Forest or a city slum. I too have lived in a slum in England, in a singularly grimy area near Paddington Station, and it was there. It is everywhere, waiting to transform us, as I said earlier; waiting to transform poverty into wealth, squalor into magnificence, tedium into sport, fear into recognition, hatred and bigotry into understanding. That is the gift of childhood, and perhaps it is life's greatest gift.

PART TWO

ADOLESCENCE

THE ART OF
TRANSFORMATION

INSOFAR AS ADOLESCENCE is related to the biological fact of puberty, I cannot think of a single culture I know that handles this crucial stage of life more abysmally than we do. The consequences of our folly are to be seen all around us in the violence, neurosis, and loneliness of our youth, our adults, and our aged, some of whom never even approach the fullness and richness of life that could have been theirs had their adolescence been handled with more wisdom, understanding, and gentle respect. It is bad enough for a young girl to be so ignorant of her own body that the "first blood" should fill her with terror rather than joy, with thoughts of sickness and death rather than of health and of life. Yet that is how it still is for many, and this kind of ignorance would be even more widespread if parental control were as inviolable as some parents would like. It should be a criminal offense that this natural, wholesome, and utterly wonderful signal of the transformation of a young body into something else should be used to further that extraordinary argument that the body and all bodily functions, particularly those pertaining to sexual activity, are to be associated with dirt and impurity, if not with sin.

Happily, this extreme position is less common than it was, but it is still with us in the general disapproval of premarital sex that permeates our society. And it is the same for boys as for girls, although for the male child, his introduction to sexual maturity is far less spectacular, being so gradual that it is almost imperceptible. However, it is so imperceptible that not a few boys, and I was one of them, are taught that sex is dirty, dangerous, and to be avoided even before they have any clear idea of what is meant by the word. Like girls, many boys, sexually aware or sexually ignorant, still grow through adolescence and youth into adulthood with their sexual maturity hanging over them like some secret and loathsome specter, rather than as an overt source of pride and a public symbol of their approaching social responsibility.

In other cultures, where each stage of life is seen as having its own contribution to make to the well-being of society, adolescence is no exception. Instead of individual curiosity in sexual activity being treated as shameful, it is encouraged to flower into exuberance, and that individual exuberance in sexual potency is then transformed into joy with the realization of the individual's wider social significance as a life-giver, responsible for no less than the continuity of society itself. What a contrast with our way of doing things is the Mbuti way of dealing with this stage of life.

Akidinimba, familiarly known to the Mbuti boys as "Bouncy Breasts," prolonged her freedom as a child for as long as she could; but when she entered adolescence, rather late in life for an Mbuti girl, she did so with unparalleled zest. This delighted the boys while discomfiting some of the less well-endowed girls. Akidinimba had her final fling as an utterly flirtatious, dazzling beauty. But when she entered the adult state of marriage it was not with regret, not with misgivings about any supposed tedium of the marital life that lay ahead, and not with any pretense at a sudden conversion from her irrepressible joy in her body to some kind of adult solemnity and reticence. Far from it. She flung herself into marriage with the same joy that was hers as a child and as a youth, augmented by her new awareness of both her power and her responsibility as a potential giver of life.

So it is with Mbuti adolescents. Like Akidinimba they become transformed; they become all that they have learned to be and have already become, only more so, in keeping with their new-found sexual potency. They discover that each stage of life is rich, but that the next stage is even richer; nothing is lost. That is the magic of transformation, as distinct from mere transition.

Adolescence is generally considered to be the time of life between childhood and maturity that extends from age fourteen to twenty-five in males and from twelve to twenty in females. It is the period in which we are, or should be, prepared for sexual maturity and adult social responsibility. Just *when* the passage from childhood to adulthood occurs varies enormously from society to society, however. In one African society, for example, adolescence seems to be compressed into a one-month period; in another it lasts for three months. In both cases there follows a brief period that is not yet adulthood, even though mature behavior is expected in all respects except those that must await the completion of bodily growth. This period can be usefully referred to as "youth." So for our purposes here, since its social significance is so crucial, the definition of adolescence is modified to refer to the span of time between childhood and sexual maturity. "Youth" is used to refer to the period between the close of puberty and the completion of the process of physical growth.

In cultures such as those of the Ituri villages and the Mbuti, the period of transformation from childhood to sexual and social maturity is often highly formalized in rites of passage, generally accompanied by ritual initiation. These rites are frequently among the most important in the life of the society; the focus is as much on the social good as upon the good of individual participants, for with this transformation from childhood to young adulthood there is a corresponding and vital transformation of an individual being into a social being.

One of the most important occasions for such rites is the onset of puberty or sexual awareness. The rites that accompany puberty instruct the individual in the orderly predictable control of his or her new sexual potential as a reproducer and prepare him for the responsibilities of marriage. In small-scale societies the child usually knows all there is to be known about sex by this time, and so needs little further instruction; but he will be taught that there are certain restrictions that he must observe, and, perhaps through allegory, it will be explained *why* these are necessary and how they operate for the good of society at large. The child begins to see himself as a creative part of a much wider world than the one he has known up to that point, and it is as a creative, productive entity that he enters youth and maturity. He associates sexuality with sociality; he respects his new power and is respected for it. Throughout the process of initiation he is encouraged to see himself as now belonging to a much wider unit than merely that of the family, lineage, or clan. He is encouraged to see himself not only as a part of the total society of the present, but also as a part of the past and of the future.

In adolescence, then, especially in traditional societies, the individual is now pulled in one direction by the needs of society and in another by the enormous security afforded by his family. The pull is both affective and effective, for up to this point his emotional life has largely been built upon kinship and the family has effectively provided for him. It is no easy matter to leave such security, and in traditional societies whose social organization is based on kinship, the pull in that direction is all the more powerful. This is not so with hunter-gatherer societies, such as the Mbuti, whose progressively expanding concept of family causes biological kinship to become secondary to sociological kinship from an early age, so that by the time the children reach puberty they have, in a very real sense, become a part of society at large. But it is true of more complex societies, such as those of farmers or cattle herders. In these societies the nuclear family or extended family or even the lineage is likely to be an effective economic cooperative group, linked with others by marriage or proximity but always distinct. There is a much narrower sense of the "us" as distinct from the "others." Yet, in adolescence, it is the others that the child must now join. So puberty rites almost invariably involve an initial act of separation, the dramatic removal of the child from his family; the child may be given a visible symbol of that separation which he will carry for the rest of his life. It may for boys be the removal of the foreskin, or for girls the removal of the tip of the clitoris; or it may be some form of scarification or tattoo, the removal of two front teeth or some other demonstrable evidence of transformation, such as some mandatory form of dress or ornamentation.

Following the act of separation there is a period of limbo during which the individual is neither child nor adult, often neither male nor female, animal nor human. It is as though the individual is once again in the womb, being transformed from one thing into another. This period may be passed in a special initiation school, often well removed from the homes of the children. Usually the sexes are segregated. In that school the novice is prepared for his new life as a fully social being. He probably knows, as he does with sex, the practical aspects of how things are done, how cattle are tended, how fields are cleared and planted and harvested; his instruction during this period is of much more profound significance. He is taught that on emergence from this period of limbo he will have a new social personality, a new economic responsibility, a new political power, and, above all, a new spiritual being; and he will have been shown how all these aspects of his life, of his new self, interlock and make of him a single integrated whole.

The third aspect of any rite of passage is reincorporation, but in a new capacity. I have seen one such rite in which boys are symbolically reborn, passing through a tunnel made of bark cloth and representing the womb, emerging through the legs of a man who stands astride the mouth of the tunnel. The symbolism is very clear, removing all ambivalence, and from that moment onward, even though the boy may only be three months older than when he left childhood, he is now considered a man, treated like a man, and expected to behave as such. The following brief period of youth, ending with marriage, merely gives him time to develop his physical self, attaining full growth, and time to find his mate for life.

Although the *elima* involves both boys and girls, which is uncommon, and occurs among a people who emphasize the social rather than the biological family, which means that separation is less necessary, the Mbuti puberty festival, briefly mentioned in Part One, highlights much of what I have been saying about puberty rites so far. It is public recognition of puberty and sexual maturity. It is of particular interest, however, because it not only begins with focus on the female, it continues to focus on her and on the concept of motherhood throughout the entire month of the festival. Puberty in boys makes no sudden appearance, it just sneaks up rather gradually. For girls it is different. The first menstruation is nothing if not dramatic. It is an unequivocal demonstration of transformation from girlhood into womanhood, so the Mbuti use it as a signal for the *elima* to take place. The festival is relatively informal, but the three ritual stages are clearly there, starting with the separation of the girls (they generally wait for more than one girl "to see the blood") from their parents. They are provided with a house of their own, the *elima* house, which is not secluded but built right in the camp. The food they eat is prepared by themselves or the camp at large, but *not* from the family hearth. From the very first day, dramatic changes in dress and ornamentation visibly separate them from their former childhood. They emerge from the *elima* house, white with clay rubbed into their skin, dressed and adorned as *bamelima*, no longer as *miki*—children.

Then follows the period of preparation, which for them is primarily preparation for motherhood just as for boys it is preparation for fatherhood. Here, perhaps, is as good an example as any of "a fully integrated self" emerging from adolescence. The participants in this rite of passage are very young girls and boys, some perhaps not quite yet in their teens. They have already played at sex and very likely begun to play with it, but in the knowledge that a girl who has not yet menstruated is not likely to give birth to a child, which for the Mbuti is the crucial issue. Now, however, the girl does have that potential, so sex, while still play, must be controlled in order that conception does not result. How this is achieved is not as important here as the fact that it *is* achieved, and there is no known or recorded instance of an *elima* girl becoming pregnant, let alone giving birth. Both boys and girls have been well instructed in the responsibilities that accompany childbirth, and in the flush of youth they are neither ready for nor do they want such responsibilities. Their controls to prevent conception are exerted voluntarily and, as I understand it, mostly without even thinking. So sexual activity is still play, without any deeper significance attached to it. But it takes place in a different way. It occurs either in the *elima* house, which is probably where the controls are first learned and practiced, or if it takes place during one of the periodic sorties of the girls, the couple, rather than wait until they return to the camp (which is preferred), carefully choose a place; it does not happen just anywhere because it *cannot* just happen anywhere. Each couple chooses a place that to them is *ekimi*, or good, and therefore free of all *akami*. That means that the possibility of conception, which would be *akami*, is also absent. Now even in sex play, hitherto nothing more than a somewhat riotous frolic, the notion of the sacred plays a part, and religious concepts are utilized to bring about the desired result—fully satisfactory cohabitation without conception. In the period of youth that follows the close of puberty each couple discovers for themselves the parts of the forest and the times of day that are sacred to the sexual act. The pleasure of the act, they say, becomes correspondingly intense, only to be surpassed when a couple makes the decision to have a child, which may be several years following the *elima*. When they do, they discover the ecstasy of creation, one of the most sacred acts of all, and recognize that it is achieved only when the conscious objective of the act is reproduction, which is within the bounds of marriage. Any sexual act without this objective is subject to the *elima* restrictions, and perhaps because of that (I do not know) is mere pleasure and secular rather than sacred. However, the Mbuti make it clear that it is not merely the physiological restrictions on the nature of the extramarital embrace, but what is absent from the mind and intent that is responsible for the lesser intensity of the experience.

At exactly the time of their participation in the *elima*, boys and girls alike are first introduced to a totally new, largely antiphonal song form that requires a great deal of cooperation between the two sexes and within each group and calls for a new and high level of creative expression, especially from the girls. Taking this all into account it is clear that for the Mbuti, adolescence is the art of transformation from a consuming condition to a creative condition, not only in terms of reproduction but in economic, political, and religious terms.

There are a number of vital differences between the *elima* and the *nkumbi*, the corresponding rite of passage practiced by the neighboring peoples around the Ituri, all of whom are farmers, fishers, or both. The most obvious is the fact that the puberty rite for village girls is separate and private, whereas that for boys, the *nkumbi*, is public and the occasion for a major ritual. Since males do not manifest any immediate physiological change that can be recognized as a clear-cut signal for the *nkumbi* to take place, and since the idea seems to be to prepare them in advance of puberty, boys between the ages of nine and eleven, give or take a year at either end, are selected once every three years according to their physical, mental and social readiness. But whereas the same basic procedure is followed of separation, preparation, and reincorporation, over a three-month period, and although girls are totally excluded, the focus is not on the boys alone; rather it is on the adult society into which they are about to move. For the boys it is a time of transformation; for the rest of society it is a time of reification of the social norms and religious values, a time of purification in readiness to welcome the youths when they emerge among the adults.

The symbols are unmistakable; the underlying concepts are as clear as, if not clearer than, any written language could ever make them. Mothers shave their boys' heads as a sign of their sons' approaching death as children. The boys' families shave their heads as a sign of mourning. When perhaps a month of ritual dancing has sufficiently prepared and purified the village and initiated a long period of abstention and strict adherence to the moral code, the ritual priest seeks out the boys he feels are ready, marked by their shaven heads, and literally seizes them and drags them away from their families. From the village they are carried or marched to the initiation camp that has been constructed in the adjoining forest, which, for the villagers, is a place of death. Immediately on arrival the boys are circumcised, although on certain occasions a boy may be circumcised just prior to being led into the camp, but never in sight of women or noninitiates. In any event, the operation, which may seem crude to Western eyes, is expert. The ritual doctor sees to it that each boy feels no more pain than he can stand. The moment the boy is about to break down, the doctor deftly finishes the cutting and wraps the wound in a herbal medicine pasted onto a fresh leaf. The boy is then made to sit down with the others, if he is not the first, and immediately has to start singing one of the *nkumbi* songs. Since the initiation camp is always within earshot of the village, he already knows the songs by heart, but within seconds of his circumcision and being made to sing, he is beaten with a switch for not singing "properly." The beating hurts no more than a mosquito bite, but it is so aggravating and so unexpected, coming at just the kind of moment when as a child the boy would have run to his mother or father for comfort, that it effectively takes the boy's mind off the much greater pain between his legs until the medicine has had a chance to begin the healing process.

But those beatings are just a prelude, and these initiations have often been described as savage and brutal because of the constant ordeals of increasing severity that the boys have to undergo. Yet not once have I seen cruelty, for not once have I seen a boy tested beyond the limits of his endurance. Every boy knows that he is being taught what he must know if he is to survive satisfactorily as an adult, and he knows that his fathers and grandfathers, back into the distant past, have undergone exactly the same ordeals, step by step, and that like them he will in three short months be transformed into responsible adulthood and that when he finally emerges from the *nkumbi* camp it will be with all the honor and respect due to any man.

Separation from the family is reinforced by compelling each boy to ridicule some family member, usually his father. His body is painted with white clay every day, another sign of mourning, as a reminder that he is socially dead. Some of the ordeals he undergoes are based on women's activities, such as planting corn. At best that is a backbreaking task in a forest field, but in the *nkumbi* camp it is doubly so, and the boys are kept at it, bobbing up and down at the crouch as they move around the camp, until they are ready to drop. In this way they come to consider how fortunate they are not to be women, and begin to *want*, consciously, to become men. Similarly they are made to imitate various animals until they cultivate a real sense of being and desire to be other than animal. Growing up is seen as being a question of will and volition just as much of mere aging. All this time the boys may eat only vegetable foods, untouched and uncooked by any hands other than those of adult males. They may have been born of women, but the womb of the *nkumbi* camp is entirely male. I have known boys defer the choice of becoming male by not entering the *nkumbi*, but never for long. In other parts of the world a boy may, if he wishes, opt to become a girl; but if he does so, he must be ready to accept a woman's full responsibilities, other than for childbirth. If he does that, then he is assured of an honored position in that society as a woman.

Toward the end of the three-month period of preparation the boys are dressed daily in skirts made of fronds from the raffia palm as symbolic of their virility, for it is up the erect palm tree that the white sap rises so freely, providing several gallons of palm wine each day, once cut. So dressed, but with a leaf mask in his mouth to mark his limbo state, each boy is armed with a whip and taken into the village, where he is expected to beat the girl of his choice. This is the reverse of the *elima* practice where it is the girls who beat the boys, but otherwise it is the same preliminary courtship ritual; it in no way amounts to betrothal, but it is the first sign the boy gives of his intent to settle down to more serious courtship, leading to betrothal and ultimately to marriage. "Romantic love" is far from absent in later life, but at this stage, when the boys have not yet experienced their full sexual potential, a very special groundwork is being laid on which romantic love will be built. The courtship rituals and other sexually symbolic activities of the *nkumbi*, because they occur prior to the fullness of sexual experience, are dominated by feelings of respect, responsibility, and mutuality that are, to this moment, the individual's only experience of "love." It is upon this bedrock of Platonic, or social, love that the adolescents are taught to build that particular expression of love that is sexual. Insofar as love of any kind demands mutual respect and consideration, responsibility and control, then for the boys and girls in these societies, adolescence is a time for learning how to love in the fullest sense.

During all this time, after the excitement of "opening" the *nkumbi*, the village has resumed its normal daily life, only with extra attention to avoiding conflict and offenses of any kind. All those who come to help celebrate the "opening" return to their own villages as soon as the circumcisions are all done. But when the boys are ready for their "coming out," the village again becomes host to visitors from neighboring villages, and there is further ritual dancing to make sure that the village is a fit place for the young men to enter and begin their new life. One morning, shortly after dawn, the boys, dressed in their *kifa* skirts but invisible because they are surrounded by a tightly packed mass of men, slowly progress from the camp into the village where the house of the "father of the initiation" has been prepared to receive them. It takes them until midday, and during this time a battle is waged between the women and the men. They say it used to be fought with bows and arrows, but now it is fought only with stones, sticks, and occasionally with burning logs seized from the ever-smoldering household fires. It is a ritual battle, but a reminder that one of the major areas of potential conflict is that of the male/female relationship. This is particularly true in societies such as this where political authority lies primarily in the hands of the men. Once every three years the women have an opportunity to vent their displeasure, if they feel any, and with such degree of physical violence as they see fit. The men are little able to defend themselves, since they have to stay close to the boys to conceal and protect them, and minor injuries are not uncommon.

At noon the procession reaches the center of the village. The boys lie flat on the ground, face down, and are instantly covered with plantain leaves so that they are invisible. They stay in the leafy mound while the initiation camp and everything in it that touched their childhood is set on fire. Everything must be utterly destroyed. There must be nothing left; no flames, no smoke, not even a wind that could blow the ashes into the village and reinfect them with their past. When the fire has done its work, a blast on a trumpet made from an elephant tusk announces the death of childhood, and the boys are removed from the leaves and led hastily into the house where they will stay for their last three days in limbo.

Now, instead of being painted white, they are painted half-white and half-black, as a sign of their approaching reentry into life. Each boy in turn comes out and dances in front of the assembled villagers. Ideally, each village with which the boy as an adult is likely to have any connections should be represented, and each village, through its representative, must make a public gift to the boy as he dances his "coming out of the womb" dance, signifying that he is accepted as a man, without qualification. When he has been thus accepted by all the villagers, the boy then has to dance in front of each house in his own village, where more likely than not he will spend the rest of his life; and each household must similarly accept him by publicly making a symbolic gift. The nature of the gifts and the manner of giving betray the readiness or hesitancy with which any boy is accepted by any one village or household. When all the boys have danced, which usually takes three days, all is over but the final rite.

On that day, in the dark before dawn, the boys are taken down to the river and bathed. Their bodies are anointed with palm oil. The oil palm is the symbol of continuity and wealth, for it persists from generation to generation, unlike the raffia palm. After being dressed in new bark cloth in the manner of adults, they slowly proceed up through the village, walking on a carpet of plantain leaves. The plantain is the symbol of success and survival, for when these village farmers first moved into the forest from the grasslands, they found that only the plantain could grow readily in an otherwise hostile environment, with a minimum of land clearing and preparation. Each boy holds a plantain leaf to the side of his face that is nearest to where the initiation camp lay; he must not even look in the direction of his childhood. Outside the house of the father of the initiation, stools have been set, one for each initiate. These are the stools on which adults sit in their *baraza*, or meeting place. Still standing on plantain leaves the initiates line up in front of the stools, their leaf face-shields are taken away from them, and they sit down and are young men. They stay there on public display for an hour or two, perhaps singing a few initiation songs, and then without any further ceremony it is all over. They just get up, pick up their stools, and start wandering around the village, but as men, not as children. Each youth must now build his own house and start living on his own until he marries. There is great family pride in the boy's accomplishment and his family will help him, but he now belongs to the village and the society as a whole, not just to them.

The last remaining vestiges of the boys' lost childhood are

the *kifa* skirts, which were not burned with the camp because they were worn for the boys' coming-out dance. These skirts are found the next day, perhaps on a tall pole erected in the village or else strung around trees in the forest.

One of the many things this description has not been able to cover is what goes on in the village during this three-month period, though I hinted at it when referring to this being a period of abstention and morality. It is something more positive than abstention or adherence, however; it is an active reinforcement of the way of the ancestors, the way of life. There are those general rules, common to nearly every society, corresponding remarkably closely to the ancient Hebrew Ten Commandments, and each adult will make additional rules for himself, particularly if related to one of the boys. These voluntary acts of sacrifice or penance often involve abstention from a favorite food or from palm wine, and the "father" by thus purifying himself helps to bring even greater purity (and power) to the boys. This is all so that the boys can be reborn without danger of the infection of evil. Any adult transgression against the moral code during this period is considered a grave crime, since it directly threatens the life of the boys. This effectively reinforces the moral code, but it also provides an opportunity for the code to be modified, once every three years, in light of changing circumstances. Similarly, the *nkumbi* provides an opportunity for political authority to be realigned in the host village, since the man chosen to be "father of the *nkumbi*" will occupy a position of extreme respect until the next *nkumbi*. It also allows for conflicts to be brought into the open and settled amicably, since any other form of settlement, particularly if violent, would again be a crime against the *nkumbi*. And just as major areas of potential conflict, such as that between male and female, are made overt and explicit in rituals of rebellion and rituals of reversal, so the potential for conflict between neighboring villages is reduced by the necessity for cooperation that an initiation in any one village involves. In fact the *nkumbi* is probably the only regular and major occasion which does bring the villages together, since each village is otherwise virtually autonomous and self-sufficient, with no central chieftainship in the traditional sense.

The *nkumbi* is also of vital importance in the religious area. Once initiated, an individual falls directly under supernatural sanctions, and wrongdoing, even if undetected by the villagers, will be detected and punished by the ancestral spirits. Thus, participation in the *nkumbi* guarantees pretty firm adherence to the moral code in adult life, making for an order without law and without physical coercion. Most important of all, the religious power of the *nkumbi* has made a single political unit out of a circle of adjoining but otherwise vastly different peoples, all immigrants from different parts of central Africa. Some are Sudanic-speaking, others Bantu-speaking. On immigration they competed with each other for land, and each society was virtually, though briefly, at war with its neighbors. Faced with a common enemy, first in the form of the Arab slave traders, then of Belgian colonial power, there was a powerful political incentive to unity, but no political means of achieving it. The *nkumbi* became the means by providing a common body of religious belief and practice acceptable to all. One by one those tribes who did not already practice initiation in that form adopted it, with minor variations, until the circle was complete. Thus, despite considerable continuing linguistic and cultural differences, this one dramatic common ritual has provided a symbol of unity that led to a sense of community both political and religious.

The significance of the *nkumbi* obviously extends far beyond the mere initiation of boys into adulthood. It involves the total adult society, not just the initiates and their teachers. While the boys are learning the adult values by which they will soon have to guide their lives, the adults are putting extra effort into the proper practice of those values. It is thus a cooperative effort, and of course cooperation, rather than competition, is one of the main values that characterize adult life in any such village society in the Ituri Forest. Through song, dance, and submission to ordeals, the boys learn other adult social values such as interdependence, equality, the acceptance and sharing of responsibility, mutual respect between all categories of human kind, regardless of age, gender, family, or even tribal affiliation. Many of these and other values learned at this time reinforce values already learned in childhood; others are new, being specific to adulthood, but *none* of the values learned in childhood are now contradicted. Physical childhood was ended with the act of circumcision, but the values remain alive, augmented and enriched by all that goes on in the camp as the boys learn how to be responsible adults. Then in one dramatic final ritual their limbo status is equally sharply ended, and they are men in their own eyes and in the eyes of all the world around them.

Perhaps the most remarkable, and most important, thing about this rite of passage is the way the boys learn the true significance of their approaching sexual maturity, the *full* meaning of "love." The boys learn that the sexual act (and proper abstinence from it) can be an onerous responsibility just as it can be one of the greatest joys. Dances and ordeals lend weight to what might otherwise be ineffective intellectual argument. In dance they learn that the sexual act can be a sometimes unwelcome chore; in song they give voice to the ecstasy they can expect to experience at other times. And the very fact that they themselves are the center of all this elaborate ritual drama, the focus of attention for the entire society, the cause of a manifestation of pomp and ceremony unmatched by any other, is all an indirect, subtle, but powerful, lesson in the social responsibilities and consequences of parenthood. Part of the initiates' training has indeed been to witness and participate in the criticism of their own parents, whom they are made to ridicule for real and imaginary inadequacies in *their* handling of parenthood. The boys may be forced to watch while the teachers ridicule the sexual excesses, abuses, or inadequacies of their fathers or mothers (rarely) and to listen while their entire families are held up to scorn, even in the presence of their fathers and older brothers, for failure to contribute generously enough to the *nkumbi*, for not spending enough time in the camp helping with the duties of teaching and supervising their own children. And while their own parents generally refrain from praising them, tending rather to criticize them and subject them to even stronger discipline, the boys see that whenever they succeed in doing something well, it is *other* adults in the camp who are always eager to claim them, saying, "See? He is *my* child, *I* taught him how to be a man. He will be a son to me in my old age."

And as well as being set dramatically and firmly in its

domestic, economic, and political context, the sexual act is consecrated in the rich religious symbolism that runs through the *nkumbi* from start to finish. The symbols appear at every turn of everyday life, constantly reminding the individual of the sacred as well as secular consequences of any sexual relationship. Ultimately, for the Mbuti at least, it is this sacred connotation that converts the sexual act from being one of pleasure to being one of joy and ecstasy, augmented, rather than diminished, by a ready acknowledgment of all the social responsibilities and consequences involved. Here lies the significance of adolescence being made the signal for this major rite of passage; the growth of children into youth and adulthood is seen as part of the continued growth of society at large. The reproductive act is related to the ongoing social process of which every initiate is a part, and the boys are all made aware that, in a sense, their individual growth is as incidental as their individual pleasure or pain. If they are allowed any sense of self-importance it is only as parts of the greater whole; and then they learn that it is only as parts of the greater whole that they can fully realize the full potential of sex. By timing this stage of social development to coincide with the physical maturation of the adolescent, the rite achieves what is virtually a transformation from one state of being to another, both social and physical.

In Western societies adolescence does not directly mark the individual's entry into adulthood, but it is generally considered at least as the beginning of training for adult responsibility. The years spent in high school can be compared with the *nkumbi* rite of passage. However, as a rite, the passage through high school achieves transition rather than transformation. It seems to encourage change rather than growth by treating sexual growth as something quite separate and distinct from physical, intellectual, or spiritual growth. Indeed, in many schools spiritual growth is treated either as an extracurricular option or left to the discretion of parents who probably went through a similar educational process. In this way adolescence, instead of integrating a whole being, may become a traumatically disintegrative experience. The formal, if not ritual, preparation of our adolescents for adulthood is most often restricted to physical and intellectual training. Thus, at the very best, even given the most concerned parents in the world, the adolescent is likely to be treated as though he or she is two or more distinct, unrelated entities, one physical and one spiritual, each pursuing its own course, rather than as though he were one, single, united, integrated, vital whole.

One of the major differences between the high school and the *nkumbi* is the element of choice. For the participant in the *nkumbi*, there is only one kind of school. We in Western society can choose between public and private schools, day or boarding, free or costly, near or distant. We tend to regard freedom of choice as a sign of progress, yet whatever else it does, in this case it divides rather than unites both the world of the adult and that of the child according to inclination, wealth, religion, politics, or territorial considerations. Even next-door neighbors may be divided in more ways than one on this single issue. Given freedom of choice and opportunity, it may be that only poverty or isolation will compel all the children of a community, village, or county to go to the same school and thus provide the adults of that community with an opportunity to manifest any kind of joint concern with the process of education and socialization. Even then adult participation is fragmented and restricted, for there is still the major difference between the two systems, that is, that in ours, our teachers are a highly specialized and tiny segment of any community with whom the adolescents mostly will have had little contact before and have equally little after their schooling is over.

Such differences notwithstanding, adolescence in both societies is accompanied by a rigorous system of formal education that separates the child from his past, prepares him for adulthood, then restores him to society. In following those three stages of a rite of passage, we shall find that for most of *us*, however diverse our backgrounds, the nature of the separation is often traumatic, and permanent rather than temporary. Similarly the period of limbo is different in highly significant ways. That the values learned are different is to be expected, given the contextual difference; what we should question is the process of teaching and learning itself. And when we leave school and are restored to society, how well fitted are we for adulthood, how efficiently are we truly reincorporated by comparison with the Ituri system? Have we become what the system intended? Is this what we want? Has our full potential been properly exploited?

The British public school today is perhaps less of a strange creature now than it was before World War II, which is when it initiated me in such an incredible way into the mysteries of adolescence and prepared me so inadequately, in many ways, for any sane, truly social kind of adult life. Not the least strange thing about the public school in Britain is that it is called public when in fact it is very private. Right there in the very name of the institution is the first of a whole gamut of inconsistencies. It is not what it says it is, in common usage. Not unlike private schools in the United States and elsewhere, public schools in Britain are ranked in a hierarchy, with Eton and Harrow at the top. Wealth and family are the main criteria for admission; acceptable parents may enter their sons' names on the waiting list at birth, if they wish. I believe that my name was entered for both, but eventually my parents gave me that questionable freedom of choice.

As we have seen, rites of passage may be characterized as consisting of three stages: separation, indoctrination (or preparation), (re)incorporation. In the first stage the individual is not only separated from the physical world to which he belonged (in this case, as a child), but also from his immediate family, and even more importantly, from his former status and individual personality. He then enters the central and generally longest part of the rite, in which he is taught all that is necessary for him to know when he is finally reincorporated back into society. This is often seen as a medial period, a period of *limbo*. In that limbo world the initiate is in between two real worlds, the worlds of childhood and adulthood, and, as we have seen in the *nkumbi*, is in a sense dead, waiting to be reborn and being nurtured and prepared for that rebirth. This framework, applied to the public school, puts it into the same perspective (in terms of its educational function) as the *nkumbi* and throws additional light on some of the things it achieves, albeit unknowingly, in the name of "education," but while concentrating on the education of the mind and the body to the cost of the equally vital development of the heart and soul, proper to this time of life.

At first glance there are certain superficial similarities between the two systems as far as separation of the child is concerned. In our society when an adolescent goes to school he is separated from his family, to a greater degree if it is a boarding school, and also from his childhood because his new school will demand very different things of him, and because he knows that he is approaching adulthood, a condition of life earnestly desired by most adolescents in our Western society. But whereas for the adolescent in the *nkumbi* the separation is temporary and involuntary, with us it tends to be permanent and voluntary. In my own case, for instance, I opted for public school when I was twelve, partly because my older brother was at a very chic, private, experimental school. I actively sought not only a territorial but a qualitative separation. I wanted to be different and, in my judgment, "better" by going to a school with greater social prestige. And although at first I chose to be a day boy rather than a boarder, perhaps because I was too scared to choose separation from my parents, the nature of the education alone began a process that was irreversible, separating me from my parents permanently in terms of education, ideals, aspirations, and life style. Some parents seek to avoid this by sending their children to the same kind of school they attended, but that has little effect, for each generation in our world has whole new vistas to deal with and assimilate, and the same school is, in fact, never the same school. More startling still is the fact that more of our adolescents expect and *want* a permanent separation. They call it "freedom" and claim the right to "do their own thing." And, indeed, most parents would agree that, however painful, separation at this stage of life is essential in order to teach their children "to stand on their own feet." The conscious objective of separation in the Mbuti society or Ituri village is very different. At adolescence the child is separated from his parents, not so that he can do his own thing, but so that he can learn how to extend a familiar and satisfying pattern of interdependency to all the other adults in his society. Once his social horizons have been enlarged in this way, he is restored to his family, for now the whole community has become his family. He has been socialized.

Our system not only separates the adolescent from his family, however; it also separates him from some or even all of his former peers. I went to a school where I did not know a single one of the other boys. Every friendship made as a child was broken. But even more serious than this separation of the adolescent from his former peers is the form of separation that our school system effects according to caste, class, religion, race, economic and political factors, totally at variance with the nominal value of equality that receives such generous publicity. Since this is not how most of us think about our school system, and is certainly not what it consciously sets out to be, let me revert to the schooling that I knew; the data are of course specific to one culture at one time, but it is not the data that concern us, it is the process.

British culture did not impose class segregation, it merely allowed for it; class discrimination for the wealthy in particular became a voluntary factor. The matter of choice is crucial. In a sense I, as well as my parents, chose my separation from the "lower" classes in my adolescence. This was a hierarchical distinction, very different from the distinction of caste, which is strictly hereditary. "Family," hence an aspect of caste, was involved, but so was wealth, which is a major determinant of class. In being separated from boys from my former school who did not choose or could not afford to go to public school, I felt myself placed above them. Similarly, my former friends, the gardener, cook, parlor maids, even my nannies, were now separated from me, permanently and irrevocably, by much more than geographical distance or any temporary condition of limbo. They were all beneath me, to be dealt with courteously, justly, properly, but *differently* from my "equals." And now look at just one way in which this was accomplished.

Dress and ornamentation seem to be among the few universals by which we can begin to understand human and social behavior. Everywhere, dress in some form is used to signal both individual and group distinctions. The reason I chose Westminster rather than Eton or Harrow, other than to be separated from my brother, was that I liked its school uniform. At Eton new boys had to wear an Eton suit, long dark gray or black trousers surmounted by an Eton jacket which is cut off above the waist, leaving both front and rear end totally unprotected; and a huge starched collar unlike anything worn by anyone else. I had been made to wear Eton suits as Sunday dress when I was quite a small child, so I wanted nothing to do with childish dress. Harrow was distinguished, in my mind, by the fact that its uniform was dominated by a ridiculous-looking hat called the boater. I later came to associate the boater with the more vulgar music halls, but then I think my prime association was with a lot of uncouth youths of no academic distinction, in hot pursuit of some ugly, unfriendly, and violent sport. There was nothing to attract me there. At Westminster, however, although new boys normally wore Eton suits, if they were of a certain height they were allowed to graduate immediately to the tails and top hat worn by senior boys at Eton. That fulfilled all my requirements; for tails and top hat were very specifically adult. But I was within half an inch of the height requirement for new boys to wear them. I think it was Gardener who suggested padding in the heels of my socks. With double-thickness soles added to my shoes, I visited the school tailor who measured me and pronounced me ready for tails. There was an uncomfortable moment when he examined my shoes and discovered my real height. But rather than condemn me to Etons he congratulated me on my determination. My family and friends similarly congratulated me on this achievement, more than they did for passing the school's entrance examination. In this way, through my choice of dress, I learned that deceit, if not dishonesty, was an acceptable, even commendable adult value.

The contrast between the nudity of the *baganza*, the *nkumbi* initiation boys, and a boy only a year or so older dressed in tails and top hat, tells a story of its own. The *baganza* are given no opportunity to dissemble; stark naked, the *nkumbi* boys can only use their bodies with honesty. I quickly learned to use mine dishonestly. I used it, by the way I was allowed to dress and adorn it, to complete and heighten the separation between myself, my family, my former friends, and those whom I now began to perceive as somehow inferior.

Tails and top hat are directly associated with both class and wealth, and I found that I could do all manner of things that I could not do when dressed otherwise. I could gain admission to adult movies; I could travel first class on a third-class ticket, or even without any ticket at all; I could expect, even demand deference that I would never have been given in any other form of dress. The system not only allowed this to happen, it encouraged it. Even when discovered by an unimpressed ticket inspector on a train, or by an overzealous tobacconist when trying to buy cigarettes while underage, I was commended rather than denounced: "You are a *real* young gentleman, you are." And indeed that is what I was becoming in my early adolescence. I was being separated from my honesty, from respect for my true self.

Quite obviously, the psychological and other educational advantages of nudity could not be had in a London climate. The choice of uniform for the school was not arbitrary, and it was intended to have some significance other than mere clothing. We have to consider the *possibility* that however unconsciously, it was indeed part of the system that Westminster boys should learn deceit, and should learn to consider themselves as superior, different, separate. If so, then in the period of limbo we should find these qualities being taught to the boys; and so they were. The values and qualities were different from those taught in the *nkumbi*, but the process and even some of the techniques by which we learned things during our period of limbo were much the same. We learned from and used our uniform just as the *baganza* boys did from their nudity. In a sense it united us as a class distinct from others.

However, unlike the unity created among the *baganza* that persists throughout their lives and, in fact, unites them with all the elders and adults of their society who have "seen" the *nkumbi* and been naked before each other, our unity was limited and ephemeral. It united us beyond the limbo world only with a tiny fragment of our society, the union of "Old Boys," and with a wider but still small and much divided "class." And within our limbo world the very dress that was the symbol of this fragile unity was used to divide us. Seniors were divided from juniors, as I mentioned, by dressing the one in tails and the other in Etons. Scholars wore gowns. Monitors (prefects) wore wing collars. All that was mandated by the system, consistent with the hierarchical and non-egalitarian actuality of life, in accord with fact, if not with theory. But then there were voluntary manipulations of dress that further contributed to the fragmentation of our frangible adolescent community.

The *baganza* can do little with their uniform of nakedness to manifest individual or subgroup identity. In nearly all our Western schools we can and do use dress this way. At Westminster, the quality of tailoring could be used to demonstrate economic status. Choice of material, style of cut, and manner of wearing the clothing associated the individual with other kinds of social grouping; the individual could even set himself apart by the manner in which he swung the compulsory umbrella, or the way he rolled it. We all used our freedom in these respects to manifest our individuality, each seeking to set himself apart from the others in some tiny way. For most of us, those remained private ways by which we demonstrated our identity to ourselves. But outwardly, our uniform and our freedom afforded us the most opportunity for self-expression in the trousers we wore. These could be plain or patterned, feathered or striped, the stripes could be solid or pin, wide or narrow; the color of the cloth could be anything from a fairly dark gray to black. These were choices we had to make; the school did not make them for us. And since we had to have several changes of clothes we had to choose between keeping to one outward form or selecting a variety of forms, representing a variety of identities.

The social consequences, at least within that limbo community, were enormous. Because of the limited number of variations possible, our trousers united us in groups, outwardly visible unities. We recognized kindred spirits by the trousers they wore, and we signaled our interests and our "character" to each other by the angle at which we wore our top hats, the way we twirled our umbrellas, the way we adjusted our tails as we sat down. This was serious, social business. The faint pinstripers and umbrella twirlers with whom

I found myself associated (these distinctions were often verbalized and used as terms of praise or abuse) were mostly both artistically and academically oriented. Imagine, then, the dismay on days when I discovered that all I had left to wear was the feather stripe, and thus found myself outwardly allied to a rather stuffy group of nonentities given to contact sports. Would they then expect me to join them in their rough-and-tumble in Dean's Yard? Would pinstripe friends think me disloyal? Of course, when I tried signaling that no, I was still loyal, by twirling my umbrella even more vigorously, they both told me to stop acting like a faggot, a word that at that time had no meaning for me at all. At one stage, to protect myself from an older boy, a solid-striper, I took to wearing solid-striped trousers, and he became my protector instead of my bully. Then people had other things to say that I did not understand. And of course we all observed with care what kind of trousers our teachers wore . . . there was another avenue of political manipulation open to us. We were indeed being initiated into the mysteries of a certain form of political life, as well as into the subtleties of economic power and class discrimination. By change of attire, at first unconsciously, then consciously, the individual learned to shift his loyalties with infinite subtlety, playing one group against another to his own advantage. Given the inevitable and constant ongoing change in the sartorial scene, he learned to mistrust outward professions of loyalty, visible or verbal. Our limbo world became a world of chameleons; like the "public" school, we were not what we seemed to be. But the crucial question that nags is whether we were not, after all, just like the *baganza*, learning exactly those attitudes and values necessary for us in our particular social context?

The two forms of initiation have many other elements in common insofar as the process and the techniques employed are concerned. Both use uniform to outwardly symbolize separation from the narrow confines of family, though for me, at Westminster, tails and top hats proved positively lethal to my concept of kinship. In both schools there is an appeal to vanity followed by ridicule. We certainly met with ridicule once we stepped beyond the precincts of the abbey, not so much from adults as from boys of our age wearing a more "normal" form of dress. In both schools there are moments of kindness, and in both schools that kindness is all too often followed by alienation. Above all in both schools there are ordeals that appear insuperable, but which in fact are within everyone's capacity for endurance. These are fundamental ways of learning; they teach at a gut level and affect us more profoundly, at this stage of life, than most intellectual instruction. The important difference here is not so much in what is being taught and learned as in the fact that in the *nkumbi* these vital techniques are all exercised by the teachers. They frequently used to ask me about my own *"nkumbi"* and were shocked and astounded when I told them that in my *nkumbi*, called public school, it was the *baganza*, the boys themselves, who controlled the ridicule, the alienation of one from the others, the tears and the pain, and who themselves devised the ordeals they inflicted on each other. "Did you have no teachers?" they asked. Then when I told them that our teachers were not kinsmen or friends, or even known to our families, and that they only taught our minds and trained our bodies in sports and games and didn't teach our hearts or spirit, they understood, I think, why we seem as cold to them as we do.

Their reaction to other aspects of my own rite of passage at public school was equally instructive. I stressed the excellence of Westminster for the academic training it gave us, but the *nkumbi* teachers were quick to point out that, at least as I had described it, the school seemed to concentrate on imparting knowledge rather than on developing the intellectual ability to understand: "If we taught like that our boys would learn nothing," they said. In the *nkumbi* the boys are taught in riddles, in songs and dances, where the inner meaning is carefully hidden so that each boy has to discover it for himself, and so discover the truth *within* himself. And so the *nkumbi* teachers sought to find out what it was that as a boy I had learned from the dances and songs I had been taught. The closest I could get to their concept of dancing was playing football. They were not interested in the physical skills that developed, nor the good health the activity allegedly induces; they wanted to know what the Westminster *baganza* were learning while playing football. They saw it as comparable with some of their ordeals that demand concentration, coordination, and considerable physical stamina. What they did not like was the competitive element and the physical damage that sometimes results. They were frankly disgusted at what I could tell them of boxing, picking up on two elements particularly significant for them, namely, that blood is often drawn, even expected by the spectators, and that one of the boxers actually "lost." It was bad enough for them that in football the boys *could* injure each other, it was worse that in boxing they were *expected* to injure each other. Was this what the teachers at Westminster wanted their boys to learn? Even fencing, which I thought might appeal to them because of its almost balletlike quality, they rejected as unthinkable, for even though the sport took great pains to avoid any danger of injury, it openly encouraged the values, not only of aggression and of doing bodily injury, but of killing. They asked me if any of these "dances" taught any agility or skill that I had not seen them teach their boys through dances and ordeals that were noncompetitive, so that nobody "lost," and the symbolism of which was related to all the positive values of their society, which did not include injury and murder.

New boys at Westminster were given the choice of joining either the Boy Scouts or the O.T.C. (Officers' Training Corps). Although already thoroughly nonviolent by nature I opted for the O.T.C., again because of that trivial thing, dress. Boy Scouts were not only called "Boy," they had to wear short trousers, appropriate to childhood. Boys who joined the O.T.C. wore adult uniforms. The O.T.C. did not involve the violence of the so-called "playing field," and to me at that tender age the rifle was a symbol of adulthood more than of slaughter. But the O.T.C. was anything but tender. Within about two weeks one boy was hospitalized and died. We had been out on night maneuvers and some of us supposedly guarding an imaginary flank had got stuck waist-deep in a quagmire. Through various ordeals, the *baganza* learn to deal with physical hardship, discomfort, even danger just as effectively, but without ever for a moment being endangered. Further, their ordeals all operate within a symbolic framework that relates directly to what they know will be the realities of their adult life. I doubt if any of us in that quagmire recognized any symbolism or believed for a moment that we would ever in real (adult) life be soldiers, guarding any flank, or in any other quagmire. The exercise related in no way to any reality that we could imagine.

Even the daily activities of the O.T.C. camp were mostly dysfunctional, or at best taught things that could have been better taught in other ways. There was a lot of drudgery; polishing boots and shining brass and cleaning rifles, washing dishes, cleaning potatoes. This might have been intended as a healthy lesson for boys who normally left such chores to servants, but some of us had already been taught that lesson in childhood by wise parents. What it succeeded in doing was to make very clear the difference between work and play, the one being a punishment, the other a reward. In this way we were effectively taught that work is undesirable, that our goal should be play. One of the really cunning things about the *nkumbi* activities was that the distinction between work and play was effectively blurred; both became equally desirable under certain circumstances and equally undesirable under others. Ultimately, the distinction is almost abolished, either activity being equally pleasurable in its right place. The O.T.C. camp taught us something very different, and none of it seemed to have a right place, to be in any way desirable.

It might be argued that at the very least Westminster was teaching the boys discipline and that hardship was an essential ingredient in this. Hardship and discipline were prominent elements in the life of the *nkumbi* initiates also, but apart from the fact that they were at all times carefully controlled by the teachers, there was one other highly significant difference; every moment of the *nkumbi*, every lesson, every ordeal, every song, was part of a sacred ritual and was clearly and overtly an act of consecration. There, "discipline" always had a purpose that the boys could clearly see and led to a goal they wanted to achieve. To teach a boy "discipline" the word used was closer to "wisdom"; he was taught to follow, and to *want* to follow, a way of life that was sacred. Even when being beaten with a thorn switch, the boys were aware of the symbolism both of the beating and of the thorns. When being touched lightly on the arms with tiny sticks or daubed with white clay, the pleasure or displeasure at the sensation was secondary and the symbolism was paramount. Had this been the case at Westminster, then the otherwise incomprehensible and senseless ordeals we suffered, the locker room flagellation with wet towels, the caning by monitors, even the caning by teachers, might have made sense and provided an incentive for us more gladly to follow the way of *our* ancestors. But despite the richness and sacredness of the world around us, bursting with symbols begging to be put to use, these were systematically ignored or secularized, as though Spirit were something shameful and to be rigidly excluded from adolescence, as though the yearnings of an adolescent heart were either childish or improper. Even our rituals, including daily prayers, were secularized by this overwhelming subjugation of Spirit.

There was one ritual, however, that still had a touch of sanctity about it, and it was the only one of which the *nkumbi* teachers approved when I told them about it. It was called "handing," and it took place in the ancient school hall which somehow, for the boys at least, was even more of a sacred place than the abbey. Appropriately, it was just called "School." At the far end of this huge hall there was a raised dais, in the center of which stood a table, the drawer of which faced the assembly. The drawer was always partly open and out of it protruded two birches. Handing took place when a boy had committed a particularly heinous crime, some breach of etiquette. What we called etiquette, or good manners, was after all not all that dissimilar from "the way of the ancestors" . . . it was part of *our* sacred and any breach of it was equivalent to sacrilege. The entire school was assembled for the ritual. In this way it was made public rather than private, as a caning by the headmaster in his study would have been; and it was made both official and sacred by having the handing in School. Further, unlike any other ordeals or punishments, this was clearly a ritual with high symbolic content. The miscreant was called up to the dais, his offense was made public, and the headmaster then lightly touched him on each hand with one of the birches, and that was that. The effect was powerful; the boy was never again regarded in quite the same way, and the handing carried with it unmistakable ostracism.

Handing was such a rare ritual that you could go through your whole school career without seeing one take place, though that table was always there, with the sacred birches sticking out of the drawer, to remind you of your obligation to the "way," every time you went into the hall. So it was right that the whole school should be assembled there, in the ancestral hall, every day after the last class. The occasion was called "Latin prayers," and for me it was the most sacred moment of each day, more sacred by far than the school "service" which took place every morning in the abbey, technically the school chapel. "Prayer" has a much more direct relationship to the concept of Spirit than does the word "service," particularly if referred to as "morning service" rather than "divine service." Language was the second factor that helped convey special sanctity to Latin prayers. Latin was, after all, the language of the early Church, and despite the Reformation, Westminster School remained a Roman Catholic institution for some time and even after conversion retained some old Catholic rituals. Grace before and after meals was always said in Latin, and the evening prayers, in School, were said and sung in Latin. And thirdly the place was sacred and for us, filled with the ancestral spirit. During the morning service the abbey was exclusively ours, but though it too was a sacred place, that sanctity was somehow violated by the subsequent admission of the general public, the uninitiated. School was never violated in this way; like the *nkumbi* camp, noninitiates were ideally never allowed within its walls. It was particularly sacred because it was ours, and because it was filled with symbols of our ancestry, of the special community that we had joined. But it was typical of Westminster that it seemed to go out of its way to desacralize Latin prayers and treat that daily event as though it were nothing more than another quaint secular formality by which we showed how different we were from everyone else. Prayers there may have been; of worship there was nothing. If anything, Latin prayers corresponded most closely to the annual secular ritual of the Latin play, rather than to the morning service in the abbey during which at least some nominal exhortation to higher things was occasionally offered.

One other special school activity, generally considered to be highly secular, was also traditionally held in School. Since everything that takes place in a sacred place, as in the *nkumbi* camp, is to some extent sacralized and acquires a sacred power of its own, so perhaps did the Pancake Greaze, unlikely as that might seem. But just as everything the vulnerable adolescent learns in the sacred *nkumbi* camp is taken to construct a model of the ideal and sacred way in which adult life should be lived, so then must we consider what kind of ideal adult behavior the Greaze symbolized, since it was singled out with handing and Latin prayers for the honor of being held in School every Shrove Tuesday according to centuries-old custom full of hidden ritual and symbolic elements. At the time of the Reformation, the universities of Oxford and Cambridge, and three public schools, Eton, Winchester, and Westminster, received special permission to continue to hold their services in Latin. At Westminster, the senior boys occupied the upper end of the great hall, formerly the monks' dormitory, and the junior boys the lower. The Upper School was divided from the Under School by a large curtain hung from a metal bar high up under the fifteenth-century hammer beam roof. Here, every year on Shrove Tuesday, the ritual Greaze takes place, with the entire student population, Upper and Under, fighting for a pancake that the school chef tossed over the bar, the curtain (no longer used) drawn. Each form, or class, elects one representative, usually its biggest, toughest, and roughest member. Since mine was a very junior class with little chance of winning the Greaze, it was decided to take the opportunity to victimize its two youngest fellows, both pinstripers. Luckily, the other boy was smaller and weaker than me, so he was elected. Our peers openly enjoyed the prospect of his humiliation and probable injury, and laughed at the thought of the pain he would certainly suffer in a battle that, if ritual, was far from controlled. There was more cruelty in this malice alone than I have ever seen in the entire course of any *nkumbi*.

When the day arrived the whole school was assembled in the ancient hall, the ancestral birches as prominent as ever at the far (Upper) end. The teachers wore their gowns, we wore our tails, and the Greazers wore whatever they felt would best protect them from their fellow initiates. The contestants gathered in a circle under the central bar, and then the school chef entered in full uniform, his white hat seeming taller than ever. He carried his frying pan as though it were the royal scepter. At a signal from the headmaster he eyed the bar above him, took a few practice swings like a golfer, then slung the pancake up in a great arc so that it crossed over the bar, from the Upper side of School to the Under, into the center of the waiting circle of Greazers. Even as it fell they were leaping for it, tearing it to shreds, then fighting each other to get the largest hunk they could. Sharing was as far from their mind as was food or the upcoming religious festival of Lent. That was at least consistent with the rest of our adolescent education, as was the highly competitive nature of the event, its aggressivity and even its violence. Our class representative was completely submerged in the kicking, clawing, scratching, biting mountain of British adolescence.

Eventually, an end was called and those who had managed to get and hold on to a recognizable lump of pancake lined up to have it weighed. There were approving laughs and cheers as contestants revealed where they had hidden their bit of dough, safe from the scrimmage; another consistent manifestation of the value of deceit or trickery. The victor was awarded one guinea and the admiration, envy, or hostility of his fellows. There was anything but the equalization that *nkumbi* teachers see as the proper ritual objective, anything but cooperation or sharing or mutual concern. However, again we have to ask ourselves whether, nonetheless, the Pancake Greaze did not teach us the values necessary to us in our society just as effectively as the *nkumbi* prepares the *baganza* for their world. But even if we do each learn the values appropriate to our society, there is a world of difference in the manner of learning.

The adolescent is perfectly capable of reason, and should be prepared for intellectual development. But the symbols we feed him are mostly in the form of words, and words, written or spoken, come from outside. In this way we learn what others tell us, and although the values we learn by listening or reading are reinforced by the sports and games that form the other prime instrument of learning at most schools, they are still external, coming to us from the outside. It is through symbols other than words, symbols that he can see or hear or taste or touch, that the *nkumbi* initiate learns. There are no clear verbal definitions, no written or oral examinations.

Whether the boys have learned correctly or not is tested against their behavior toward each other, their teachers, and the symbols themselves. They each make their own way to the same truth, each making it *his* own truth. At school I did, or did not do, what I was told; the *nkumbi* initiate does what he *feels* to be right, and although each may feel slightly different, the net result is the same degree of conformity that is necessary in any society, and that we achieve through law. In adult life, perhaps partly as a result of our way of dealing with adolescence, social order for us rests on a law that is external to the individual; we are coerced into social behavior. In the Ituri, and in other similar societies, the same degree of social order is achieved without law, without even the threat of physical coercion, because each individual is impelled to social behavior from within, having learned to feel that way and to *want* to feel that way.

When, not long out of adolescence myself, I first saw the girls of the *elima* rolling the round fruits of the gardenia down from their bare shoulders, bouncing them off their upturned young breasts, and throwing them back onto their shoulders again, I was mildly shocked at such public display, at such sport being made of the human body. Then when I saw Akidinimba and others like her flaunting their nubility, tossing their breasts up and down, swinging them from side to side, waving them like flags at the male youths, I thought I was witness to that legendary (and quite nonexistent) primitive promiscuity. Similar behavior among the male Mbuti adolescents could equally easily be mistaken for uncontrolled, indiscriminate sexuality, if not perversion. But at variance with this interpretation of erotic play and dance were the equally observable, highly mature, socially responsible, interpersonal and intergroup relationships that invariably accompanied this behavior. Premarital sexual relationships, following the pattern established by play and dance, were similarly far from promiscuous; despite considerable freedom of choice in some respects, as to the act itself, there was careful control at all times. Far from diminishing pleasure in either the relationship or the act, the control (learned during the *elima* and the *nkumbi* schoolings) transformed the pleasure into something even higher and more intense; just as the joys of play and dance are greatest when shared with others, so it is, the young Mbuti discover, with this wonderful new form of self-expression. Although performed in private, the sexual act, in sentiment, becomes communal; an immense, exultant testimony to man's potential for sociality. Sex and sociality become inextricably bound together, each lending new wonder to the other, and in such a society, at adolescence, children, youths, adults, and elders all join in helping adolescents celebrate their new-found power.

At Westminster our young bodies were ready, however unprepared our minds. Many, like me, had been so effectively isolated in childhood that we knew nothing of the realities of sexual activity until summoned for a private, fifteen-minute talk on "the facts of life." My parents, as had most others, opted for my housemaster to undertake this distasteful chore. Now just consider the social implications and once again see how the tiniest details can have profound significance. It is significant in itself that for me this should be one of the most vivid memories of my school days.

Shortly after coming to Westminster I was sitting in a French class, looking through the sooty old skylights at the buttresses of the abbey, flying high above. A message was delivered to the French master asking for me to be excused and sent to my housemaster. When this was announced there was a titter of laughter that I did not understand. Note the conjunction of the sacred abbey, the profane ridicule, linked together by a message summoning me to my initiation into the mysteries of sex. My housemaster sat me down in his study and reminded me that I had just turned thirteen. That seemed an odd remark, so I did not respond in the hopeful little silence he left for me to fill. The seat I was in was an armchair of brown leather. His teeth were bad and he smelled of tobacco. He was *not* wearing his gown, so this was not an academic matter, nor could it have anything to do with the school. It was morning. I was at a loss. My housemaster continued, announcing that my parents had told him that I was uninformed as to the facts of life and had asked him to tell me about them. He left another little silence, as though he had asked me a question in class, but when again I did not respond he filled the silence with embarrassment rather than anger. The brown leather was cold, so I sat on my tails. I was still completely in the dark. Irene Fritzel had never told me that urinating in someone else's mouth was "a fact of life," and I had never heard that phrase. But then came more questions that fascinated me. Had I ever had a wet dream . . . and no, it was *not* the same as bedwetting. What about a "nocturnal emission," and that too had to be explained. When I displayed total ignorance of the phenomenon and denied ever having caused it to happen, far from explaining it, let alone its social consequence, he hurriedly ended the ordeal with an abrupt, "Well, don't worry, when it happens, just come and tell me and we'll have another talk." He raced to a full stop, gave me a note to take back to the French class, giving the time. It was 10:30 A.M. It annoys me that I cannot remember the day of the week, but I know it was spring and still chilly. He put on his gown as I left, clearly telling me that the facts of life had nothing to do with school and I should forget them at once. So I promptly went to the basement toilet and tried rubbing my legs together and everything else, as he had obligingly specified, and with a curious mixture of fear and delight the appropriate results were achieved. There was no time to go and tell the housemaster of my success so I went back to class. The French master, whose suit under his black gown was a drab brown, like the leather chair and my housemaster's teeth (very definitely secular, not sacred), read the note aloud. It was not proper for a master to wear brown. It certainly was not proper for him to be shabby and drab. I felt tainted every time that man talked to me when he was dressed like that. "Turnbull," he said, "this note says you left your housemaster at ten-thirty. It is now eleven. I presume he was telling you the facts of life and you were delayed on your way back." The class, most of whom were at least one year older than I was, broke into guffaws of laughter, and I was mortified without knowing why.

So "the system" determined that sex, like so many other worthwhile things, should become something very private and secret for me. In public it was associated with cold brown leather, drab clothing, shabbiness, bad teeth, stale tobacco breath, ridicule, mortification, and shame. But the abbey buttresses were still there, reaching into the clouds through the skylights of that ancient classroom, and that proved my avenue of escape. No thanks to the system, my first real brush with the truth of my adolescence is more happily associated with empty churches, and the Rule Water, and old Great-uncle Willie, and a tree beckoning to me through a heavy fog. Throughout this time of general growth these two sets of associations did battle, and throughout, my mind was blissfully uncontaminated by knowledge that could have connected sex with women or babies, let alone with a creative social responsibility.

It was a battle between the sacred and the profane; the sacred was private and the profane was very public, only barely concealed from adult authority. It was *directly* due to that authority that sex became something private and shameful, unnatural and debasing rather than public and joyful, responsible and ennobling. Sex was sullied by the same values we learned in other ways; deceit, violence, and competition. From most of that I was shielded until, because of the war, we were evacuated away from London and the sacred world of the abbey and Latin prayers. But then, within my first week in a school dormitory, I saw everything, starting with the gang rape of a friend of mine who did not yell for help or scream as I would have done. As he fought silently, he just cried. It was his tears, and mine as I watched, that bound us together and brought a glimmer of beauty and the real meaning of love, by its very absence, to our adolescence. For three long years this was how we learned to deal with our frightening new power, blind to the essential goodness of its nature.

While the nocturnal activity was, of course, concealed from the teachers, it was openly competitive among ourselves. It was a major means of acquiring status. There were those who engaged in entrapment, enjoying the pleasure of a brief encounter and then winning favor by reporting the incident to the authorities. There were those who boasted conquests, real or otherwise, sometimes just to harm some boy who had refused their advances. And of course there were those who acquired another kind of reputation by being willing to give themselves wherever there was advantage, competing for the patronage of the older boys; just as some out of fear competed in the same way, but for protection. It would have been good training for life in a prison. But the competitive spirit was nowhere more harmful to our understanding of the beauty and potential of adolescence than in the mornings, when in the bathroom the boys who prided themselves as being above such homosexual activity used to compete with each other to see who could splatter his sperm highest up on the white tiled wall. To me the emptiness of that act was more debasing than anything else that went on, symbolic of another emptiness that permeated our adolescence. If two boys formed a liaison, either for mutual pleasure or for protection, they were criticized for exclusivity, for selfishness, and lack of "team spirit." But far worse, if two boys formed a liaison because of mutual affection and respect, whether such a liaison was accompanied by sexual interaction or not, the two were condemned publicly and accused of all manner of perversions. Yet gang rape or splattering sperm on walls was just "good clean fun." In all these ways our first sexual experiences were systematically divorced from normal human relationships and set against the concept of sociality. Far from being acts of creation, even in our minds they were acts of destruction; in place of beauty there was ugliness.

To the child the world is full of wonder, a wonder that is felt with all the senses. Adolescence can and should add yet another dimension to this wonderment, providing another sense, another means of perception, another means for self-expression. It should make the world even more beautiful, and human relationships even more challenging and full of richness and reward. Working in harmony with all our other faculties, harnessed to the goal of social consciousness, the very special quality of adolescence can effect the transformation that makes of the child a complete being; still imperfect in some respects, still to be developed and trained and readied for adult life, but complete and integral, mind, body, and soul. Indeed it is in neglecting the inescapable relation of the generative act to soul that our manner of dealing with adolescence does the greatest harm, driving a wedge between them, just as it does between body and mind, giving the word "love" an almost exclusively physical, sexual connotation.

The kind of leap that we compel our children to make at puberty also separates them from patterns already established in childhood that could well continue, in adulthood, to impel the individual into social action rather than into a quest for individual survival. It fails to provide that transformation which is essential to reincorporation, the third stage of any rite of passage. In my case I was returned, untransformed, to the care of my parents, who had the authority to forward me on into youth, the next intermediate stage between childhood and adulthood. In normal times that would correspond to university or technical training school, and although World War II had already broken out, so it was for me, because I was too young as yet to be conscripted.

Others of my schoolfellows were not so lucky. Similarly dismembered at school, they were sent, mind, body, and soul, into the armed services and, for some of them, to an early death. A few went directly to positions waiting for them in the adult world. But all of us were forced to make the same leap into a world that was as unknown to us as we were to it. *Re*incorporation was a technical impossibility. Our families were no longer the same because our whole concept of kinship had been changed and we had been taught to be independent. Our bodies had been taught to be competitive and aggressive just as our minds had been filled with perceptions of ourselves as individuals, so our relationships with all others, even kin, were marked by distance, by latent suspicion, if not hostility, concealed by the respectable cover of "reserve." Our bodies went to different territories, universities or army camps or other places where we were to be employed or otherwise occupied; all of them unfamiliar places. "Home" was a mere transit camp at best. Since there was nothing to go back to, reincorporation was impossible, and since we had not been transformed into whole beings but rather had been fragmented, simple incorporation was equally impossible. Our various component parts were added to our new worlds like so many discrete isolates; insoluble, unblendable, incompatible. In the absence of transformation, even those of us who successfully adapted to the new world and found our individual place were in danger of succumbing to that peculiarly Western disease, terminal adolescence.

During my four years of schooling, at least the school allowed the facts of life fifteen minutes of its official and undivided attention. To the soul it gave nothing, unless by soul we mean an intellectual dogma to be argued, asserted, or denied. "Religion" was taught just like any other class and was as far removed from soul as were mathematics or chemistry; not once did it touch on Spirit, or the religious experience. Any exaltation of the soul that might occur was as aberrant and as unmentionable as its physical counterpart, the orgasm. While I quickly recognized that the latter was a shameful thing never to be discussed, for my first year at school I did continue to think that the former was respectable. And before we were evacuated from London, I did find exaltation of the soul in the proximity of that glorious abbey, in the sound of the great organ, the echo of the muted voices of visiting pilgrims; the cool, smooth touch of marble monuments, and the smell of antiquity. It all gave me a sense of belonging, as we adolescents took possession of our abbey and truly made it ours for thirty minutes of each day. And to have a sense of belonging you have to have a sense of who and what you are; it was at least a start. It could have been put to good use if only those of us who felt this (and I think most felt *something*) had been encouraged to carry those precious moments with us into the rest of the day; but the system ignored this brush with Spirit, and for most of us it remained imprisoned in the abbey.

The waste of opportunity was widespread, for I felt the same sense of the sacred elsewhere, as is the way with adolescents. I could invoke it by walking around the cloisters, or sometimes it just came to me in a moment of need, as it did when it rescued me and raised me above the mortification suffered in that French class, coming to me then in the form of all those buttresses and pinnacles seen through dirty classroom skylights. Even in that horrendous O.T.C. camp, I felt the presence of a transforming exaltation of Spirit that momentarily reduced the most sordid and brutal antics of my companions to insignificance. There, it was the dark line of the forest that began at the foot of the soggy fields where our infantile army was encamped. There were religious symbols all around us that similarly, passively, offered themselves to all our senses, inviting us to feel, to explore, to experience, and to exult in what we discovered. And as adolescents we were ready for just such experiences and exultation. But there was no one to point the way. Surrounded as we were, at Westminster, by symbols of higher reality, religious and social, the "system" did nothing to encourage us to recognize them for what they were. We were, on the contrary, taught to reduce them all to the lowest level of empirical reality; Spirit was systematically annihilated.

For various obscure reasons I was selected for early enrollment into the confirmation class. I was later told that this was where our souls were dealt with, but at the time I thought I was volunteering for a class in religious history that, being given after hours, offered other opportunities. I was duly confirmed, with much pomp, in Westminster Abbey, as a fully instructed member of the Church—a church to which I did not belong—and the only piece of positive instruction that I now remember receiving in preparation for confirmation was that none of us should put grease on our hair out of deference to the bishop's hands. The only confirmation that was achieved was to confirm my intuitive belief that Church and Spirit had little to do with each other. Like sex, music, and anything else that evoked a sense of goodness and beauty, Spirit became private, carefully concealed and separated from the rest of me so that it would not be profaned by others. And, as with all those wonderful creative elements, the school swept soul under the carpet as soon as it appeared, as though anything that we discovered to be beautiful was shameful evidence of our childishness, our weakness, our refusal to grow up and "behave like adults."

Now since much of this is so obviously specific to a certain time and place, we have to be careful to continue to sift out the general principles at work. Right here the one that concerns us is that in every society areas of conflict are predictable and can be turned to the benefit of society, if properly controlled and exploited. We are in one such area here, that of the generation gap, but there is much more to it than meets the eye. It is more than that childhood and adolescence are *not* the same thing for each succeeding generation, so that adults cannot with real justification claim to understand their children simply because they themselves have been through both childhood and adolescence, least of all in our rapidly changing modern world. Part of the conflict, and a much more significant part and one that in many cultures comes to the fore during adolescence, is that basic and frighteningly crucial conflict between the individual and society. Childhood was spent in exploration, in the process of becoming. In adolescence the child's individuality is taking on a very definite and distinctive form and rapidly asserting itself with all the vigor that comes with sexual maturity. But, as we have seen, adolescence in other cultures is also a time for transformation; a time for individuality, caught in all the freshness of its first flush, to be expanded, even exploded, into the infinitely greater richness of sociality. Yet even there adolescent individuality is likely to rebel, perceiving this transformation to be a diminution rather than an expansion of self. There is nothing wrong with such rebellion; it demonstrates, rather, an acute awareness of the critical issue at stake: is life to be lived for the greater or lesser good? The *nkumbi* provided ritualized ways of dealing with this conflict, just as all other forms of conflict were dealt with (and largely averted) by their regular and ritual manifestation in the same society.

At Westminster and, from what I can gather, at other public schools, and from what I can observe here in the United States at schools of all kinds throughout the nation, one part of the process is at work but not the other. The adolescent feels the conflict, senses its nature, but is not given socially acceptable, let alone beneficial, ways of dealing with it, ritual or otherwise. It is as though we are unaware of what is happening, for we concern ourselves only with the symptom, mistaking it for the sickness. The least harmful manifestation of this conflict takes the form of dress, dress that is bizarre and usually offensive to the adult norms of the time; perhaps smoking and drinking come next, a protest against continued refusal to allow the norms of adult behavior to apply; then drug-taking and membership in exotic cults, perhaps an unconscious search by the social self for community rather than isolation. Any or all of these manifestations are usually combined with flouting all established sexual norms; a desperate attempt to discover love. The adult world manifests enormous concern at this phenomenon, as though it were something new, unusual, unpredictable, unnatural, and unhealthy. This widespread concern among parents and educators is focused on the physical and mental health of the adolescents, who are perceived to be in danger. Judges in juvenile courts see another danger, to society itself; they see the beginnings of a life of crime or, at best, of social irresponsibility. They seek to re-solve the problem, to cure the sickness, by repressing the symptoms. They deny access to cigarettes, drink, and drugs, enforce conformity of dress, and take legal steps to prevent adolescents from joining "unacceptable" religious cults. And in so doing they repress often healthy social yearnings, of which these are sadly mistaken expressions. In fact these yearnings, which some perceive as unbridled sexual license, may well be forlorn attempts to express a capacity for love in what adolescents so tragically believe to be its highest and purest form, for they have found it lacking in other forms.

Many of us have indulged at one time or another in acts of rebellion, but the anthropologist is not interested in the indi-vidual or the acts as such; he wants to know the social signifi-cance, if any, of the behavior. The clue lies in the values that are flaunted or upheld rather than in the law or rule that is transgressed. At Westminster a soul mate joined me in a campaign of petty larceny during which we acquired no small amount of skill in cat burglary and lock-picking. We stole with equal dispassion from boys, masters, and servants, and from the school store. But when it came to distributing the booty across the countryside, as we did, booty from "the good guys" was buried with elaborate pomp, even wrapped like a gift, lovingly placed in parts of the country that to the two of us were the most beautiful, and usually in the dead of night, a time that to us was most sacred. The ritual and symbolic ele-ments, in retrospect, are clear and undeniable. There were even ritual feasts. Booty from "the bad guys," however, was buried with scorn, in cold and shallow graves, or placed under unfeeling stones where it could easily be discovered by any predator, and often buried in daytime. Even at that early age, for all of us, the symbolic process is at work, a vital means of communication that we all too easily overlook. Most of the adolescent behavior that is so puzzling to adults would be immediately comprehensible if only they searched for the proper symbolic key. But it has to be sought. My friend and I, unknowingly, even set ours down on paper, in the form of a map of all our treasure troves. But when we were ultimately discovered, a discovery we had to force, the significance of the map was ignored. We offered it with a sort of educational treasure hunt in mind, in which everyone would participate. That was merely taken as adding insult to injury.

Our sinking opinion of adulthood and diminished respect for authority were confirmed when the only concern of adult authority was to restore the material goods to the rightful owners with a minimum of publicity, a scrupulously correct assessment of financial damages (we buried some things in the waters of a very lovely lake), and a maximum of punishment. The glorious ritual climax that we had planned, that would have brought into the open the values of goodness and beauty triumphant over those of badness and ugliness, never materialized. It was hardly a satisfactory conclusion to the episode for either of us; as a rebellion it was a failure and we were regarded more or less as common thieves. My friend chose to leave the school, I chose to be beaten and to stay for another year of more clandestine rebellion. But at least the two of us had clarified our own perceptions of self and of the essential (for us) distinction between right and wrong, good and bad, the beautiful and the ugly. What we could not find in school in what we were taught by a seemingly unfeeling and unsympathetic adult world, we found in our own way; and in our own way we compelled others to participate in our ritual, trying to make them aware of the all-pervasive emptiness we felt so deeply within.

In adolescence we are in many ways like empty but organic receptacles, fully formed though still growing, waiting to be filled. And like receptacles we are capable at that stage of life of receiving with all our being, becoming one with what is within us. Sexual and spiritual awareness as modes of experience are just as valid as physical and intellectual awareness; and like those other modes of apprehension they can be turned in any direction, inward or outward, restricted to the individual self or encouraged to expand and encompass the infinitely greater social self. They can be poured into the empty receptacle, to work the wonder of transformation, or spilled upon the ground, leaving us empty and unfulfilled. Education and socialization can be accomplished in the solitude of the rational domain, but it is the intensity that these other modes of perception can bring to each and every experience that gives such education an inner significance, endowing it with a vital force. It is this intensity of perception, together with integrity of being, that can make of human society a living, thriving, truly loving, joyously full and exuberant organism, rather than a cold, mechanical, empty theoretical concept. That is the magic of transformation, and that is the potential of adolescence.

PART THREE

YOUTH

THE ART OF REASON

FOR MANY IN WESTERN CULTURES youth is a stage of life that is both confused and confusing. This may in part be because we do not make the clear distinction between adolescence and youth that other cultures do. We use the term as though it had everything to do with age and little or nothing to do with social responsibility or the educational process; in this way adolescents may be referred to as "youths," and so may many of those compelled at an early age to engage in the adult activity of working for a living. If we were to make the distinction it would probably be that adolescence is spent in high school, and youth, for those with the inclination or the good fortune to have that opportunity, in college. But in other cultures adolescence is specifically that period of time that covers puberty, and is just the first step from childhood toward adulthood. That step is carefully guided with all the problems and potential of sexual maturity in mind, and directed toward a transformation of the total being from individual into social awareness. In such a system youth is a necessary second step before true, socially responsible adulthood can be reached. In youth the brain is virtually fully developed, it has been exercised during adolescence and taught how to retain knowledge. That may be enough to equip youth for working for a living, but not for *earning* that living, other cultures tell us. Youth is that time, however long or short, given to developing the art of reason, the power by which we convert mere knowledge to wisdom. Knowledge in itself is of limited use; the art of reason is the art of right application of knowledge. This is perhaps best seen by taking some examples from India, where I was told the following story.

Two young Buddhist monks set out to search for a great sage from whom they could learn. They traveled in many lands before they found the one they sought. When they found him he was already old and was surrounded by many disciples. He welcomed the two friends and asked each one why he had traveled so far in search of a teacher. The one said, "I have come to learn from you; I will be your disciple; teach me all you know." The sage smiled and said, "In that case you may stay, and I will teach you all I know."

The other young monk said, "I came to be with you." The sage seemed not to hear him at first, then got up to leave, and as he was leaving said, "You may also stay."

The two young monks shared a cell, and together they attended all the gatherings of the disciples and listened to all the discourses of the great sage. The one engaged the sage in learned discussion of the scriptures, and the sage taught him all that was in the commentaries and the arts of debate and of reason. The other never took any active part in the discussions. To him the sage said nothing.

After some years the old sage called the two to the sacred tree under which he always held his discourses. He told them that he had given his last discourse and that he was going to devote his remaining years to the pursuit of Nirvana. Both were dismayed and asked what they should do. To the one he said, "You came to learn, and I have taught you all I know. Go back to the world and teach others to be learned; none are as well versed as you in the art of reason."

To the other he said, "You came to be with me. You have become me. Stay and help others to be wise."

Reason and wisdom each have their place, this tells us, and the two should not be confused. Youth is the time to learn the art of reason; old age is the time to practice the art of being, which is being wise, unless wisdom touches us sooner. It cannot be taught. Reason has its limitations, and perhaps the art of reason is the art of recognizing its limitations and leaving

oneself open to the wisdom that comes in other ways, through
other arts. Whereas adolescence can be defined for any culture
in terms of physiology, and specifically in terms of sexual potential, youth is a more elusive category.

Just as in the Ituri Forest the end of adolescence does not
plunge the child-that-was immediately into the full economic
responsibilities of adulthood, so high school is followed, for
those who can afford it at least, by a period that precedes the
assumption of adult responsibility of any kind. More than for
the forest dweller, for the schoolboy there are many skills still
to be learned, and the intellect has yet to be developed in a
special manner to provide for a rational way of dealing with
our complex world. But if in our childhood and adolescence
we have not learned other modes of awareness, if we have not
become fully integrated beings, and if we persist in dissociat-
ing reason from these other faculties, these other modes of
knowing and understanding, then we remain fettered by the
limitations of reason and cease to grow.

For an example of how youth is dealt with in another culture, we are going to have to leave the Ituri, for the most part,
and it is worth asking why this is so. Does this imply that the
Mbuti and their village neighbors either have no more to learn
or do not have the capacity for learning more? Far from it.
The apparent parting of the ways occurs entirely because of
the contextual difference that leads adolescence and youth to
be regarded as a single stage of life in the forest, but requires a
distinction in our own and some other societies. For one thing,
the one context is literate and the other is nonliterate, which
merely means that in a literate society the individual has yet
another skill to learn, another set of symbols to master; his
training takes longer. On top of this is the dominant economic
factor. In a subsistence society the necessary skills are all
learned at an early age by the daily observation of adults performing those skills; all that is required is that the body reach
adult capacity in that respect. Further, in such a small-scale
society there are not only fewer skills to be learned, there is
much less division of labor, and most individuals can and do
learn all the necessary skills, economic and political, in an
ongoing educational process that starts at birth. In our highly
specialized society much of adult life is not observable by the

young, and even if it were possible it would not be desirable for any one person to learn more than a few skills, and even these often require prolonged, specialized training.

Some basic economic skills can just as easily be learned in childhood in our society as in the Ituri, as many a child can testify, having begun to help support his family by the sweat of his hands while still at school. Political and social skills come less easily; the family does not provide an adequate model as it does in the forest. A complex theoretical system has to be learned so that all the intricacies of interpersonal and intergroup relationships can be mastered. At the school level we barely make a start at this, but through teaching the skill of writing and reading we provide the means by which the student, given the will and inclination and the time, can pursue such understanding later.

While for some, youth involves a direct passage from adolescence and high school into the labor market, with little chance for developing full intellectual potential regardless of their ability; others go through the intermediate stage of attending technical training schools or universities. Much of what is taught at university, and the manner of teaching, amounts to little more than technical training and thus, however necessarily, curtails full intellectual development. That is the price we have to pay for the specialization that characterizes our society, in which even the art of reason comes to be considered a specialized skill, appropriate and useful for some and not for others. It is certainly true that eggheads can be just as impoverished and partially developed as the semiliterate street sweeper, if not more so.

We cannot begin to consider all these variables, but at least we should be aware of them while we limit our focus of attention on youth to that segment that goes to a university or through some comparable training in the art of reason. As with schools for adolescents we should try to see what it is that these universities and colleges achieve, not for the individual, but for society at large. Very different from the *nkumbi* or high school, the university, like the public school, is isolated from the rest of society, does not impose restrictions on public or familial behavior during schooling, does not go to the public and demand that it reassess and modify or reify the social norms, and does not demand public consent and approval before the degree is conferred. However, all this does not mean that the institution contributes less to society than the *nkumbi*, which does all of these things; it merely suggests that its contribution may be different in kind and different in intent, and that what may consciously be intended may be very different from what is effected.

But before looking at our society we shall look at two types of universities in India, both firmly within the Hindu culture. The first shares some of the characteristics of social consciousness with the *nkumbi*, but is also related to the second, the more modern Indian university, which in turn forms a bridge with our own system. The three together show us some of the major ways in which youth may be prepared for adult responsibility. This was brought home all the more forcibly to me because when I went to India, shortly after it won its independence, I considered myself fully adult. I had served in the Royal Navy during the war, and had graduated from Oxford University, from where I was encouraged to go to India for graduate studies. I had not yet even thought of ever visiting Africa, so I was unaware of how inadequate was my training in childhood and adolescence, and I certainly thought that Oxford had taught me all that I needed to know during my youth. Wartime service was, for me, more than sufficient evidence of my adulthood, for I had, while undergoing all these stages of life, still learned virtually nothing about social responsibility and was concerned exclusively with my individual rather than my social self. I went to India, then, merely in pursuit of further knowledge, almost as though it were a technical training school that would qualify me to earn my living. And a training school it was.

The art of reason is an ancient one in India, and within two months of my arrival at Banaras Hindu University, in 1949, I discovered that in spite of an Oxford education, I was far from qualified to conduct the postgraduate research in Indian social philosophy for which I had been awarded a grant. Two visiting scholars, one from Madras and one from Calcutta, engaged in a *shastrarth* at one of the *ashrams*, or religious communities, in the city. A *shastrarth* is essentially a public debate, with the public voting in the event that neither scholar concedes defeat. This particular debate concerned the interpretation of a single Sanskrit word, and most of it was incomprehensible to me. I felt prompted to learn more about the debate from the students who formed each teacher's retinue and who were expected to engage in a debate of their own after each session, as part of their training. They accepted my inquiry with courtesy and interest, but first they demanded my credentials and the name of my teacher. I named Sir S. Radhakrishnan, who had been the Spalding Professor of Oriental Philosophy at Oxford, and Professor B. L. Atreya, who was head of the Department of Indian Religion and Philosophy at Banaras Hindu University, and who was supervising my doctoral studies. Satisfied, they then asked to know *my* position with respect to this obscure Sanskrit term, which I have ever since blotted from my memory. When they saw that I did not even know the word, they inquired why I wasted my time attending the *shastrarth*, or theirs by seeking to engage them in discussion since I knew less than a child. They suggested that I go back to school and learn some basic facts before I attempted to reason. Of course they were absolutely right. Just as reason comes before wisdom, so knowledge comes before reason. The acquisition of knowledge is one of the mechanical skills we learn at school; what we do with that knowledge depends to a large extent on how well we learn the art of reason during youth. These young students were part of an ancient tradition in which youth is a time set aside for learning how to deal rationally not only with facts but with existence itself.

Traditional Hindu culture recognizes four stages of life. The first, unexpectedly, is not childhood, but youth. Until youth, after all, you are not a whole person in mind, body, and spirit, so you cannot truly be said to be alive (how close the Hindu is to the Mbuti in this). That first stage is known as *brahmacharya*, a period of celibacy and, ideally, of intensive education in a religious school away from home. It starts in the student's tenth year or so and lasts for ten years. Then comes the second stage of life, *gṛhastha*, during which one raises a family and performs worldly duties. Once parents have seen their children established in life, they reach the third stage of life, *vanaprastha*, in which they live separately but not necessarily as anchorites, gradually ridding themselves not only of worldly possessions, but of all attachment to material wealth and considerations. When that has been achieved, they are ready to enter the final stage of life, *sannyas*, in which they live as religious mendicants, free of attachment, totally dependent for material sustenance on the charity of others.

The Hindu child's socialization begins in earnest at about the age of five when he undergoes the *vidyarambha* ritual, which marks his entry into the educational system. The major aspect of the ritual is that it introduces him to the worship of Sarasvati, the Goddess of Learning. Incidentally, it would be more consistent with Hindu thought if we substituted the words "sacred symbol" for "goddess" or "god," but I shall retain the English usage because of its connotations of that which is sacred. However, it does not necessarily imply an external force, but rather an internal one. The boy also now participates in the worship of the guardian deities (symbols) of his family (unity), already knowing full well at five that these are all but aspects of the one divinity, the one absolute reality. This ritual is relatively recent, the earliest references to it not being much more than a thousand years old; it probably arose at a time when the classical language of the scriptures was no longer a widely spoken language, so the child needed a primary education to prepare him for his real education as a youth. This has something to say about the much neglected role of classical languages in our own educational system; they are the original vehicle of much that is or was sacred in our lives, and perhaps their neglect represents a neglect of the sacred.

For the traditional Hindu, youth, or *brahmacharya*, begins around the age of ten with a ritual known as *upanayana*, which rather literally means the handing over of a youth to his teacher. The ritual is almost universally known outside India, and to a large extent in India itself, as "the Sacred Thread" ceremony, which refers only to one not overly significant part of the ritual, for the sacred thread with which the boy is invested is no more than a symbolic replacement of the cloth with which the upper part of the body must be covered during the performance of any worship.

The ritual, being a true rite of passage, opens with a break-fast that the boy shares with his mother *before* he bathes, a reversal of the norm, at other time an impurity. This separates him from his childhood and its associated lack of discipline and responsibility. His head is then shaved and he is bathed, a further separation from the past. He is then invested with a *kaupina* with which to cover his private parts, and a three-stranded girdle to hold up the *kaupina;* sexual power is thus associated with intellectual power and both are sacralized by the ritual. As this is being done he is told that the girdle repre-sents the three *vedas* (scriptures) and will protect his chastity and purity. Finally, in this ritual of separation, the boy is given the cloth with which to cover the upper part of his body so that he may participate in subsequent rituals and achieve both spiritual and intellectual growth. Since this cloth is an integral part of any ritual performance, and since the sacred thread that represents the ritual robe is worn at all times, it may be said that *any* act performed by anyone wearing the sacred thread thereby is in a sense ritualized, the sacred con-stantly being brought to bear on the otherwise profane.

The boy is then ready to make his first offering to the sacred fire, while being exhorted to be as brilliant and powerful as the flame in both his scholarship and his spiritual strength. This part of the rite places the student under the divine pro-tection of Savitri. He then stands on a stone to emphasize the need for strength of purpose and determination (there was a stone at Westminster on which only monitors could stand). The boy's future teacher then asks the boy who his teacher is, and when the candidate names his teacher he is told that on the contrary, he is now "the pupil of the gods," that the teacher is merely the intermediary. The teacher, placing his hand above the boy's heart, prays that there shall be total com-munion and harmony between them during the years that follow, and then initiates him into the *gayatri mantra,* a simple but magnificent prayer to the sun with which the boy from now onward will welcome the dawn every day of his life.

He is then invested with a staff with which to begin his journey on the road to knowledge and wisdom. He will use this staff during his life at school, such as when walking through a forest trail or while performing some service for the teacher, herding cattle or buffalo; it is another reminder of the conjunction of the sacred and the profane. In anticipation of the final stage of life, that of a religious mendicant or *sannyasin*, the boy/student must now beg for his first food, as a youth, from his family. I have seen more than one occasion on which a boy was obliged to beg throughout the village, and had anyone refused him food it would have been a sure indication that they thought him unworthy. In this way the interdependence between the individual, his family, and society at large is made plain. In some of the more orthodox schools the students may eat only food they have begged, reminding them constantly of their dependence upon as well as their responsibility toward others. After three further days there is a final rite in which the teacher assumes the role of the boy's father. The separation is complete and the youth now begins the long period of *brahmacharya*, which may take place in a remote, highly orthodox school known as a *gurukula* or in a less orthodox village school. Some villages, those with wealthy patrons who established schools there with a well-endowed faculty of learned pandits, became centers of learning where even higher education was free to all comers, provided only that they had academic ability and were ready to accept the discipline. Today, the government of India has all but brought all these schools, together with the many others financed and run privately by individuals, missions, or other groups, into a more or less centralized system of education. Not many orthodox *gurukula* are left, and they either have to conform to government standards, or students have to wait until they have completed their minimum required education before embarking on the very special education offered at these ancient institutions, where they are not merely filled with knowledge, but taught the art of reason.

Gurukula are sometimes known as "forest universities" because of their preference for seclusion and isolation from the material, man-made world. On my first visit to India from Oxford, I myself stayed at one, not so much as a student as because while high up in the Himalayas, following the pilgrim route that crosses from the source of the Jumna to the source of the Ganga, I was suddenly struck with a violent attack of hepatitis and only just had enough strength to get back down to a *gurukula* in the Himalayan foothills, where the Ganga is a raging torrent compressed between forested mountainsides rising steeply on both sides. This *ashram*, or religious community, was more than a university. It was a rest home for any who wanted to get away from the world for a while; it was also a stopping place for pilgrims taking the more conventional route to the source of the Ganga, at Gangotri. It was also a hospital. It cared for mind, body, and soul. I was received almost as though I had been expected and carried to a stone cell higher up the mountainside, where I was cared for until fit enough to begin to move around on my own. The cell was one of the many in which the students lived. There was just enough room for one bed, a simple wooden board with a clean piece of cloth for a mattress. For a student this would double as a chair and a desk; the small table that was the only other item of furniture was only to hold a bowl of water for washing. A piece of string served as a line on which the student could hang his one change of clothes, a single length of cloth, after washing in the icy Ganga each morning. The open window space had wooden shutters, and was barred against the larger monkeys who used to come and sit outside and watch me as I lay there, oblivious to the intense discomfort, on that hard wooden board. By the time I was better, I had learned that the Spartan cell, in its simplicity, offered a much greater comfort than physical. I had not set out to test the rigors of a *gurukula* education; in fact, I knew next to nothing about the institution at that time; but I came to recognize that far from being a life of deprivation, which is how we so often picture the life of the ascetic, it was a life of a different kind of luxury—fulfillment.

Here was a place in modern India, established and run in the full tradition of the ancient *gurukula*, not only aware that times had changed and present-day needs were in many respects different from those of yesterday, but actively meeting those needs. The students who came here were different from students at the well-known urban universities of India, primarily because they had taken the full vows of *brahmacharya* and also had chosen an education that joined, rather than separated, body and soul. Some of them intended at the end of their schooling to bypass the next stage of life, *gṛhastha*, renouncing marriage and the obligations of family and home, and pass from youth directly to the final stage of life, *sannyas*, in which they would become religious mendicants. For them the final years at the *gurukula* would serve as their stage of *vanaprastha*, and they would live in isolation in one of those small stone cells on the wooded mountainside.

Others of the *brahmachari* go back to remote rural villages and themselves become teachers. Still others return to wealthy homes in major cities and become businessmen, or go on to a formal university and acquire a professional degree. But wherever they go and whatever they do, they bring something with them that few others have. The reverse flow is equally varied, consisting largely of adults who seek to recapture something they lost during their youth, or something they had never acquired. There would be nothing particularly strange about finding a cabinet minister sitting in the assembly hall beside a beggar from the streets of a nearby town and a student from some other school or university. Every *gurukula* that I have seen has this quality of being both in the world and beyond it, and not one of them makes any demand for payment. Those who can contribute to the finances do so; they are no more welcome and no less welcome than those who can contribute nothing, even for their food, let alone their instruction. Only one thing is demanded, and that is devotion.

These *gurukula* are no easy havens for the lazy, irresponsible, or unsuccessful, for the devotion demanded involves an acceptance that this is a place of arduous preparation for life; it is arduous for the young *brahmachari* students and it is arduous for the teachers, themselves celibate *sannyasi* who live, if anything, under an even more rigorous discipline than the students. As soon as I was well enough I was required to participate, as part of my "cure." At the time I did not realize that I was considered as being in need of curing from more than hepatitis. At first I thought the discipline would be both overly rigorous and distasteful; for one thing it was set out on an instruction sheet for newcomers and despotically seemed to seek to control every waking moment. The day's activities started at four A.M. in the assembly hall, with *japa* (recitation of the name of god) and meditation. This was followed by various exercises in yoga, with only fifteen minutes of rest, and then a period of silence (*mauna*) and prayer. The assembly concluded with an hour of chanting and study of the Bhagavad Gita, one of the greatest and most popular of Hindu scriptures. From seven to eight A.M. everyone was required to perform *nishkamya seva*, or "selfless service," silently serving the needs of the *ashram*, however menial, or attending to individuals unable to care for themselves.

The next twelve hours were devoted to study of all the major subjects taught to youths in any school, and in service to the *ashram*. All the chores were taken care of by the students; there were no servants, unless it could be said that we were all servants. Whereas the first four hours of the day and the last two (spent in communal prayer, scriptural discussion, or *kirtan*, the singing of sacred songs) were focused directly on spiritual development, the twelve intervening hours involved the body and mind as well. Certain times were set aside for individual study, which we could do wherever we liked, in the library, in our cells, or in the woods, or on a rock on the banks of the Ganga. It became second nature to match our choice of place to our mood, so that intellectual study became a physical and emotional satisfaction as well.

At other times the head of the *ashram* was available for private discussion, as were other teachers, and there was a time when students who wished could join in some debate in the assembly hall. For the advanced students these debates were compulsory, and they learned that part of the art of reason lies in recognition of the need, even while disputing, for a total absence of competition, in the presumption that both disputants are in search of the same truth and are helping each other rather than competing.

There were also classes, held on a regular basis as part of a well-planned curriculum, which were attended by the less advanced students. As described it sounds as though the day were divided into sacred and secular activities, and it could be so described with justification; but it was during the secular activities that the religious ideals of the Hindu way of life became a living reality, without the students even being aware of it at first. And through the discipline that all accepted, youths learned to live life in a way that integrated their whole being as a single, vital entity in which there was no place for a division into sacred and secular; the segregation of their lives into separate and isolated economic, political, and religious segments became unthinkable.

As I have mentioned, *brahmacharya*, or the stage of youth, is a period of celibacy. The *gurukula* isolated from towns and villages fosters the practice of celibacy by removing youth from the temptations that arise from the explosion of energy and creativity that gives youth its unique potential. In sharp contrast to our own attitude, celibacy is thought of as a freedom rather than as a constraint. The vital force of the body, the force of life, is associated with spiritual force, so the very effort toward abstinence unites mind, body, and spirit, something that focusing on one aspect to the exclusion of others can never do. We in the West tend to think of celibacy as a goal in itself rather than as part of a coordinated approach to living life to the very fullest. In the framework of Hindu belief it is the effort that is important, and the emphasis on celibacy makes most sense to youth. To them celibacy appears not as a deprivation but as an opportunity, all the more real because of the reality of the power the youth feel within their young selves. The rigorous discipline helps make the attainment of celibacy easier in the *gurukula* than elsewhere. A carefully supervised diet avoids those foods classified in the Hindu system as *tamasic*, or likely to arouse passion of any kind, but these are mere mechanical aids. The focus is on encouraging the effort rather than on demanding achievement, and the encouragement is given, as is proper for youth, through the art of reason, by providing the rational incentive of growth into a full being rather than a partial being. And there is absolutely no question that the youths, few of whom attain absolute celibacy at first, themselves find that the reward for making the effort more than justifies the effort. They find that the closer they come to achievement the greater the freedom and fulfillment of their total being.

Even outside the *gurukula* there are a number of pressures and incentives that help boys and girls to desire and achieve a degree of celibacy quite remarkable by comparison with the school system I knew. One important factor is that *upanayana*, which is when the period of celibacy begins, takes place just at the age of puberty, prior to the awakening of sexual desire.

Remember that part of *upanayana* ritual requires that the boy be encircled by a girdle that will not only continue to stand as a symbol of his chastity, but which is thought and believed to bring divine aid to that end. No pretense is made that chastity comes easily. The exhortations to be chaste during youth, made during this ritual, are followed immediately by the youth's introduction to scriptures, teaching, and discussions that fully explain the rationale.

There is a correspondence here between the essentially, even prescriptively celibate system of the Hindu during youth, and the essentially and prescriptively noncelibate system of the forest Mbuti and villagers. Both systems demand restraint, be it the restraint practiced by the Mbuti youths in embrace, or the coitus interruptus practiced by village youths, or the abstinence practiced by the young *brahmachari*. Yet in none of these societies is this restraint coerced by threat of physical punishment, no sanctions are invoked to compel it, and it is for most of us so remarkable that we need to know how it is achieved in the absence of coercion. It is the *gurukula* system that has really shown us the answer, for our nagging disbelief that youth can exercise such remarkable control arises mainly from the fact that we insist on referring to it as restraint, and some would even go so far as to say repression. There is something much more positive at work; it is the formidable combination of the value of the social good with a powerful sense of religious belief. Both the African and the Hindu systems clearly demand some measure of control over the sexual urge and sexual activity during youth; they manifest control in different ways and supply different rationales through different systems of belief, but in all cases the overriding value is the supremacy of the social good (perhaps the Hindu might say the greater self) over the individual good (the lesser self). That is a splendid value, most of us will agree, but how can it be so strongly held that in the absence of any other form of coercion it results in a form of self-control among mere youths that few adults could hope to achieve, even if they wished to? This of course ignores the possibility that the voluntary exercise of such control is specifically one of the great potentials of youth, especially if it is taught the art of reason.

Once again we have to confront the creative potential of the conjunction of sex and Spirit. The adolescent, I believe, senses this conjunction, he feels the affinity between the sexual and the spiritual experience, but he cannot yet rationalize it. Just as during adolescence his experience should be developed rather than repressed or ignored, so it should be heightened and given a more rational sense of direction in youth. Our culture has unknowingly deprived us of a great deal by placing so much emphasis on adulthood, and by abrogating to adulthood both the power and the glory of living. In other societies every stage of life has its own special power, its own special abilities, and its own contribution to make. For the adolescent in many other societies, the sexual experience is a glorious sensation, a feeling of greatness that in childhood, with its own glory, had never been known. For the adult it is an act performed consciously and rationally; it is an act of doing, rather than of feeling or thinking, and as an adult, in most societies, one is expected to perform it with a clear recognition of the social consequences. What is the nature of the act for the youth, and more precisely, wherein lies his desire for the sexual experience? Although it may not seem likely at the moment, the question is as applicable to the young celibate, *brahmachari*, as it is to the lusty Mbuti youth, and the answer is the same for both.

For the majority of youths it is not primarily a desire for proximity to another human being; at that stage of life, such proximity is more a means to an end. The desire to "know" (what an apt and rich archaic term that is!) another person more fully comes with adulthood and is evidence of our sociality. Before that comes the natural desire to explore one's own human body and test its potential, and for most of us this results in an agreeable experience. For some it may happen first by accident, without prior desire, but the pleasure leads to a desire for repetition. In the absence of constraints, as among the Mbuti, a youth may experiment with different ways of inducing that pleasurable feeling by coupling with others. This not only increases the pleasure but generally results in more effective orgasm, both of which lead to the realization that various forms of sexual activity are indeed other ways of "knowing," about oneself and about others. But still the initial experience, and the one that dominates throughout youth, is one of pleasure. At its height this pleasure has been described as ecstasy and regarded as unique and supreme. The former it may be, the latter it certainly is not, and to understand that we have to lower our cultural barriers, but not so very far, and use that mode of knowing we call imagination.

A sunset or a mountain vista or a seascape are all often described as "breathtaking." It is a cliché, but it persists because it is apt. I am not being flippant when I say that sexual activity is also, quite literally, breathtaking, for I see a vital relationship suggested by the use of that same symbol in such apparently different contexts. They are both more than just "beautiful" experiences; both involve the taking of the breath of life. There are those who without any sexual manipulation or conscious volition are brought to the point of orgasm by other "breathtaking" experiences. A sudden death or an act of violence can do it, but though related that is not what I am thinking of. Two things can almost do it for me; music and immersion in unsullied nature. But for this to happen it requires the right frame of mind, or perhaps they induce it until the right point is reached. That frame of mind is one of respect. Respect is another rich word that we abuse in daily usage. For me it implies both distance and proximity, fear and joy; it brings us into contact with the unknown. Now if the ecstatic experience can be found as readily in a landscape as in copulation, any youth aware of this has a ready alternative to sexual activity in his search for and delight in pleasure. If his values or those of his society militate against any particular form of sex, or even against all forms of the act, he is deprived of nothing if he has learned the art of cultivating the right frame of mind. I know of no value system that discourages youth from looking at sunsets or making music; I know of some that encourage it (or its equivalent). I know that at Westminster the notion would have been ridiculed, most particularly if placed in such a context. Even my imagination cannot conjure up a very lifelike picture of my housemaster telling me to go and look at the trees in Dean's Yard any time I felt a sexual urge, or take a walk around the cloisters, or go and sit alone in the abbey, or go and play some Bach. Had we but known it, any of those things might have worked; they would certainly have been no less effective than his palpably empty threat of physical and mental debilitation.

Now that I have seen other ways, just to think of Teleabo Kengé in that forest clearing at night, dancing with the forest and dancing with the moon, is ecstasy enough for me, just as it was for him in the full prime of his hot-blooded youth. But then the Mbuti live in a natural world, filled with the beauty and power and awe of nature, and awe is the corollary of respect. And the Mbuti make music day and night, another source of ecstasy for them, and again a literally breathtaking experience, as they fill their lungs with air and expel it in sacred sound that makes the whole body vibrate like the musical instrument it is, creating not just sound but joining with others to create harmony, a harmony as binding and as intimate as any act of copulation.

The *gurukula* students need and deserve no special commendation for their celibacy or restraint; there is no celibacy and there is no restraint. Like the Mbuti, they have *their* form of *molimo*, just as Westminster could have had its *molimo* (and what a *molimo* it would have been, in the abbey or in the ancient school hall; the dormitories would have become dull places indeed!). If you look again at the schedule of daily activities for the *gurukula* you will find two hours of the morning that could be classified as "ecstatic" and two (*gita* and *seva*) that could be classified as semiecstatic, and the last two in the evening again as ecstatic. That means that a student's day is made up of six hours of sleep, twelve hours of study, and six hours of ecstasy. Many forgo two hours of sleep and boost their intake of ecstasy to eight hours. During a *molimo* the Mbuti enjoy from eight to ten hours of ecstasy every night for a minimum of one month. This ritual is repeated, sometimes more than once a year, throughout their lives. For the *gurukula* student the rigorous schedule ends with the termination of their ten or so years at school, but the daily rituals their religious belief enjoins fill each day with moments of ecstasy thereafter, beginning every day with that glorious welcome to the rising sun, the *gayatri*.

I can see it now as plainly as I saw it thirty years ago, every day I was at Banaras, for two years. Young and old go down to the water's edge at dawn and stand there, each alone in his inner self, but all together as one greater Self. One by one, as they feel ready, they walk out into the water until they stand waist-deep. Some stand there for half an hour. It is their time of *japa, mauna,* and *mantra.* Then as the sun rises above the green fields on the far side of the Ganga, its first rays reaching across and touching with warmth the ancient palaces and temples of Banaras, thousands of pairs of hands, cupped together like begging bowls, raise the water to the sky, and thousands of voices recite the sacred *gayatri mantra* so silently you feel rather than hear it. As they let the water trickle back into the holy river the sun catches it, and a million sunlit drops add their beauty to the beauty of the sound of the temple bells and the voices of devotees singing *kirtan,* all in one single greeting to another day of life. And a fragrant incense hangs in the air, binding the sound of beauty with the sight and touch and taste of beauty; the bells become drops of water, the drops of water become human beings in all their goodness, and human beings in all their goodness become the sun rising in the sky. Is that ecstasy enough at the beginning of every day of youth, every day of adulthood, and every day of old age? And what might we have been if we had been taught such an art as this?

Some of us have been; some learn it elsewhere, perhaps in the home or in church or in the fields and the woods or by the sea. But here we are discussing university systems, and such teaching is rare in our academic training and rare in the life of our youth. Yet it is an essential part of the art of reason; it is part of the knowledge on which reason feeds, the knowledge of ecstasy. It is the art of reason to relate this moment of ecstasy to every other moment of the day, and as dull as it may seem, the teaching of social responsibility is one way it does this. Perhaps it sounds a little less dull if we remember that *nishkamya seva,* selfless service, is the bridge, built in the *gurukula* daily round, that links what I perhaps wrongly classified as the ecstatic and academic parts of the day. It does not mean that every human relationship could or should be ecstatic or anything even approaching it, and the *gurukula* ideal certainly tells you that you are going about it in a very wrong way if, as you are cleaning out someone's night pot, you congratulate yourself on your social consciousness, or even think of it. What is taught, in very rational terms, is simply that except for the recluse, whose path is probably the most difficult of all, *it is only in relationship with others* that the self can be fulfilled, by becoming more than its isolated individual self. And the Hindu scriptures, as with the scriptures of the other great religions of the world, are basically a blueprint for social organization and a recommendation for those who want to live well and fully of the exercise of social responsibility.

It would seem unreasonable, and to some unnecessary, for the high ideals of the *gurukula,* its unbending yet welcome (because it is so satisfying) discipline, to pervade any modern institution of higher learning in India, even in Banaras, perhaps its holiest city; both kinds of university seem to exist for very different purposes. But perhaps we should question this. For instance, for those who are puzzled as to why Hindu India with its lofty ideals of nonviolence should be so prone to a bloodthirstiness and violence that on occasion matches any found in the less overtly idealistic Western world, the answer might well be found in the deemphasis on social and religious ideals in the modern Indian university. Similarly, it is there that the answer might be found as to how India, with its ancient teachings of oneness of Self, known down to the poorest and most illiterate of villagers, and its emphasis on those essentially social qualities of compassion and consideration, can nonetheless tolerate the poverty, misery, sickness, and premature death of so many millions of its masses. It may also explain how so many of the Western-educated middle and upper classes seem to take refuge in the Hindu doctrine that all is illusion and do next to nothing to put the lofty humanitarian ideals, about which they are always ready to boast, into practice. Many Westerners going to India expect somehow to find it a "spiritual" country, its people a "spiritual" people. They certainly find an all-pervasive addiction to ritual behavior, but many are hard put to discover any spirituality as they look upon the juxtaposition of incredible wealth and abject poverty; and the higher they look on the social scale, the greater the discrepancy they find between what is preached and what is practiced. And whereas it may be true that the blue-collar Hindu is probably more conscious of his religion and more knowledgeable about his system of belief and values than most blue-collar workers in the Western world today, this does not mean that he is necessarily any more spiritual. Although Banaras may be the holiest city in India, for instance, it is also surely one of the filthiest in the world, one of the most squalid, impoverished, and not without its quota of corruption, vice, and perversion. Banaras is a good deal cleaner today than it was thirty years ago; there is less human urine and excreta lying about in the streets and alleys, though plenty can still be found along the railway tracks, along the sacred Ghats where the morning *gayatri* ritual takes place, and in disused open spaces such as those surrounding churches, temples, and the more expensive hotels. But more beggars than ever squawk at you from tongueless throats, or poke at you with mutilated stumps of arms or legs, or whine at you from their wooden trolleys if they have no arms or legs. More hawkers swindle you, more opulent shopkeepers sell you more defective goods and still make you feel you are being blessed, eating houses still give you dysentery free of charge, police now watch as you are being robbed, and touts tout for any kind of vice you can imagine at cut-rate prices. I think that every disease known to man must be in the air you breathe in Banaras, but for me that city is still one of the most beautiful I know, for the old system *does* still work; the high ideals are still alive. Spirit permeates every horrid hovel, wafting inward from the Ghat steps every morning with the incense and the bells and the sunlit drops of water and the sound of the *gayatri*. It is often difficult to *see* this Spirit at work, particularly when one is being robbed or clawed at or when trying to negotiate some puddle of filth; and it is not being claimed that all the rogues are angels, even though some of them do smile quite winningly and make ample restitution when you catch them in their roguery. If any one thing had to be named to explain the affection that so many feel for Banaras if they stay long enough to overcome their horror of the squalor, I think I would name the lack of malice or ill will, however violent the action or harmful the intent. That may not sound like much, but it is astounding in a city with these unsavory characteristics. And the explanation for the power and pervasiveness of that sense of something that seems to transform the most profane into something sacred is surely in part the overwhelming presence of all the symbols of holiness that assail the senses just as persuasively as the scriptures assail the intellect and the longing for something better assails the heart and soul.

Banaras is also the home of the famous Banaras Hindu University and of a great *ashram* that was, in a sense, my *gurukula* together with the university. It was headed by one of India's three greatest religious leaders of the day, a Bengali woman known as Anandamai Ma. At the university I practiced the art of learning; at the *ashram*, where I lived, I learned the art of being ecstatic and at the age of twenty-six went through my second adolescence, properly this time. Between the two of them I began to learn the art of reason, the proper application of knowledge. But in contrast to the *gurukula* an air of lethargy hangs over the university, unrelieved by the scent of incense, the sound of bells, or the sight of the great Ganga which flows past the furthermost and unfrequented extremity of the huge sprawling campus. Indeed, it is the relative lack of such symbols that for me characterizes the university. The city and all it stands for has been left, seven miles away, to work its own strange and wonderful way through life, though it too is faltering. The campus is laid out in the form of a series of concentric semicircles, closing in on the hub, which is not a sacred temple as one might have expected, but the secular administrative offices and bank. Radial roads, lined with trees, reach out from the hub to connect it with the various colleges, the hostels that lie behind them, and the living quarters of the faculty, the furthest removed from the invisible sacred Ganga. The university temple is hard to find; the college architecture is the equivalent of our Victorian Gothic, remotely reminiscent of the north Indian temple architecture, but most reminiscent of Indian government offices.

The symbolism that relates the university to the government is unfortunate but instructive, for of all government offices in the entire world those of India must be the most hopelessly inefficient and most dedicated to the endless pursuit of further usage of red tape. So the heavy, ornate, rose-colored buildings of the university tell me what to expect: the mindless pursuit of knowledge and indifference to the result, the greater result, in terms of the society. If there is any concern it is for the lesser self only, the individual self. I greatly fear that one day there will be a shortage of paper and string or tape in India, and that will be more catastrophic than any famine. Yet I cannot imagine a shortage of Spirit. What is lacking in the youthful students of this university, and many like it, is the dedication to the greater Self that is the core of the *gurukula*. It is as though someone has forgotten to tell them what to do with the facts with which the modern university fills their heads. The huge open fields that fill the empty spaces left by the intersecting roads are symbolic of that lack of application. A few students are dedicated to competitive sports, but that is still not a major part of university life anymore than is the art of reason. The students are mostly occupied with the pursuit of knowledge. However, the innumerable subversive attractions of the seamier side of the city are even today still given scant attention, and not just because it is seven, dusty, rather dirty miles away. This is where the home training, the childhood and adolescence of the modern Indian university students stands them in good stead.

The major similarity that links the two Indian university systems lies in the home background of the students, in the fact that their lives are already filled with symbols of the sacred that they recognize and respect without any conscious act of thought or reason. The sacred has by now become a natural part of their lives. Many of the students at Banaras have been through *upanayana* and are clothed with the ritual robe of the sacred thread, even if under a natty three-piece suit or cricket shirt. So it is not surprising to find such sophisticated, apparently Westernized students touching the feet of their teacher or blissfully urinating on the sidewalk or performing the *gayatri* while sleepily standing on the dormitory steps in the early morning. It would be very surprising to find an Oxford student doing any of these things. The major difference between the Banaras student and the *gurukula* student lies in their approach to the art of reason, in what they do with the immense body of symbolic knowledge they have acquired in childhood and adolescence. I am tempted to say that the Banaras student does nothing with it. Throughout the university there are exceptions, of course, individuals who pursue the art of reason, as defined. But other than at the Sanskrit College, there was, when I was there, no overt or sharp dedication to the sacred and social application of knowledge. At the *gurukula,* as we have seen, everything is focused on the intensive development of the individual self into the greater social Self; students sometimes see it in those direct social terms, and they sometimes see it in spiritual terms; for them both are one and ultimately the same thing. It is that total dedication to Self/Society/Spirit that is lacking both in the university and its students at Banaras, though all the foundations are there. For me the result is sad; sad because of the wasted potential, the waste of all the promise and hope that lies in youth.

The inefficiency and utter indifference that are the two qualities in which India would win any international contest are not brought into the discussion just for the sake of it. They are symptomatic of what can happen, even given the extraordinarily wise and fulfilling experience of childhood and adolescence that is the Hindu way, if youth is not encouraged to pursue that way. It is what happens in a religious society under the pressure of secularization, and it leads to more than just inefficiency and indifference; it leads to what is nothing short of criminal negligence. The lives that are lost every week, and perhaps every day, because of nothing more than the state of the roads and the condition of the public vehicles allowed to ply those roads, would be criminal in other countries. So would the lack of sanitation that claims even more lives, and so would the open, uncleaned urinals installed in the name of sanitation at the side doors of food shops and restaurants. So would the daily violence that every newspaper recounts in this land of *ahimsa,* or nonviolence. So would the ruthless and systematic exploitation of the poor, *harijan* (outcaste) or otherwise, driving them to a premature death by starvation, disease, suicide, or just plain physical exhaustion. The rational dedication to sociality and its equation with sanctity that is so much a part of the *gurukula* system simply is not a part of the modern university in India, as I saw it.

The same is surely true of most of our universities, except possibly some of those with a strong religious affiliation, appealing to specific groups with strong loyalties to specific moral systems. At Banaras Hindu University, however, youths had the advantage of the kind of background in childhood and adolescence that had already given them a strongly social orientation, particularly in their concept of Self; they had mostly learned, in the Hindu tradition, to use all modes of awareness equally, not ranking one sense above another; and above all they had from infancy onward become accustomed to recognizing and learning from the incredibly rich world of natural and man-made symbols that surrounded them. In these respects at least they entered youth far more prepared to learn the art of reason than do most of our students, whose qualifications for university entrance are for the most part measured in terms of their ability to pass tests or do well in sports. On top of this disadvantage, our universities share with any modern Indian university the hard fact of life that in today's complex, highly specialized, and technological world, unlike the youth of the Ituri Forest, our youth are nowhere near well enough equipped even with the most basic of manual or intellectual skills to make an effective contribution to the nation's economic or political life. The economic reality, for us, is so harsh that our universities too readily fall into the trap of encouraging youth to devote themselves to the pursuit of job training, physical or intellectual, rather than to the art of reason which is the right application of that training. The right application, the cultures we have examined would say, is application with concern for the greater social good, arising from awareness of what the Hindu might call the greater Self, and what the traditional African might call the reasonable or social Self. But all too often our universities take up where high (or public) school left off, continuing the process of fragmentation of self, and stressing more than ever the value of individual success. Very unlike both the *nkumbi* and the *gurukula*, at the end of youth the individual has come to see security in terms of economic competence rather than social concern; survival has become mechanical rather than organic. Compassion and caring have become almost totally dissociated from the business of earning a living; for some they may be moral requirements, but still dissociated to a large extent from "work"; for others they are luxuries to be enjoyed if and when possible, and even then the extent of this social concern may be measured by the fact that society has to offer economic incentives, so that social concern itself becomes a tax write-off.

I was lucky to go to one of those universities where social concern was taught every bit as effectively as were the academic skills to which it was nominally and firstly dedicated. Our education into the art of reason may have been more incidental and informal than with the *nkumbi* or *gurukula*, but it was nonetheless effective. Social concern was not taught as such, nor did it figure in the examinations, but that it was an inherent part of the system can be seen once we look beyond the formal academic structure and pay attention once again to those things we dismiss all too readily as trivial, insignificant, even childish. We also have to look beyond superficial impressions, however powerful, such as those that characterize life at Oxford as bordering on anarchy or portray the university as the backbone of upper-class supremacy in England. The reverse is true in both cases, for beneath the apparent air of freedom, even decadence, there is a firm underpinning of a discipline every bit as rigorous as that of the *nkumbi* or *gurukula*, and college life, when I was there, suggested that there was more to equality than mere economic equalization and compelled a very different concept of equality.

Oxford and Banaras are similar in several respects. At Oxford there is the same dramatic juxtaposition of two worlds that seem unconnected with each other's existence, though the opposition at first seems to be one of wealth and class rather than of sanctity. The city streets are used by some of the intellectual elite of the world and by the workers who labor at nearby great industrial plants. One of Oxford's most prestigious colleges is jostled by a Woolworth's, others adjoin pubs, teahouses, dressmakers, barbers, and hairdressers. The contrast is overt and explicit and is formalized in a number of ritual ways. For instance, students were expected to wear academic gowns on the streets during the daytime or at other times when (theoretically) engaged in academic pursuits.

This clearly and visibly placed them in one world, with its own value system, even its own set of rules and its own law-enforcement agency, the bowler-hatted (uniform again!) "Bullers" who patrolled the streets, teahouses, and pubs, and took the names of "young gentlemen" who concealed their academic affiliation by not wearing academic dress. The ritual clothing marked both obligations and a certain license given to youth (undergraduates) that was valid for as long as they were devoting themselves to the pursuit of responsible adulthood.

The relationship and separation between Town and Gown was also formalized in other ways. There was a pub of that name, and there were ritual confrontations by which Oxford students demonstrated the separation of the two worlds, thereby linking them. Periodically students would go on a rampage and break a shop window or commit some other minor civil disorder. Then the goal would be to steal the policeman's helmet when he came to remonstrate with them and persuade them to return to their colleges. It was a ritual confrontation and recognized to be such; it was a way by which the two worlds recognized each other and came to terms; the students limited the extent of the damage done and the city withheld the power and penalty of the law. Yet, however separate a world the university may seem (and despite the fact that although it is scattered throughout the heart of the city it still seems a totally other, isolated world), there was a strong sense of mutual responsibility; and with respect to the teaching of the art of reason, Oxford was anything but passive, in both itself and its educational system. Unlike Banaras, both the city and the university bulge with external symbols that cannot be ignored. To some extent these symbols work, as in Banaras (but in both worlds) to bring sanctity to the secular, to permeate the profane with an ideology that is far from dead. The ancient masonry, the towers and the steeples, even the pubs with their paneled walls emblazoned with college coats of arms, are as vibrant as the bells that peal and chime day and night, all serving as a constant reminder of something sacred, something carefully not defined, for each student must find the sacred for himself. The students' sacred does not at first sight seem to be social concern, and, of course, at first it usually is not. Many seem more devoted to bacchanalia than to learning; on the city's crowded streets almost any normal kind of vice is for sale; students often talk more of sport, getting drunk, and other social events than of academic subjects; but all the time, without knowing it, they are learning the art of reason. For instance, when we deliberately flaunted the inner law of the Gown and pursued some minor illegal activity in ordinary clothes, such as being out of college after the gate had closed for the night, part of the excitement and incentive was that we were to some extent abandoning the security of our privileged community and placing ourselves at the mercy of the external world to which, as adults, we would belong. We quickly learned that our immunity from the law was limited and more than counterbalanced by the very real penalties exacted by the college; we learned to appreciate privilege and to use it rather than abuse it. Even our visits to dine with friends in other colleges were lessons in social responsibility, for each college offers its own privileges and imposes its own restrictions, which guests are expected to respect. A breach of college etiquette at the dinner table can result in a form of penalty called a "sconce," which usually takes the form of a fine, payable as an excessively large tankard of strong ale. If the culprit can drink it all in one go, while standing up unaided, the "sconcer" has to pay for it. Under the guise of yet a further excuse for drinking, the student is thus in reality faced with the choice of attempting to establish his own reputation as one who can drink a sconce, of saving himself the cost, or of admitting guilt (however unwitting) by merely taking the first sip, and of restoring good relations by passing the tankard on for others to share. He thus also acknowledges his respect for the customs and privileges of others. As a means for getting youth to know and respect the complex human relationships in the world to which it will soon belong, there is nothing like channeling youthful energy into controlled ritual confrontation of its own choosing and for its own less noble motives. The alternative is to let that energy run wild or repress it altogether.

In equally indirect ways, Oxford inculcated other values that ultimately served to moderate the potential conflict between different segments of a sharply differentiated society and to remove the hostility from opposition. Both those who performed and those who were merely spectators of sports treated sports with a mixture of enthusiasm and abandon that considerably moderated the excess of competitive spirit that had been encouraged at school and that is an inherent danger of all games and most sports. It used to be said that the Oxford Eight (and they tried to train me for it once) nearly always lost to Cambridge because, since Cambridge so desperately wanted to win, the only gentlemanly thing to do was to let them do so. And so in other aspects of university life, while active and dynamic and demanding of dedication and intensive training, this absence of the rivalry and competition of the playing fields was matched by an air of leisurely relaxation. The underplaying of competition, such an important element of public school life, was a major part of the process of socialization at Oxford; we learned to work with rather than against each other.

Perhaps it was in default of the kind of prior formal training in socialization that takes place in the childhood and youth of other cultures that Oxford proceeded with English youth in such an indirect way. As a first step toward the art of reason, Oxford, like all good universities, gives its students credit for being mature and assumes that they are there to learn rather than to acquire knowledge. It does rather more than many universities in that it treats the students accordingly, grants that they already have an adequate store of knowledge (which any good British public school or high school provides), and that they are rational enough to make decisions for themselves with respect to how they intend to apply that knowledge. So it is much more than a job-training school, and to say that it prepares students for careers does it great injustice. For some students that is all it is. If that is all they want, the university leaves them to be the losers. But almost as though it recognizes that the public school system, which supplies most of its students, has not even attempted the vital task of transformation, Oxford provides opportunities in abundance for any student to become what every Mbuti or village child or *gurukula* student has become by adolescence, a fully integrated human being. In keeping with its policy of treating the students with the respect due to maturity, of mind and body at least, the university does not compel this transformation. It is too late for compulsion. On the contrary, when it occurs, the transformation is as successful as it is because the university *seems* to go to considerable lengths to give the student every opportunity for remaining as immature as, in reality, he is.

My own entry into this world illustrates a certain consistency in the educational system, but it also illustrates the element of chance that, for the youth of the Western world, so largely determines whether or not they learn the art of reason, or remain overgrown children, dedicated to self rather than society. I recognized that Westminster had given me a first-class academic education and like many students thought that the primary goal at Oxford was to add to that education, to increase my store of knowledge. But one of the advantages of the difficulties I had at school was that they made me acutely aware that the school had done a dreadful job of transformation, that something much more important to me than my mind had been stunted, and that it was waiting and wanting to grow. The sacred symbols of Oxford beckoned as much as did its libraries and lecture halls.

As a university Oxford is made up of about two dozen semi-independent colleges that are both residences and centers of learning. The bigger colleges, with larger faculties, offer tutors in almost every discipline that can be studied at the university. So you might choose a college because some outstanding scholar in your chosen field is one of the dons, or tutors. Or you might choose a college because of family connections or economic considerations, for if a college has no tutor in your subject you are attached to one in another college. Right away, even before you enter the university, there are a number of decisions to be made, and you have to make them yourself with whatever advice you care to seek from others. Your training in the art of reason begins even before you join the university.

I approached the problem from the vantage point of a sound academic training and total spiritual demoralization. I just took a couple of days off from school and went to Oxford and walked and walked, looking and feeling and sniffing at the air. The moment I saw Magdalen Tower and heard its excruciatingly out-of-tune chimes (I hope they never do anything about that badly diminished seventh) I knew it was for me. The old tower soared into the sky and with it soared my dislocated, earthbound spirit. Directly across the road from the entrance, the botanical gardens filled the air with a fresh scent. The college gate is virtually on the bridge that leads over the Cherwell River and out of Oxford, and being on the edge of the city, Magdalen has by far the largest grounds of any college, including a beautiful deer park. Inside the gate is a quiet yard that leads into the cloisters, on one side of which is the chapel. Through the cloisters is a large expanse of lawn backed by the imposing New Building, in fact, one of the oldest. Behind that is the deer park through which the Cherwell runs, dividing for a time into two streams that encircle a large tree-studded meadow, around which is a path known as Addison's Walk, a place where poetry and music should ever be made. Those were the symbols that I took to be reasons for choosing Magdalen.

Oxford thus at the outset allows a youth a vitally important opportunity for self-expression and self-discovery, as well as for an academic education. It may not do so consciously, but even at the conscious level it is there in the question that so many ask, students and faculty, as to why you chose this college or that. And the next step I took, the interview for admission, still further broadened the opportunity and laid the first of the many booby traps that are such an integral part of the way that Oxford teaches the art of reason and are so very comparable to many of the ordeals of the *nkumbi*. Since the president of the college was away on some important war business, I was interviewed by the vice-president over a glass or two of wine. As he did not ask me, I never thought to volunteer any information about my academic interests until the very end of the interview, when he brought the subject up almost as an afterthought. At first we had discussed the wine, but since I knew very little about it the conversation was gently turned to music and literature (French and German, not English), the deer park and meadow, and then back again to music, abbeys, and organs. From there it went, of all things, to an excited discussion of weeds. When I proved totally ignorant about weeds, on which the vice-president was an expert, he saw the opportunity for filling my young mind with a whole new vista of knowledge, and I rather think he saw an opportunity for doing something with my soul as well. Not only an expert on weeds, Bruce McFarlane was as well something of an expert in medieval history, I believe, but that subject never came up, nor did it ever come up in all the years I was to know him as he nursed me through Oxford. At the end of the interview when he saw I did not even know the name of a single Magdalen don, other than a cousin who was the dean, and that I really had no idea of what I wanted to study, he said something to the effect that if I liked Benjamin Britten's music perhaps my first tutor should be A. J. P. Taylor, who was a good friend of Britten, which in turn meant that I would be registered for Modern Greats. That is a catch basin for any student who does not know why he is at Oxford, a gallimaufry of philosophy, politics, and economics.

And so it was settled. I was to spend my time with wine, weeds, and music, and incidentally go to A. J. P. Taylor once a week and do whatever he asked me to do, which turned out to be a great deal more than I had bargained for. But before the interview concluded we reverted briefly to matters of importance, and I was given some very positive incentives not to work unduly when I arrived at Oxford the following term. I was told that I could attend lectures if I wished, Mr. Taylor would suggest some; and that I would be required to turn up for my tutorials once a week. Beyond that I would be expected to indulge in dinner parties, music, and theater. The chef and wine steward would help me with the first, and if I liked, the vice-president would help me with the others. The subject of formal dress for dinner, both in one's private rooms and in hall, was discreetly mentioned, and something about menservants, known as scouts, which the college supplied and whose duties were to bring hot water in the mornings, lay out clothes, look after rooms, and arrange with other servants for the proper serving of dinner parties. I was advised that it was wise to study hard during vacations; the implication clearly being, throughout the interview, that a good student should not waste too much time on such frivolity while in residence.

In this leisurely, informal, seemingly superficial way the trap is laid, and with his mind deliberately filled with other dreams and expectations the student is introduced to the art of reason. But the symbols were all there to guide you and teach you the art while, incidentally, you also acquire additional knowledge. The art lay in recognizing and interpreting the symbols and learning what to do with your life rather than your mind. The heavily ecclesiastical architecture that characterized not only the college buildings and libraries but some of the public toilets, the constant sound of bells ringing from college towers, the presence of academic gowns throughout the city, all suggested that the pursuit of learning had to do with the sacred, and that somehow this sacred pervaded even the most profane areas of secular life. The exceptional care and devotion lavished on college gardens showed a respect for nature that seemed to be reciprocated by the quiet and peace you felt the moment you left the hurly-burly of the crowded streets and entered through the portals of any college. The ease with which the two sharply contrasting worlds lived side by side seemed to demonstrate that opposites, far from being antithetical, may be perfectly compatible and, indeed, complementary; another healthy lesson in human relations. The very smell of antiquity compelled a sense of continuity, of growth and expansion, and the surprisingly wide diversity of mood and character provided by all the colleges was yet another constant lesson in the compatibility and complementarity of diversity. These symbols taught all these things, not by appealing to the intellect, but rather by working on all the other senses and parts of one's being. And just as all of this gave us as students a firsthand experience of the richness and value of diversity, and of a pride in belonging that had no connotations of superiority, merely of difference, so the relationship of students with their tutors gave us our first sense of belonging to an as yet remote adult world, and for me, at least, my first sense of *wanting* to belong to that world.

Between teacher and student the academic relationship was in many ways close to the *gurukula* ideal. There was a rigorous discipline, but it was not imposed, it had to be accepted. The alternative was to be totally ignored or, if your default was too blatant, you were rusticated and had to leave the enchantments conferred by residence and go home for a term, which meant working during that term as well as the ensuing vacation, if you wanted to return to the pleasures of Oxford. Your relationship was, as in the *gurukula*, much more one of equal partners in the joint adventure of discovery; at times friends, at times father and son, and at other times God and man. The God/man relationship is one of enormous distance, yet of intimate proximity; it is the very epitome of a relationship of respect with its fusion of fear and ecstasy. In the teacher/student situation this relationship does not occur in every tutorial by any means, nor does it happen to every student, for it *is* a happening, and the event is rare. It can happen when the two sit down together and listen to music; for me that was easy. Or look at weeds; that was more difficult. But it also happened to me once when my tutor interrupted my reading of a dreadful essay written in desperation in the small hours of that morning. His mind was obviously far away, and he suddenly uttered a thought that had come to him; a new thought. Something had been created, and although it had absolutely nothing to do with what I had written and was reading, I was there when the thought came and was therefore a part of it. It was not even that he was grateful to me for having driven him to think of something better than my essay, and having thus led him to have that moment of creativity. It was just something that happened while the two of us were together in the same tutorial space, and therefore it belonged equally to both of us and united us. The import of the thought was not significant; the fact that it was a newborn child, a thing of creation, made the moment what it was. This is what can happen between any teacher and student, and this is what makes it possible for the relationship to be in the nature of a joint enterprise rather than a one-way imposition of knowledge, and it is this that can help youth to flourish to its fullest creative potential. But while the relationship was not all these things at all times, there was none of that disconcerting ambivalence that marked the relationship at Westminster, none of that chameleonlike quality I had come to associate in that way with adulthood, where the intimacy of one moment was contradicted by an immeasurable distance the next. And through coming to know other dons by meeting them through one's own tutor, our experience of responsible adulthood was widened and our ideals raised even higher. As students we had access to some of the most brilliant minds in the world, both those resident at Oxford and those visiting their colleagues, at whatever level we chose to make of the relationship. The choice was ours, and if we did not make the right choice and offer something worthwhile in return, the opportunity was not offered again. We began to learn something about reciprocity, another essential ingredient of any truly social relationship.

The wide freedom of choice allowed us, however, was in part illusory, as was the overall air of relaxation. We quickly learned, rather like the boys in the *nkumbi*, that there *were* rules, however informal and underplayed, and that, like the rules of the *nkumbi*, they worked for our benefit, a benefit we could feel in ourselves as well as see in our academic progress. These rules sometimes manifested themselves in ways not at all dissimilar to the ordeals the *baganza* had to undergo.

Every tutorial was an ordeal, since however hard you had worked you knew that you were going to be told that it was nowhere near good enough. A. J. P. Taylor was by far the most demanding tutor I ever had. Even worse was the formal ordeal called "Collections." Students were assembled in the college hall, a great refectory that backed onto the chapel, as refectories should, linking body and spirit. The entire faculty sat at high table which, just as it did during the nightly dinner, symbolized the great intellectual distance that still lay between us and the amount of mutual respect that consequently was due. One by one our names were called, and in cap and gown we had to walk the length of the hall and ascend to the holy of academic holies, the high table. On my first Collection, the president of the college unnerved me by standing up and with great courtesy pulling out a chair, much as my scout would have done at a dinner party, for me to sit down at his table. He then opened with a number of pleasantries and compliments about the quality of my dinner parties, as substantiated by one don, and about my musical taste, to which another testified. With that familiar throwaway technique, just as I had fully recovered my composure and was waiting for some comment about my knowledge of weeds, he said, "Well, let's hear what your tutors have to say." A. J. P. Taylor was the first. I expected trouble, but he continued looking in the other direction as though he had not heard the president's request for a tutorial comment. Then his attention caught by a cough, all he had to say was, "Oh, Turnbull? He is the most naive student I have ever had and I doubt he will ever make anything of his studies." Then after a long pause, "But he is quite good at digging my vegetable garden and I recommend we keep him on for another term." All that is said at Collections is said in a loud voice for all your fellow students to hear. It was comparable to being whipped with a switch on the bare arms, for no evident reason, having just sung an initiation song with absolute perfection and knowing it. It stung, but it removed some of the pain you felt at the realization of how much more there was to learn, at the recognition that the receptacle was yet far from full. It took some of us a long time to realize that mere knowledge was not the point of the academic exercise.

As with the *nkumbi*, the fact that the ordeals hurt, and that their purpose and the purpose of the hurt might at the time seem incomprehensible, was part of the system. If we wanted to be considered as equals, then the lesson was that there had to be trust, if not blind faith. Something of that was also demanded in the *gurukula*, but faith was a perfectly normal part of the entire tradition there, whereas in our society, as in our human relationships, we generally expect or even require rational explanation and justification for anything demanded of us. But different from both these alternative systems was the way in which we learned discipline at Oxford. In the *nkumbi*, as in the *gurukula* to a lesser extent, it was at first imposed from without and only in time became internalized by the students. At Oxford we had to learn to discipline ourselves, drawing on whatever example of discipline we had learned through imposition at school. The compelling factor to self-discipline was not so much the formal threat of rustication (temporary expulsion) for inadequate work, for few of us ever saw that sanction invoked; it was rather that special relationship established between ourselves as students and our friends as teachers and gods . . . to be false to that relationship would have been a sacrilege.

For most of the time I had two tutors, which meant two tutorials each week. At one point I had three. Each would suggest various lectures that I might attend, given in different colleges by different dons, and seemed utterly indifferent as to whether I attended or not. And each gave me a topic for an essay, to be researched and written by the next tutorial, with a list of books to be read if I was to have a minimal understanding of the topic. I found that if I did not attend the lectures, which I tended not to do, then if my tutorials were to be anything less than nightmares I had to do the minimal reading and more. Since each tutor suggested about six books for an essay, that could mean from twelve to eighteen books a week, so rather like the *gurukula,* my days became planned almost minute by minute and acquired a rhythm and a sense of their own with the academic work being done late at night, the following morning, and perhaps early afternoon. The late afternoons and evenings being given over to the anarchy that was, without our knowing it, just as much a part of our training. Unlike the *gurukula* we were left to devise our own schedule, and like the *nkumbi* there were constant ordeals and rituals that convinced us we were not succeeding in either our work or our play, that there was still some hidden achievement expected of us. Once we learned that it was not the quantity, in work or play, but the quality that counted, the senseless quest for more knowledge and more "experiences of life" ended, and we were on our way to becoming reasonable and reasoning youths.

We found both pleasure and profit in our self-imposed discipline just as we did in the reciprocity and mutual respect demanded of us in our tutorial relationships, and this we extended from work to play. In all societies play is an important part of youth. Even in the *gurukula* the student there plays and relaxes and learns about the nonacademic side of life but with no less enthusiasm and fun than we did at Oxford, though in very different ways. But in playtime, more than anything else Oxford resembled an Mbuti hunting camp in the midst of the honey season, or during a riotous *elima,* with girls and boys chasing each other through the colleges rather than the forest, and with miraculously few of the drastic consequences that the Mbuti avoid so completely. There was certainly no evidence of chastity that I could see, in those days at least, yet despite outward appearances sexual escapades were seldom brought to the ultimate conclusion. For one thing the work/ play schedule did not encourage it and our growing sense of responsibility militated against it. I have been at many a party when just as things were beginning to get cozy, the host would announce that he was going to "sport the oak," a ritual way of saying that he was going to close the outer door, the double door that usually stood open and was, properly used, never locked when closed; there was going to be a transition from the profane to the sacred. If the host had just said, "Look, guys, I want to work, I've got a tutorial in the morning," nobody would have even heard. But "sporting the oak" is one of the ways that the student learns the art of being reasonable (which is perhaps what is meant by "being a gentleman") rather like the much more secular Westminster dormitory customary and gentlemanly prohibition on jumping into a bed that was occupied by more than two boys. But at Oxford sexual experimentation was more decorous, ritualized, and had all the connotations of the sacred. The reason for the host wanting to sport the oak was not announced, nor was it questioned. It indicated all that it had to indicate, that the host was going to enter his private and therefore exclusively sacred world. Whether it was to work or to go to bed with his girl friend or drink himself to sleep or listen to music of no import; the oak was the symbol of privacy. An enraged don coming to seek out a delinquent pupil would not enter if the oak was sported. It was further understood that you did not sport your oak merely because you wanted to read a good novel undisturbed, or even because you just wanted to get some work done. Your rooms were your private domain at all times, and if a visitor, other than the dean or your scout, was unwelcome you only had to say so. The oak was a symbol of an *inner* privacy, however you wanted to manifest it, through work, sex, or music, or whatever. And, of course, in England the oak is a sacred tree.

In these ways the reasons we learned to give to ourselves or others for almost anything we did, came to involve consideration for others, for we came to recognize the power of community at work, seeing ourselves in others whether we liked them or not. Mutual respect was no longer a courtesy, it was a necessity. And since most of us sported our oaks so seldom, that indicated that we seldom needed to retreat into our private inner world, excluding other individuals from our own individuality. Yet our inner individuality was never denied or questioned, as the ritual of sporting the oak demonstrated. It was rather that the value placed on individuality, be it in terms of character or success or whatever, was subtly changed, as were other values to which we were introduced at public school but before we had learned to assess them in light of the art of reason.

Keeping in mind the relationship of the university system to the public school system, with its connotations of class superiority and its emphasis on competition and the acquisition of knowledge, it is evident that Oxford did more than just allow the student to reassess these values; it systematically demanded such a reassessment, leaving the final judgment to the student. For me, it was particularly successful in putting class into its proper perspective. The concept of class is not a bad one at all; it is only when it becomes associated with the concept of superiority that it begins to harm the fabric of society. But at Westminster, the natural and healthy urge of the adolescent to find and express "class" as a general quality was allowed to develop into an assertion of superiority. Oxford began to undo this from the first day under the guise of doing just the opposite.

In those days students were fewer and probably wealthier than now. I had a set of two enormous rooms above the cloisters, with its own pantry the size of a small bedroom. It was almost next to the set of rooms occupied by the Prince of Wales, later Edward VIII and later still the Duke of Windsor, when he was a student at Magdalen. My scout had then been a junior scout, serving the same two staircases. He was Oxford born and bred and his name was Ming, to which Mister was never to be attached. All this sounds like an open invitation to snobbery, but the system determined otherwise. Dinner parties were expected to be given in one's rooms and, as I have said, in formal dress. The invitation cards clearly printed the detail, "Black Tie," with no option. That was no problem, it was the details of how to arrange a dinner party that caused the trauma, making it yet another ordeal comparable to that of the *nkumbi* and, at the same time, working as a ritual of reversal with respect to notions of class and superiority. In fact the ritual made you feel very inferior.

Ming advised me that four were too few for my first dinner party. It was too intimate. Ten was too ostentatious. He suggested eight, or possibly six; I settled for six. He accepted, and sent me to the chef, whose name, I think, was Butler, but we usually addressed him as Chef. He was an imposing man, kindly enough but unbending and not at all lenient. He also approved the number of six, while indicating that eight would have been more to his taste, and asked from what colleges would the young gentlemen be coming? He approved the colleges, hence the guests. What did I wish him to serve the young gentlemen? And then the ordeal began in earnest. This soup did not go very well with that fish, and surely I meant another kind of poultry before the venison? Of course I did. By the time it was over he had told me what I should have ordered and why. The fact that it was wartime and food was heavily rationed seemed in no way to affect private dinner parties at Magdalen. Everything was available, in and out of season. In time I was able to second-guess the chef to some extent, but he was always my master and commanded respect. I thought I had got the better of him once when I felt more secure about the procedure. I gave a dinner party for ten, and when he asked as usual for the names of the colleges, I said that one of the guests was not from the university. "A relative perhaps?" he asked. Looking forward to a frown, surprise, or even an outright protest, I said no, he was a Jamaican bus conductor. The chef merely continued to look interested and asked which route. "Ah!" he said, "route number two. Yes, I think I know the young gentleman. That will make ten."

The menu fixed, I then had to go and ask for a consultation with Bond. Bond was the wine steward, and in his private room, beside the Junior Common Room buttery, a selected few could, uninvited, help themselves to the ever-full decanters of sherry, Madeira, or port, or ask for special wines or vintages if these did not content them. Bond sat on his high stool at his high wooden desk like a scrivener, and with a quill pen he unobtrusively entered the total amount consumed so that later you could be billed. But it was so unobtrusive that you felt he was giving you of his own wine, as in a way he was, for he had chosen every bottle himself; the payment was more like an offering to his holy temple. His thin black hair was always tightly plastered down (or else it was a toupee) and his mustache was waxed. At the outset of a consultation he wanted to know what menu you had chosen, recognizing the chef's hand and making that plain. "Oh, yes, that is a favorite of Mr. Butler," the casual use of the prefix and surname indicating that the two of them, but not you, were on the same exalted plane. He then played the same game as the chef until in time you not only came to know what wines to order with which courses, but you came to know Bond himself through his wines, much as I came to know that medieval historian through his weeds. Graduation came when you could both address Bond as "Mr. Bond" and refer to him as such when speaking with others. Consistent with the concept of ritual reversal, social graduation was also marked when you began to address your gurulike tutor by his first name. It was true ritual and all were equalized. And if we go along with Levi-Strauss that rituals do indeed serve to equalize, whereas games serve to create inequality, even the more bizarre rituals of youth take on new significance.

Some such instructive rituals were more in the nature of rituals of rebellion. At Westminster, the Pancake Greaze *could* have been a ritual of rebellion, and a very good one if the headmaster had been substituted for the pancake, or if his authority had been better symbolized than by that soggy lump of dough. But it was not; the symbols were ambiguous and Spirit was missing. There was no ritual of rebellion, so the rebellion took other and more dangerous forms. Far from equalizing us it divided us into an unequal hierarchy of superiority and inferiority. At Oxford it is well known that undergraduates climb steeples and crown these sacred symbols with the profane chamber pot. Such acts are generally considered pranks rather than rituals, but it would be instructive to make a study of exactly which monuments are so crowned, with what, and in what current social context. It might then be revealed that these rebellious acts are more than exuberant pranks of high-spirited youth, which is how they are most easily and most often dismissed. Steeple-climbing and crowning, because it is a recognizably special act, frequently repeated on different occasions but with the same sequence of events, might only be a secular custom. It becomes a ritual if it has symbolic content and in this way relates to and contributes to a general and sacred social order. Individual pranks are not rituals, they are merely customary behavior, but in some cases they may be converted into something very much like rituals of rebellion or reversal. In this way the individual act becomes a social act, and underlying individual resentment or feud may be turned to social advantage and made to express and reify the social order.

For example, that is not what a number of us thought as we hurled empty beer bottles at one of the senior dons from the roof of cloisters, one wartime night. We were angry with him for having made us undertake fire-watching duty, and instead of watching for incendiaries, since there were no enemy planes in the sky, we drank beer. When the don in the dark quadrangle below reminded us of our social responsibility, we pelted him with the bottles. He did not say a word but simply disappeared into the fireless night leaving us to think we had won a victory. The next day, in sobriety, we expected to be chastised for our lack of civic duty, or for doing a stupid and dangerous thing; an empty bottle thrown from a height can be a lethal weapon. But no, that is not the Oxford way. The art of reason intervened and a story circulated that certain students drank *beer* after dinner, not wine or liqueur, and it was made plain that the inevitable fine was not punishment but payment for damage done by the empty bottles to the dons' fine bowling green, a sacred area if ever there was one, and which the cloisters encircled.

Similarly, when some of us tried to blow up the dean as he slept one night, the consequences were not what we intended or expected. We hoped to achieve some minor damage and major notoriety and attract attention to quite unjustified claims that the dean was not giving due respect to students. Three of us crossed the lawn to New Building in the dead of night, armed with gunpowder obtained either from fireworks or shotgun shells, I forget which. We also had an electric cord with a plug at one end and two bare wires at the other. It was crude but effective. The dean was asleep in his bedroom, snoring loudly. We placed the gunpowder under his bed, heaped in a neat little pile above the bare wires, and led the electric cord into the sitting room, closed the door, pushed the plug into a socket, and fled with the explosion. The next morning the dean appeared, as large and jovial as ever, and not a word was heard of the incident by the rest of the college. Years later, over many glasses of claret in the Senior Common Room, I mentioned the occasion to the dean, still large and jovial. He insisted that the incident had never taken place. "Turnbull was always a good one for stories," he announced to the other dons. But his scout told Ming, who told me, that the following morning the dean had asked him to clear up the mess in the bedroom, saying that a storm during the night must have blown all the soot from the fireplace. I am convinced that at least we disturbed his sleep, he denied the event, we were equalized, and the social order was both maintained and reified with mutual respect, but with greater mutual awareness.

In this way even individual pranks can be shrewdly turned to advantage and, at least in function, begin to resemble some of those great tribal rituals in southern Africa where, once a year, subjects openly and under specific ritual conditions rebel against the king for a set number of days, whether they have cause or not. They are obliged to ridicule and revile him, both reminding him of his responsibility to them and demonstrating that he may normally have exclusive access to authority by virtue of his divine heritage but not to power. He then reassumes full authority but now exercises his power with added awareness. We miss much of the very real and deeper social significance of a great deal of what goes on around us daily by taking it at face value. Even through pranks, as well as by rituals and symbols, Oxford taught its students to become reasonable men and to behave in a reasonable manner.

As much as it is a great seat of learning, Oxford will always for me be a set of symbols: the ecclesiastical architecture with its inescapable connotations of the sacred jostling together with the pubs and their beery odor of profanity; the great tower clocks which at all of two dozen or more colleges chime every quarter hour at different intervals, reminding one of the constant passage of time; the cathedrals and organs; the secular pealing of belfries full of bells, ringing out Great and Little Toms in a seemingly endless effort never to repeat themselves, all in reality seeming to search for a purity of sound and reminding us of the purity to be found elsewhere. The gowns and mortarboards that were compulsory daytime wear during lectures, tutorials, and, cunningly, on the streets, reminded us that even on the street there is wisdom to be found and that reason should prevail. I found my passion for empty churches amply satisfied in the many libraries with their stained-glass windows and cathedral acoustics. Even the outside toilet for the old cloister buildings at Magdalen was so convincingly Gothic that unwary visitors could be trapped into entering it with undue respect, thinking they were entering a small chapel or shrine. It was all more than Gothic antiquity at work, it was Spirit at work, day and night, assailing all the senses, inescapable.

It was very much like the saffron robes of the *sannyasi,* or the nakedness of the *nkumbi* initiates; Oxford itself was a form of clothing that enveloped us, momentarily removing all contact with the outside world, enabling us to develop all over again, to be transformed into something new. Oxford was the forest world of the Mbuti, an all-nourishing womb, though perhaps with a slightly higher proportion of still-born infants than the womb of the forest hunters. It was like both the *nkumbi* and the *gurukula* in that it gave its students the respect due to beautiful, well-crafted, but empty vessels waiting to be filled, and in that it constantly led us to think that we had reached our capacity, only to remind us that we were still far from full.

Given what it had to work with, Oxford would have been unfaithful to its own ideals and traditions if it had tried to remake the individual, if it had ritually ordained a transformation as does the *nkumbi.* What makes that particular university so great is not just the academic quality of its faculty, nor even their ability to create the most fruitful kind of relationship between student and teacher, for not all of them succeed or even try. Its greatness lies just as much in the opportunity it fosters, through the examples it provides, ritual and otherwise, for the individual to accept social responsibility and awareness as a natural system rather than as an intellectual construct or plain legal obligation. Under such a system, social responsibility and concern become a way of life rather than mere adherence to a rational or "moral" code of behavior. It is when youth begins to detect this and experience it fully through the symbols and rituals that surround it that it learns the art of reason, for without experience there would be no reason. The art lies in first learning how to experience with one's whole being, just as one learns in adolescence how to acquire knowledge with one's whole being, learning how to love by being whole. Then is youth ready, by joining the wholeness of experience to the wholeness of knowing, to find wisdom, the true art of reason, through self-fulfillment in social action, in concern for other selves. It is a sad comment on our social system, if it be true, that it is often said that the streets and ghettos of our world are often better teachers in this respect than our universities.

PART FOUR

ADULTHOOD

THE ART OF DOING

FOR MOST OF US, if we are run-of-the-mill adults, adulthood is associated with work more than with play, and for many of us work is little more than drudgery, an obligation we fulfill in order to get enough money to keep us alive. For only a lucky few is work such an integral part of life that the distinction between work and play vanishes, both becoming no more than different ways of manifesting our full potential for the art of living. During childhood, adolescence, and youth we are encouraged to regard adulthood not only as providing us with a model of ideal human behavior, but as the most blessed stage of life, to be desired as devoutly as it is to be emulated. Yet, the moment we get there we begin to bemoan our lost youth and talk with sorrow about "the innocence of childhood." We quickly come to resent adulthood and the demand it imposes upon us that we work to support ourselves instead of being supported by others; as though that were an infringement of our freedom, as though there should, in an ideal society, be some way of getting through life without working.

In other cultures there *is* such a way. It is really quite simple. In such cultures "work" is seen merely as doing whatever you are doing at that particular moment in your life, providing it is socially approved (although people in such cultures would be the first to define stealing as a thief's "work"). Thus the playful pastimes of a child are its "work," just as adolescents are doing their "work" when they tentatively explore that potent new world of sexual activity. Youths are no harder at work when studying their books than when they gaze at the stars in the night sky and try to understand the why and wherefore of the universe and their place in it. The adult, then, is working not only when tilling the fields but when embracing his wife, for in such cultures making love is a very real part of the "work" that is expected of adults. The nearest translation to this alternative view of work is "duty," but again for many of us that has the unfortunate connotation of being an obligation that is imposed from outside, and usually an unwelcome obligation that we would rather do without. But elsewhere the urge to "do one's duty" comes from within, almost selfishly, as the only means by which full self-expression can be found. When, in our youth, we look forward to adulthood as that time of life when there will be so much "to do," we are right, and the tragedy is that in our Western industrial cultures we too often limit our concept of "doing" to what becomes an economic burden, supporting ourselves and our families and leaving everyone else to do the same as best they can.

The arts of becoming, of transformation, and of reason all sound much more attractive than "the art of doing," which has a depressingly dull ring to it. At first sight our nine-to-five world seems, in its manner of doing, remote from that of the adult Mbuti who spend their afternoons singing honey songs or dancing ritual reversal dances, or playing with children or just dozing; or that of the Hindu mothers consecrating the household by lighting butter lamps and decorating the threshold with intricate symbolic patterns. Many a Western male would envy the Ituri farmers or fishermen whose work includes spending so much time each day under a Mabondo tree, drinking the fresh wine with their families and friends. But the similarities with our own society are much greater than is at first seen, and before we even begin to explore the art of "doing" we must come to recognize that, in the sense in which we are going to use that word, the Mbuti singing a honey song, the villager drinking palm wine, the Hindu mother lighting a butter lamp, are all doing the same thing as

the factory worker at his conveyor belt and the urban house-
wife at her chores.

We get to the heart of the matter when we look to see what
they are "doing" in the sense of what they are *accomplishing*,
and specifically what they are accomplishing for society at
large. When the adult Mbuti men and women sing their
honey songs, they do so with all the sense of enjoyment and
fun that characterizes play and relaxation. We often expend
a lot of energy while "relaxing"; they expend a lot while singing and dancing. Similarly, when we are working we may
expend no physical energy worth mention, and in many jobs
almost as little expenditure of mental energy is demanded, it
may seem. We associate "work" with earning a living, which
for us means making money without which, however acquired, we cannot survive in our society. In this sense virtually
any Mbuti "play" activities can perfectly well be described
as work, for in all those activities they are doing something,
accomplishing something, that is vitally necessary for their
survival. The musical and dance forms in themselves not only
recreate models of ideal behavior proper to the honey season
or to the relationship between the sexes, they *demand* the appropriate forms of cooperation, and anyone who does not cooperate without good reason is subject to the informal but
powerful sanction of ostracism.

In the neighboring villages the drinkers of palm wine are
even more obviously having a good time, thoroughly enjoying
what they are doing. The men in their society are the political authority; there is no single chief or headman who
rules, though there are elders and headmen who advise. Common consent provides the authority to issue an edict recom-
mending a certain course of action or making a judgment on
some individual act of negligence or irresponsibility. In such
discussions personal opinions and self-interest are bound to
arise, however strongly it has been taught in the *nkumbi* that
the social good must always take precedence over the individual good. However, if you have been drinking palm wine
you can always claim that your own lack of social responsibility, or anyone else's during the discussions, was due to having drunk too much. It is an excuse you cannot use too often,
as you will then be reminded that it is also your responsibility

not to drink too much. While apparently busily engaged in the pursuit of euphoria, the village men are conducting vital business in a way that minimizes the danger of conflict. To keep your wits about you while drinking palm wine is hard work, and the men take it seriously.

In the same way, the Hindu woman finds great personal satisfaction and joy as she consecrates her home in daily ritual. But in fact it is a manifestation of her power in another society that also has the appearance of being male-dominated, and we have seen the vital, indispensable importance of maintaining the overall and all-pervasive system of sacred symbols in the Hindu educational system. She is at work for society just as much then as she is when performing all her more secular household chores, and there are some who find the chores more relaxing and enjoyable than what they see as the tedium of filling butter lamps with oil and preparing chalk and rice and drawing those intricate designs on the doorstep. All these things are ways of working in that they are clearly recognized as essential contributions to the preservation of social order. The acceptance and conscious awareness of social responsibility for all our actions, at work and play, underline all other criteria of adulthood. The art that some of us find in doing whatever we do with equal enjoyment and fun and satisfaction is the art of making sacred and social that which is otherwise secular and individual. Social systems other than ours prescribe that this shall be so; our system leaves it to chance, opportunity, and individual will and ability. If the five stages of existence that we have arbitrarily chosen as the framework for looking at the process of living can indeed be characterized as we have done (childhood, adolescence, youth, adulthood, and old age), then now is the time to look for some purpose to the process.

Is adulthood, the art of doing, merely a question of using one's capacities, much as a wound-up clock uses its cogs without any further incentive than that provided by the mainspring? Even the best of clocks has the capacity to go slow or fast, but its purpose, the purpose with which we endow it, is for it to keep correct time, to work as efficiently as possible. Adults, fully developed as they are, have the same capacity to regulate their lives so as to live them in the most efficient manner possible. Let that be purpose enough for the moment, but let it be the absolute minimum requirement for the proper art of doing, else we countenance irresponsibility as well as inefficiency. When such irresponsibility arises in society it is most often due to the improper development and integration of the adult's full being during the three previous stages of existence; the social clockmaker was careless. Social irresponsibility certainly strikes me as being irrational, for sociality is the only rational way of living that we know. If we merely wish to survive without using our whole being, just eating and breathing, sleeping and waking (and copulating), then we survive, we do not live. And when, as happens in some segments of our society, copulation becomes a form of entertainment and the major source of pleasure or "fun," the pleasure is actually diminished and hope for true sociality recedes.

To consider the art of doing we have to consider when we begin doing, what we do, and how we do it. For some societies who classify the various stages of life more clearly than we do, the "when" is no problem. Entry into each stage is signaled by some kind of marker; such markers may be dramatic rites of passage, as with the *nkumbi*, or some achievement (the first spoken word for some marks the transition from infancy to childhood), or the acceptance of some specific obligation, such as earning your own living. The Mbuti become adult when they get married; the choices of what to do are strictly limited, all but the rare individual entering into an active life of hunting and gathering which both directly and indirectly contributes to the social good. There is nothing remarkable about that. What *is* remarkable is the "how." Hunting and gathering may be the only possible form of subsistence available to them in their environment and at their technological level, and as such is a survival technique rather than an expression of the *art* of doing. What is not determined, except perhaps in structural terms, is that they hunt and gather in such a way as to compel the most intensive and all-inclusive participation of the entire society, and distribute the spoils in such a way as to ensure that all have an equal and adequate share regardless of the extent and nature of their input. The complexities of their rules of hunting and division go far beyond what is "determined" in terms of technology or the law of supply and demand. The "how" of their hunting is classically social, and conscious social concern characterizes the "how" of just about everything else they do. This is not because of their adherence to some kind of social theory; the facts come before the theory, and the facts in their experience demonstrate that, for them, mutual concern is the most efficient way of living and allows the fullest freedom for individual development and expression. In isolation there may be growth of a sort, but only in relationship with others can there be full development.

Not far away from the Mbuti there are pastoral peoples who establish very clear and unambivalent markers for the transition from each stage of life to the next, not just for adulthood. For both entry into and exit from adulthood the moment of transition is marked by a ritual battle between the youths and their adult fathers. Rather like the battle of the sexes at the end of *nkumbi*, this battle can reach varying degrees of physical violence, indicating the degree of friction between the adjacent generations; but it is always essentially ritual in nature, controlled. The fathers, after all, resent their sons' growing up and assuming the role that has for so long belonged to them, and forcing them that much closer to death. So the resentment is both natural and understandable, and as if recognizing the principle of adjacent generational hostility, this potential source of conflict is made overt, ritualized, and expelled, literally, by its very expression. The same public ritual that advances their sons, the youths, into adulthood advances them into old age and, eventually, to death. But not for one moment is the continuity broken, nor is any ambivalence allowed. With the transfer of status, moreover, comes a full and unequivocal transfer of social responsibility, each stage of life having its own specific area of authority and power.

For the student at the *gurukula*, entry into adulthood takes place at the end of his period of schooling, when he has a choice of leaving the celibate state of *brahmacharya* and entering the stage of *grhastha* by marrying and becoming, as the term implies, a "householder." The use of that particular term indicates clearly that the marital state itself is not what marks an adult, but his condition as a householder, or homemaker, with all its attendant social responsibilities. The young adult

may make the choice of remaining as a *brahmachari* and devoting his life to the spiritual quest. If we continue to define
adulthood with respect to the proper exercise of social responsibility there are many who might or do say that such self-
advancement, even for spiritual purposes, is more selfish than
social. That is something we shall tackle shortly, for many do
make that choice, and not only in India.

For those lacking the unequivocal system of the Mbuti, or
that of societies with age-set systems and their clear rituals
of transition, or without clearly defined social roles laid out,
as in the socialist state or as ordained by an accepted religious
belief system, there is considerable ambivalence as to when
one becomes an adult, just as there is considerable choice as to
what one does when that happy state is achieved, and how one
does it. And so there is a plurality of markers. In countries
that demand a period of national service, the donning of a
military uniform is taken as a sign of entry into manhood;
however, although it is undoubtedly a form of social service,
it does not necessarily involve any sense of social responsibility. The draft dodger who dodges out of true conviction as to
the evils of war may be more socially responsible, more truly
adult, than the individual who joins a service merely because
he sees no alternative.

For many of us marriage is considered a marker for adulthood, but one may also achieve general acceptance as an adult
by earning a living, regardless of marriage or effective social
responsibility. There is a lot of ambivalence here, since a
young boy barely past puberty may be compelled to support
his parental family if his father is sick, out of work, or dead,
and if he has no older brothers; he may have all this economic
responsibility, be a wage earner, yet not have adult status.
Alternatively, a young couple may marry long before they
can make any effective contribution, economic or political, to
social life. And there are some societies in which adulthood
may be reached without ever marrying or assuming economic
or political roles, but through reaching a certain level of
spiritual development. Obviously, adulthood is no one single
thing, but it can usefully be described as the assumption of
an active, constructive role in the furtherance of the social
order. In this sense the child laborer is not an adult, for he

only fulfills a partial role, he is not as yet equipped to serve the wider society fully.

Perhaps the one thing underlying all these measures of adulthood is the qualification we have introduced that whatever one does, it should be done with a *conscious* sense of social responsibility. National service is seen to operate in the interests of national security; marriage just as plainly and with less ambivalence is essential if there is to be continuity both of the nation and of the social order as we know it; earning a living contributes to the national economy; these are all forms of social service, but any of them can be undertaken with anything but a sense of social responsibility and with the total absence of social concern. Since we are raising social consciousness almost to the level of the sacred, as an ideal, we shall later be looking for evidence of the same sacred ideal in our own society by classifying three major ways of truly adult doing as spiritual, religious, and secular. These categories work well in other societies, and by trying to use them in our own context, we may well find an unexpected truth. The sacred can appear in many guises and work toward a diversity of goals.

Consider the Mbuti belief that God made all living things to be immortal and perfect, and that so they were until an Mbuti first hunted and killed an animal for his own personal satisfaction, both for the excitement of the hunt and the filling of the stomach. From that moment onward, because of man's original sin, they say, all living things were condemned to die. If only they could find a way of surviving without killing, say these hunters, they might regain their immortality. A pretty story; but it is believed, and the belief serves to reduce the killing of game to an absolute minimum, which is of both ecological and social significance. And Mbuti never kill each other. Many African societies have comparable beliefs that directly support social attitudes and behavior. By dismissing such "stories" as folk tales, as myths or legends, we blind ourselves to the extent of the conscious sociality of such peoples. Similarly, when we dismiss certain beliefs and practices as "superstition" we dismiss evidence of intense social concern.

It is a simple fact that in the tribal context there are no

orphans and no old people who do not have a useful place in everyday life, except for those who become so infirm as to be unable to move or talk. But even then they are put to use, in a sense, just as their ultimate death is turned to social advantage. Here again, a system of religious belief provides a rationale for social action, and unless we understand that we can never fully assess the pervasiveness and power of sociality in such societies. The institution of witchcraft, which we so often deride as primitive superstition, comes into play here. In many African societies, when someone sickens or dies there is concern for the individual among those most closely related, but for the whole of society the sickness reawakens a concern with their own mortality and responsibility for mortality. Sickness or death are turned to advantage by making the occasion one for a communal probe into social behavior. A witch hunt is, in fact, a systematic investigation, through a public hearing, into all social relationships involving the victim of the sickness or death. Was her husband unfaithful, her son lacking in the performance of his duties; were her friends uncooperative or was she herself any of these things? Accusations are reciprocal, and before long just about every unsocial or hostile act that has occurred in that society since the last outbreak of witchcraft (sickness or death) is brought into the open. But unlike our own versions of witchcraft the wrongdoers are not dramatically put to death. Most often more than one wrongdoer is discovered, and they are chastised for their lack of social responsibility and compelled to make some amends to those of the victim's family who are themselves not found guilty. Economic restitution or recompense is minor and incidental to the major objective, which is to restore the ideal of cooperation and harmony in the community. The sickness was taken as a symbol of disharmony, of a crack in the social order, because of a sickness in the society itself. No particular blame is attached, seldom are any individuals held under any cloud of suspicion of ill intent; it is seen more as a question of carelessness. Nor are those found responsible (rather than guilty) by virtue of their irresponsibility branded in any way as criminals, for just as man is mortal so he is recognized to be fallible. The death is made use of to remind everyone of this fallibility and of its consequences. If the social norm were not restored, then society would die in a very real way.

This emphasis on constant social responsibility is further seen in the way others than the sick or the dead, but who also appear to be less than useful to society, are incorporated and made use of. The cripple, the fool, the homosexual, the epileptic, the murderer, all those whom we in our society so carefully segregate and keep apart are incorporated in all but the most exceptional case. Such exceptions are rare and usually involve an indisputably and continued *willful* disregard for the social good. Individual aberrance, be it sickness or crime, can be dealt with without the isolation or the destruction of the individual and in ways more beneficial to society, these people find. It is only the action that consciously and intentionally threatens society as a whole that is considered a true crime, and that is more in the nature of a sin. The success of such a system is surely seen in the fact already referred to that these societies have no such institution as our omnipresent police force and penal system, which is the major means by which we compel social order. In the smaller, more homogeneous tribal society, belief and faith more than physical force are the compelling factors, and from childhood onward every individual's experience is of the efficacy of the system; every individual's experience is that success and security lie in sociality rather than individuality.

Now that we have more evidence to support the suggestion that the most effective marker of adulthood is the acceptance and manifestation of effective social responsibility, we can better deal with the issue of what to do in adulthood. It helps to separate different ways of doing, of manifesting social concern. We have already suggested at least three different approaches to social action that may be defined as spiritual, religious, and secular. We have seen something of all three at work in Africa, but for the moment they are more easily further explored within the more homogeneous socioreligious tradition of India and Tibet. The difference I choose to make between spiritual and religious approaches will, I hope, become evident and significant, though it may be valid only in this partial context.

The spiritual orientation to adulthood is most clearly seen

when a young *brahmachari*, at the end of his *gurukula* training, chooses to perpetuate his vows of celibacy, to renounce
the intermediate stages of *grhastha* and *vanaprastha* and enter
directly into the final stage of renunciation and become a
sannyasi. This can be done at any age, but when done by a
youth it appears to many not only to be a renunciation of
worldly life but a renunciation of all social responsibility.
Even worse, these critics will say, by further vows that he
must take, the *sannyasi* is forbidden to own property or to
work for a living; he must beg daily for his food. Thus he survives, if he survives, only by the grace, kindness and effort of
others. Even in India there are many who consider the *sannyasi* as parasites. The accusation seems even more valid, on
the face of it, when the *sannyasi* goes into seclusion with the
stated intent of pursuing his own individual salvation through
meditation and self-realization. Many retreat high into the
mountains or into remote forests where they are totally inaccessible, even to pilgrims who might otherwise seek them
out as inspiration for their own more humble efforts on be-
half of society. Even the accepted belief that upon achievement of *mokśa* ("release from the round of life and death")
he leaves the world for good, not even returning to teach if
he so chooses, seems to support the allegation. But this is only
if we ignore the important Hindu doctrine of *maya*, or illusion.
This cannot be properly used, as some try to use it, to justify
the apparent selfishness of a recluse by saying that since everything is illusion except the self, there is no need for social
concern because in reality there is nobody else to be concerned about. Gautama Buddha was a Hindu, and he left
behind a legacy of social service and dedication to humanity
unparalleled in the world. It is more that our *concept* of our
selves and of the world is illusory, and the social contribution
of the recluse becomes more comprehensible, as does the concept of illusion, in light of a rather charming Hindu parable
in which it is said that the Absolute, Cosmic Consciousness,
God, or whatever term we choose to use, got rather bored with
being God, being infinite possibility without manifestation,
so he manifested himself as a pig. That was much more fun,
but after a while he became rather lonely. So he divided himself and made manifest a sow. That was more fun still, and

before long there were lots of little piglets. The parents told the piglets that it was all a sort of divine comedy, a game of make-believe, that really they were all one and the same God, manifestations of the one eternal truth. Whether the piglets believed their parents or not is uncertain, but they all went ahead and made a whole lot of other piglets, which in turn reproduced yet again. The first piglets told their children what their parents had told *them*, but after several generations the minds of pigs and piglets were so engrossed with other things that the story lost its interest and eventually parents never bothered to tell the story at all. Which is why we no longer recognize our own divinity; we are too busy thinking that we are pigs and enjoying it.

Self-realization is a means by which the illusion may be shattered and our true nature, our one-ness, rediscovered, according to the Hindu belief. It is the spiritual equivalent of the social doctrine that the good (reality) of society lies in the good of all, not just in the good of the individual. Essential to the acceptance of recluses as being socially responsible is the belief that their achievement of this realization, even their effort toward it, in itself brings others closer to the same realization. The *sannyasi* is in the position of the second generation piglet; he *believes* what he has been told, but unlike the piglet he wants to *know* if it is really true, and chooses the only way of finding out. It is really a rational and logical decision, especially for those who do not particularly enjoy being piglets.

The recluse can be seen as practicing the art of doing, of fulfilling his socially responsible adulthood, in a very real way by his single-pointed concentration on the achievement of power, or Spirit. But the spiritual approach is not limited to the recluses by any means, and few of them are totally removed from contact with the outside world. They are scattered all over the subcontinent of India, as though by design, as if to be accessible to all rather than to just a few. In the cities of India just as in the countryside there are centers of spiritual power that are also centers of secular social power, though they indulge in no recognized form of social action. Others do involve themselves directly with society, through hospitals, clinics, and schools that they run, and by offering food and

shelter to any that seek them out. Those that do not engage
in social action operate in much the same way as the mountain recluse except for two things; they are much more readily
accessible, and in each center, under the guidance or inspiration of a single teacher, there are generally a number of disciples, *sannyasi* and otherwise, similarly engaged in the quest
for Spirit. It was in one such *ashram* that I lived in Banaras
for the two years during which I was attached to the university. Its power was very much like that of Oxford: in itself
it was a symbol of all the great things that a human community can be; its ritual life induced a sense of respect for humanity regardless of caste or class, all the more convincingly
for being in such contrast with the secular squalor and poverty
beyond its walls, the caste prejudice, corruption, and lack of
concern. The *ashram* did not need to undertake any form of
social action, it simply had to be there.

Today the *ashram* that was my *gurukula* is changed. The
annual flooding of the Ganga has washed away most of the
front of the building, high as it is above water level. The only
part of my old room left standing is now without a roof, and
is used as a small open-air terrace where people gather in the
cool of the evening. More significantly, thanks to numerous
wealthy devotees there are some fine new buildings and a
free hospital for the poor. But the source of power is gone.
Anandamai Ma is still alive, but she is constantly on the
move, uninvolved with the social work being done in her
name; content in her old age with being rather than doing.
When I tried to find her on a recent trip, her body eluded me.
She had always just left for somewhere else. Then I realized
that really it did not matter; what had to happen happened
thirty years ago. I found her power still present, but it was
inside me.

This spiritual approach to life, then, might be held to be
more appropriately relegated to old age, where the art of
living is the art of being. There is a connection, but nonetheless these rather extreme examples show the potential of the
spiritual approach to adulthood, divorced from anything that
would normally be called social action, and we might well
compare them with other examples of monastic life in different parts of the world. But when we come to monastic life,

while much of it is indeed best regarded as spiritual doing, we are again dealing with an extreme example that seems too far removed from the norm to have much relevance in our everyday world. Yet it is but a short step from this apparently remote and exclusive way of life to many manifestations of the spiritual approach to adulthood more familiar to us. The invocation of Spirit by a choir, or by a poet, a painter, a musician, can all be considered as legitimate forms of adult life under this heading, and once we are aware of it and know what to look for, the spiritual element is likely to appear even in the most secular forms of doing. And since we are more familiar with monasteries than we are with *ashrams* and mountaintop recluses I would like to pursue them, but as an illustration of the religious rather than spiritual approach to adult life.

Tibet, of all countries in the world at any time in the history of man, has developed the monastic ideal and the institution of monasticism to their utmost with respect to their direct and conscious application to the everyday needs of society. Some pretty compelling ecological factors are at work, for Tibet has been faced with the same problem as other parts of the world, namely, a population growth that could not be matched readily by territorial expansion. The topography of Tibet, however, while it hems the people in and tends to keep others out, is unique and offered a unique solution to the problem. The arable valleys, encircled by ice-clad mountains, are fertile, and those in the central region are veritable hothouses in summer. Food yield is high, and even in the neighboring uplands that are less suitable for agriculture, there is good grazing for livestock. The farms can be worked efficiently with a minimum of labor, and since inheritance is in the male line, the practice of polyandry can be seen as a response to the danger of constantly subdividing farm lands among all the sons of any one landowner or landuser (since once again the land is considered public rather than private property). So also can the monastic institution be seen as a response to the same situation, offering youths and adults alike an incentive to leave the land and providing them with alternative ways of "doing." The population of some monasteries, prior to the latest Chinese invasion (for such invasions have been periodic over centuries of history), could number up to ten thousand or more, and there were sometimes several monasteries in one neighborhood.

The ordinary Tibetan farming family is probably as well integrated as any. As we saw in Africa, so here every age level has its own area of responsibility so that mutual cooperation is a sheer necessity, there is nothing virtuous about it. Similarly, every aspect of the individual self is fully integrated in the adult. Tibetans that I have met, from eastern, central, and southern Tibet, are not afraid to express their emotions with enthusiasm and candor. At times it can be quite frightening, and the only correct and acceptable response is to be equally enthusiastic and candid. As might be expected, manners vary with class, and Tibetan society includes aristocrats as well as farmers, monks as well as traders and brigands. Brigands form a very special class that is as efficiently integrated into the overall society as any other. I never had much to do with them in my very limited experience, but the traders, who used to ply the long caravan routes between central Tibet and India, and the farmers are among the lustiest people I have ever met. They enjoy life fully and richly with all the vigor of their massive frames. They enjoy smoking, drinking, and having sex. There are special brothels in Lhasa (or there were; this is all prior to the Chinese invasion) painted yellow in honor and fond recollection of their patronage by the sixth Dalai Lama in the seventeenth century; and certainly a Tibetan brothel is unlike any that I have known anywhere else in the world. I used one as a convenient and convivial meeting place without even knowing that it had other uses, and it was used in this way by many traders who did not take advantage of its other attractions. It was there that I met two or three brigands drinking *chang* amicably with traders they had robbed a week or two earlier. I suspect at least one aristocrat of patronizing it, but I never met any monks there. It had all the atmosphere of a good Scottish country pub at its best, though the waitresses were rather more plentiful and attentive.

Yet in such a place, just as in the marketplace, or while walking beside a caravan of laden yak, or in a monastery, these full-blooded men can be found twirling prayer wheels, counting a rosary, or muttering sacred *mantra*. Prayer banners can be seen stuck in the piles of broken guns and other weapons that are the shrines of bandits who have renounced their worldly life and taken to a life of religious quest and service. Given the presence of religion at these extremes, it is not surprising to see the scented smoke of a ritual fire rising from every rooftop in an isolated farming community at the beginning of each day. Religion, not in mere formal or ritual observance, but as a living, spiritual entity, is present everywhere. It is a vital part of the hustle and bustle of the active, adult world of doing just as much as it is a part of the contemplative life of the monks, or the academic life of the monastic students. In a Tibetan family the husband and wife share in the ritual manifestations of their faith, and the children and the aged participate.

Part of becoming an adult is, indeed, getting married and raising a family; part of becoming an adult is also, certainly, getting a living from the land, or by trading, or by ruling, or by banditry. But part of becoming an adult is just as importantly the assumption of specific ritual responsibilities that are thought of primarily as ensuring the prosperity of the nation as a whole, *not* just the well-being of the family, let alone the individual. In fact the Tibetan goes about salvation very differently from both the Christian and the Hindu. The focus is not on striving to achieve eternal life during this one single incarnation, or on succeeding through retreat into an inner self and renunciation of the world. It is achieved, whatever "it" is (and the Tibetans do not bother themselves with that speculation unless they are scholars or of the highest order of monks), by living this life in this world as fully as possible, each man according to his own nature, the prime watchwords being moderation and compassion. Moderation in no way lessens the fullness with which life can be lived; on the contrary, it makes that fullness possible, for excessive indulgence or denial are both equally destructive. And compassion, for the Tibetans, is no less lusty than any other quality they exhibit. It is an intense caring for family, friends, neighbors, and strangers. You would feel resentful if you did not see the smoke and smell the juniper burning on your neighbor's rooftop as the sun rose over your valley, for it would threaten your own success that day and that of everyone else. I was never more reminded of this utterly beautiful matinal greeting to life than in the middle of the Ituri Forest, during the *molimo mangbo* of the Mbuti, when they greeted death in a nocturnal song of joy as the smoke curled upward into the great forest from their sacred hearth. The similarity goes much further than the mere use of fire and smoke as symbols, further even than the shared joy and fullness of life. The most significant element the two rituals share, in this context, is the voluntary subjugation of the individual self to the infinitely greater communal self, and the shared sense that the communal self is in turn an integral part of the whole universe. The pity is that belief cannot easily be described and faith cannot be described at all: both have to be experienced before they can be known.

In the high Tibetan valleys, as in the equatorial forest, it is plain enough that all derive benefit from mutual cooperation; there is no necessity to like your neighbor, let alone to love him; but to care about him and for him, yes, there is every necessity. There is an equally obvious necessity, only slightly less compelling, to care about the herders who roam the uplands and the traders who constantly traverse the nation, providing a sort of mobile market as well as bringing and taking news. Certainly the monastery, however humble or grand, is seen as an essential and central part of this mutual welfare system, for it is often an example of social security at its best. It is more rewarding, when thinking of the alleged wealth of Tibetan monasteries, to think of their less exotic granaries and storage houses. It is from the monastic granary that the farmers may get their seed for the coming year and their food in times of hunger, and the wherewithal to honor a religious festival that will bring together everyone in the valley as one single, vital, social, religious and spiritual community. These festivals are times at which problems can be discussed, disputes settled, and harmony restored; the same basic function as the African "witch hunt" we looked at briefly. The coffer similarly provides the means for buying such necessities as have to be imported by the traders when cash is not otherwise available to the farmer.

Even with respect to the brigands the Tibetan farmer is

content to see them as an integral part of the total society, playing an important role, however inadvertently, in the redistribution of wealth. The aristocracy equally fulfills a vital function, providing for continuity in the business of governing such a remote and geographically fragmented nation; and it also provides a healthy counterweight to the economic and political power of the monasteries.

Monasteries as a vehicle for a successful adulthood, are open to a significant proportion of the nation, and much of what we had to say about the *gurukula* system in India applies despite the fact that the Tibetan monastery, unlike the *gurukula*, is so actively and directly involved with almost every aspect of the social order. The monasteries are places of education, and it is to the monastery that the child goes for whatever instruction he needs. Far from running away from school, which is the tendency in our society, the Tibetan child often runs away *to* school, seeking admission without parental approval long before he is ready. This does not mean that he is running away from his home, however; it just means that he wants to grow as full and as robust as his parents and he knows that the monastery is the place where such growth takes place, a place of fun and excitement for the child. In the more remote areas it is the monk who will come to the home or village and provide instruction there. Some families even retain monks as resident teachers. The further you choose to go with your education, the greater the discipline imposed on you, so education is not to be undertaken lightly or as a matter of course. In the same way that in the Ituri you have to *want* to become a man, so in Tibet you have to *want* to acquire an education. As with the *gurukula*, payment is generally in the form of service to your teacher and to the monastery. The difference between the two systems is that not all who go to the Tibetan monastery go there for education or for their personal spiritual development. They may go as children from large families who cannot adequately support them. They may go as youths for whom there will be no land to farm. They may go as adults who have been unsuccessful as farmers or traders, and they may go as brigands who feel that the law of averages is working against them and that it is better to be a live monk than a dead brigand. From all these

categories of life there also come those who have made a conscious decision to pursue the religious life, and they are many;
but whereas they are immediately subjected to a number of
vows, including celibacy, the others are not. There is a large
body of lay monks for whom not even the vow of celibacy is
obligatory. Whereas the student may perform service for his
teacher, these others are more in the nature of servants; even
in a small monastery the chores are many, especially in the
absence of Western technology with its convenient sources of
energy, running water, and an almost instantaneous com-
munications system. For some monasteries, just the carrying
of water alone may require the full-time employment of a
number of lay monks.

Since the monastery would be unable to function without
such service, the lay monks are seen as fulfilling a perfectly
legitimate and honorable role, with no stigma attached to the
fact that they have taken only the minimal vows and made
only the minimal sacrifices in their personal lives. They too
are subject to a high degree of discipline and are expected to
participate in the religious life of the monastery as part of the
congregation. Even as lay monks a certain status attaches to
them in the minds of the farmers and others, because of their
proximity and service to these religious and spiritual centers.

The monastery is regarded as the source of material social
security, but not necessarily primarily or exclusively so. By
the very fact that each monastery contains a number, perhaps
thousands, of monks devoted to religion, to constantly maintaining the continuity between the mortal and the immortal,
between man and God, each monastery is fulfilling a vital
function. For if Chenresig, the protective deity of Tibet, were
to become separated from Tibet, the country and the people
would cease to be. Thus the lusty farmers, traders, herders,
aristocrats, and brigands actively encourage as many of their
number as are willing to join a monastery to do so, and to
actively work to keep Chenresig close at all times, so that they
can give their full attention to the business of material living,
prayer wheel in hand. If ever adulthood was a time of doing, it is in Tibet, where there are many widely different ways
of doing, yet where all are seen as equally valid and as equally
necessary to each other in terms of the common good. And in

Tibet, adult life, however practiced, all revolves around the monastery, the sacred symbols of which pervade the secular life of the population at every level.

In all of this there has been little or no reference to the great supernatural powers that Tibetans are traditionally supposed to manifest. While there are indeed Tibetan monasteries and hermitages much like those described for India, one of the major points of using the Tibetan example has been to suggest that the religious approach to adulthood, the religious "how" of what to do whatever you are doing, is no less valid than the spiritual way. This is surely no more graphically seen than in the difference between a mountainside hermit secluded from all humanity, sitting in still and silent meditation, and the lusty Tibetan trader swinging his mechanical prayer wheel which, he trusts, will send his prayers out with every revolution while he is thinking of when he will next be able to visit that brothel and drink some *chang* with his friends. The Tibetan woman greeting the morning with the burning of juniper wood is somewhere between the two, as is the Hindu woman lighting the butter lamps at the household shrine, as is the Mbuti woman guarding the door of the *elima* house, and as is any other mother suckling her newborn child. For woman is power, and whatever she does is touched with power.

I am not relegating religion, as distinct from Spirit, to mere mechanical performance of ritual; but I am distinguishing between ritual behavior, associated as it is with religious belief, and the direct unmediated manifestation of power which is the spiritual way of doing, of serving society. Through their dedication to ritual, and by leaving the manifestations of power to the few who possess it, the Tibetans dedicate their whole lives to the social good so clearly demanded by their religious beliefs. But their ritual behavior would be an empty thing if there were no such thing as power. Nor is it by accident that in Tibet spiritual power, religious (ecclesiastical) power, and political power are almost coterminous, for political and religious power go hand in hand as complementary manifestations of the same supreme power that I call Spirit and that others may call sociality. A life that is lacking in belief cannot make effective use of ritual, and a life without ritual cannot practice the religious way of doing, of living.

India, the birthplace of Buddhism, provides an example of the third variation, the secular approach to doing. It springs from the same source, outwardly very similar to the other two ways of doing, but with a secular focus. Whereas the way of the Hindu *sannyasi* we described earlier tends to be seclusive and the Tibetan way inclusive, the Buddhist way could almost be described as intrusive. As with the other two ways all three elements are combined, all are ways of performing social service, of manifesting social responsibility; the difference is mainly a question of the primary focus or conscious objective or intent. The *ashram* of Sri Aurobindo, one of India's greatest spiritual leaders of modern times, and once one of preindependence India's greatest freedom fighters, systematically combines all the elements in what is essentially a secular approach to adult action. Again, the approach rests on the concept of power, and attempts to maximize that power and concentrate it, at first in a few individuals and eventually to release it for the common good. Like other monastic communities it has been accused of being parasitical and escapist. Even a casual visit to the *ashram* in Pondicherry should convince the skeptic that whatever else it may be, it is neither of these two things. Even thirty years ago when I first visited it, and when Sri Aurobindo was still alive and a source of direct spiritual power, the *ashram* was run like a business. The businesslike atmosphere even extended to the way the meditation sessions were run and the annual *darshan* (public appearance) was organized. The tone was secular rather than spiritual or religious, yet Spirit and religion were equally present. The atmosphere, or tone, appeared to be what it was because of the conscious goals of the community, their overt dedication to the task of building a new society which they believed could only be done by creating a new, fuller, more complete kind of human being. They were engaged in another form of transformation. In a sense they were invoking Spirit power, but at the same time they were reaching up toward it, for merely to bring the Divine down to earth was not enough to effect the complete social transformation they sought; only individuals could be transformed that way. Man had to raise himself to meet the Divine halfway, by perfecting his mind, his body, and his soul to the utmost limits of his capacity. So perfected, he would still be incomplete and imperfect; the empty vessel would have been filled to the last drop, and the last drop that would complete the work of perfection would be Divine Spirit. Divine is their term, but I am glad of the excuse to use it.

Today Sri Aurobindo and the Mother, the active female manifestation of his passive male power, are both dead. The Mother was almost as powerful a physical being as he was. At the time I was first there I was very much a skeptic, but to be with either of them for more than a minute was enough to give me a violent headache. A headache is hardly a spiritual experience, you might say, but it was certainly evidence of some kind of power. At *darshan* Sri Aurobindo did not speak to anyone, he just sat there. It was when his eyes caught mine that my worst headache began, a pressure that at first was not painful, but which grew stronger the closer I got to the man. We had all been shepherded into the audience room in a long, orderly line, as though we were queuing for admission to a movie, and we were presented with a small flower each to put on the ground in front of Sri Aurobindo when we got to the head of the queue, with instructions not to pause or try to look or say anything, but to pass right on. I thought it was going to be a rather bad movie until I finally got up to the top of the stairs and into the far end of the room. It was more than the absolute silence as the long line steadily and slowly inched its way forward. It had something to do with the motion itself; the line did not start and stop, gaps appearing and then closing up; it flowed, and as the line flowed forward something flowed back. There was nothing designed to create any kind of visual effect, no exotic music, no chanting, nothing to tell the senses that anything unusual was happening except for that flow.

Then, although I had intended to behave according to the rules and regulations, my curiosity got the better of me and I moved my head slightly to one side to look ahead. That broke the flow, but only for an instant, because that was when my eyes met those of Sri Aurobindo. The gentle flow, which I can best describe as being like what I feel when I sink into a deep hot bath, stopped for a frightening instant, then, instead of the whole body being gently warmed, my head suddenly started to boil. The flow came through his eyes, but the power, like the heat of an open furnace, came from his whole body and being. For the life of me I could not look away, even when I was right in front of the man. My head wanted to burst from a pressure that seemed to come from both inside and outside at the same time. And once I got out I went straight to my room with a violent, painful headache that lasted twenty-four hours. I even took my temperature; it was perfectly normal.

This is not the place to attempt any explanation; the incident serves to illustrate that even for a skeptic the power was real. Hypnosis is too easy an answer, unless hypnosis is possible by long distance, with the source both out of sight and out of mind over a period of thirty years. The Mother was not much less powerful, though I disliked her from the start. She was a nag, dictatorial, unyielding, unreceptive, even aggressive; yet she was a small woman, soft and gentle, persuasive and kind. She confused me. I had many conversations with the Mother, and they were worse than anything any of my tutors at Oxford ever put me through. Sri Aurobindo made me feel with my whole body and being; the Mother made me think and reason as I had never done before. But I flunked the third discipline of physical exercise.

The *ashram* insisted on intensive physical training as part of the daily routine. There was calisthenics every morning, as well as tennis and swimming and other body-building activities. There was intellectual training as well, with both private and group discussions of various teachings and philosophies. And there were sessions of meditation and concentration that were no less exhausting. The reasoning was simple enough, that if the power is to descend, the body has to be fit in all respects and strong enough to withstand that power; but the followers of Sri Aurobindo seek to go even further and rise up and enter into the power rather than merely have it descend into them; and that is a corporate effort in every sense, not an individual enterprise.

The *ashram* also demanded of its members an active life of service to the community, which began to take over the town of Pondicherry block by block, tending to all its own needs in an efficient, systematic, and responsible way. It is the same today, thirty years later; if anything it is even more dynamic. Sri Aurobindo and the Mother are buried in the central court-yard, their tomb topped by a raised marble table perpetually covered with bright fresh flowers, brought by devotees who arrange and rearrange the floral carpet so that it is never static. It reminded me of that steady flow of warmth and power at the *darshan*. But the devotees are not devoted to a memory and they come not so much to pay respects to the dead as to be revitalized by the living. The work of transformation is continuing, and the *ashram* community, now larger than it ever was, is working with even greater intensity to create a new society that will be a communal source of power. Whether it will succeed or not, whether it *can* succeed or not, is irrele-vant for our purposes; Sri Aurobindo *ashram* stands as an example of corporate, secular, social action, or adulthood.

With these examples in mind of the highly diverse ways in which adulthood is approached in other cultures, we should be able to look more critically and constructively at our own way of doing things. Our world is so much more complex, the range of choices we are all faced with so infinitely greater, that comparison between it and the culture we have been looking at is not easy. However, if we look at some of the ma-jor markers by which we normally recognize and accept the onset of adulthood, and keep in mind the crucial criterion of the art of doing as being the art of living adult life with active concern for others, we have a sound starting point.

It is best, perhaps, to start with the western marker of mili-tary national service, for many *ashram* communities see youth as being conscripted into another form of national service. The youthful Tibetans when they undertake a stint at the local monastery can be said to be performing a kind of na-tional service, for as they consciously see it, by their worship and prayer and right effort they are helping to keep Tibet under the divine protection of Chenresig. So also with the *gurukula* student, perfecting himself in terms of conscious de-votion to the ideal of selflessness, he is seen as preparing for socially responsible adulthood before he undertakes his re-sponsibilities as a householder by invoking a divine consciousness that will, all believe, be to the benefit of mankind. To many a Westerner that may seem nonsensical and impractical; but we cannot deny the consciousness and the intent, and that is what we are concerned with for the moment. Many tribal cultures have a form of national service more directly comparable with our own when, again prior to marriage, youth and young adults are segregated and given certain tasks of obvious national/tribal importance. They are not infrequently trained and organized in such a manner as to be ready to serve as an army if the nation is attacked. And having been so trained, with no war to fight they are set about other tasks, such as herding cattle over vast distances and difficult terrain, tasks appropriate to the vigor of that time of life. To them this is just as consciously and as effectively a way of serving the nation as is the task of realizing the ultimate unity of all Self for the *gurukula* student, or the concerted, strictly disciplined performance of communal ritual, combined with individual devotion, by which a vast body of youthful monks seek to invoke the protective spirit of Chenresig for the good of the Tibetan nation. What of this conscious sense of devotion to the good of society at large can we see in our form of national service? I can best answer for myself, for I certainly saw this as indisputable evidence of my adulthood.

My national service was during World War II, so in many respects it is unlike that of peacetime conscripts. In a way it should have been easier, easier at least to manifest some social concern when the life of the nation was at stake than when the contingency seems to be but a remote possibility. It was not that way for me at all, nor for most of my friends at Oxford (which had not yet had time to work its socializing magic) who joined the services at the same time as I did. Not once during this critical time did anyone ever talk to me in terms of social obligation, and it never crossed my mind that I had such an obligation. All my past experience and everything that I had been taught at school told me that my prime responsibility was to myself. This was modified only by recognition that all of us were expected to act in such a way as to conform to our station in life. So although I had already developed strong feelings about nonviolence and deeply wanted to be a conscientious objector (which showed *some* social concern), my family and friends would not even discuss the possibility with me, dismissing it as unthinkable, improper, embarrassing. It was not a question of patriotism or civic duty, for there were plenty of viable alternatives to combat duty, some of them a great deal more dangerous. The dismissal was in terms of "what people would think." Any lack of morality that I might have shown at Westminster was nothing, in my mind, to the way in which I finally succumbed to what people might think.

I had managed to squeeze in a year at Oxford, but it was not enough to complete my adolescence, let alone equip me with the youthful art of reason; I had to go back to Oxford for that after my trial bout with adulthood in national service. At this point I was certainly anything but socialized. But a lure was held out that appealed to other values. It was made known to me, and this is the way that I was recruited, that youths of my age (seventeen) who volunteered for the Royal Navy would be given very special consideration, coming from Oxford, and within six months we would have our commissions. Following that, I was given to understand, we would join the wardroom of some ship or naval base and continue, in navy tradition, to live pretty much as we had been trained to live at Oxford. The most prominent factors outlined as part of the recruitment drive involved the high quality of food and drink, and the proper use of formal dress. Nothing of social responsibility.

After cursory training at an Oxford boathouse a large number of us were sent, as ordinary seamen, to a naval training base at Ipswich. There we were separated from the rest of the trainees and housed in special quarters and treated very preferentially in every respect. This was my first real introduction to a democratic society in which, it was evident, family, class, and wealth all spelled power and privilege. It was not exactly an introduction to a socially responsible adulthood.

After as little as two or three months, including a very brief stint afloat, we were all packed off to the officers' training base, H.M.S. *King Alfred*, where we attended classes and had numerous consultations with our tailors about the new uniforms we would soon be wearing. The only ones who did not graduate were not from Oxford University. Again, during all this training, the focus of attention was exclusively on the technology we were expected to master. There was not one word about *why* we were doing all this, and there was no evidence that any of my friends, anymore than I, even considered the question. There was one ritual that did serve to inspire some sense of belonging to a wider social unit, however. Every morning the flag was raised to the accompaniment of the naval band playing "God Save the King" in the grandest fashion. That always brought a lump to my throat and made me think of goodness and greatness. But then, so did almost every other national anthem, and that of the Germans raised the lump even higher. It was much better music.

Inevitably, the time came when we were ready to go to sea as officers; surely by now we had reached adulthood? Not a bit of it; we were still adolescents and our retardation was written into the system as meticulously as if it had been planned. Most of us elected to join Coastal Forces rather than "big ships." It was never seriously suggested to us that our choice should be made in terms of the needs of the nation or the navy; on the contrary the criteria were consistent with those cited by the recruiting officer at Oxford. The appeal was to values such as the availability of menial service, the relative quality and quantity of food and liquor, uniform, proximity to Oxford, and in the case of Coastal Forces, the minimal amount of combat duty we could expect and the maximal amount of time spent in the comfort of our home port. The recruitment service did not tell us where our nation needed us most, or where our particular skills could best be used, and I do not remember any of us asking those questions ourselves. So it was rather as adolescents than as adults that we entered the war.

Worse than our lack of social concern was the growing lack of human concern, which is directly attributable to our participation in national service, but which would not have happened had we been better prepared during our youth. Following the invasion there were a number of dead bodies floating around the Normandy anchorage. Since our craft were low in the water and we had nothing else to do during the daytime we were given the task of pulling the bodies alongside and getting the name tags from them. This was a disagreeable task for anyone, and most of the seamen, like myself, were in their late teens or early twenties. Some of them found that if the body was sufficiently decomposed a sharp tug at the neck chain with a grappling hook would disconnect the head. If your aim was not good something else might come off, and it became a sort of macabre sport. A lot of tags were lost in the process because the neck was often stronger than the chain. When the Germans started attaching explosives to dead bodies and floating them into the anchorage, we were instructed not to make any further attempts to get tags but to blow up all floating bodies on sight. The other two officers on my ship were older than I was. They commented only on the expenditure of the ammunition, which they had to account for, and the quality of the marksmanship. This and other things drew me more and more toward the enlisted men. Most of them were volunteers, as I was, but in many ways they seemed more adult than the officers. It was they who sickened first at poking bloated bodies with grappling hooks, and ultimately they just refused to fire at any more bodies, asking if there was not another way of disposing of them. In contrast, the officers on my ship and others seemed to enjoy the target practice and used to swap stories in the ward room, over their gins and whiskies, about putrid bodies, detached limbs, and burning gasses. In my youthful naivety this did not seem like adult behavior, it was not even human. Yet there are many who claim that national service, particularly combat duty, "will make a man of you."

When the war ended and we were posted to Cuxhaven, at the mouth of the River Elbe, we had to deal with the defeated German civilians we met on the streets, on our way to the officers' club, or wherever. The easy, natural, and correct way the "uneducated" enlisted men treated the Germans made the educated officers look like animals. At this time, in the last days of the war, the civilians were on the verge of starvation, and through advanced malnutrition their reflexes were almost nil. When approached by a car, while crossing a road, they could not make up their minds which way to run, so they just froze in terror. It was a source of endless fun, for some, and the requisitioned Mercedes used by the officers was many a time driven at civilians as part of an organized sport. But what sickened me most was the behavior of my fellow officers at the elegant Allied Officers' Club in Hamburg. It had been a great hotel and the dining room had an area that jutted out over the road running along the side of the Alste Binne, a large lake in the middle of the city. The officers ordered lavish meals and competed for seats in the bay window so that they could gorge themselves in full view of the starving Germans below. The intent is not imagined, nor is it merely deduced from their conversation and laughter as they mocked those bedraggled figures standing, watching, and waiting. They chose window seats, not just to be seen, but so that from time to time they could throw some unwanted morsel out of the window and watch the Germans fight for it. The Westminster Pancake Greaze had nothing on this for animality, but the values that made such behavior possible had been taught and learned in schools like Westminster, and the values that could have made real men of us had been ignored.

In such ways national service did indeed mark the beginning of my adulthood, by all too slowly awakening some sort of social conscience. But there was one particular moment when I think the actual transition finally took place; abruptly, violently, yet with a strange beauty, ending both my adolescence and my youth before I had learned the art of being either. It happened when our flotilla was assigned to guard the eastern flank of the invasion anchorage against the nightly attacks by unmanned explosive motor boats. The Germans sent these in under radio control, then turned them loose as they reached the anchorage. They were low in the water, and once turned loose they sped around in haphazard circles until they hit each other or something else, when they exploded. Our job was to fire at them and try to explode them before they got through our line of defense and into the main anchorage. In the pitch darkness of night it was as much an exercise in maneuverability as it was in target practice, and as fast as we were, we were more than vulnerable. Within the first week one of them struck the next ship up the line from us and exploded on impact. One of my Oxford friends was the navigator; I knew the other officers well and most of the crew. Three thousand gallons of high octane gasoline and all the ammunition on board went up in one great blast, and with it went thirty-three lives, indistinguishable bits and pieces in that fountain of sparks and flame. The only person on the bridge with me was the helmsman, a taciturn seaman named Scouse McBride; we knew each other well and he also had a number of close friends on that ship. Oblivious of the other explosive motorboats milling around us, he let go of the helm and put his arm around my shoulder and gripped tight, to have something to hold onto as we watched our friends disappear—and with them something of ourselves—to reappear as flotsam the next morning.

I see this as the beginning of my adulthood because it was my first experience of two human beings needing each other, as though their existence were inseparable. I found myself holding him as tightly as he was holding me; it was as though if one of us were to let go, both would cease to be. It is the first time that I can recall that my whole being came together, with the realization that the next moment I too could be a shower of sparks. But something else was also happening; I was feeling more alive and more *fully* than I had ever felt. In contact with this violent display of mortality, I felt at one with my friend from Oxford, sparkling away in the night sky, and at one with the arm still clutching my shoulder. It was a moment of companionship with both of them, the quality of which I had never experienced before. It was a moment of fearful ecstasy, and it took me a long time to understand it. I just wish that I had learned what I learned then some other way, and that I had been initiated into adulthood other than through national service that was all too consistent with other sorry things my society had taught me.

Another generally accepted marker of adulthood in many societies is marriage, and in most societies marriage compels entry into the economic life of the society. In our society the emphasis is almost exclusively on the economic ability of the couple to survive, if we are to approve the marriage. That is not so elsewhere. The Mbuti only become fully integrated into adult life, as hunters and gatherers, when they have married; the youth may not own a hunting net until that moment. But while the male youth must have demonstrated his ability to hunt before the girl's parents readily consent to the marriage, that is not where the emphasis lies. The major focus of concern is on the readiness of both of them to want and to have children and to raise them as they should be raised. They have to have outgrown the mere physiological fascination of sex, and emotional involvement has to have been transcended by spiritual awareness. This comes about by the increasing participation of older youth in the great *molimo* festivals, and the *molimo madé*, or lesser *molimo*, is perhaps the Mbuti equivalent of national service. Marriage, as a marker of adulthood for the Mbuti, marks their spiritual readiness for adulthood, just as the presentation to his prospective in-laws of an antelope he has caught marks the groom's material readiness. Clearly, marriage in itself does not define adulthood, as the Hindu term *grhastha* shows, for the adult stage of "house-holding," as seen in Hindu thought, as with the Mbuti, demands both spiritual and material economic preparedness . . . to which they add intellectual or rational preparedness through the institution of the *gurukula* or other formal schooling. All these elements are present in the Western approach to marriage, but the readiness for spiritual responsibility is minimal. While spiritual readiness for the sacred state of marriage is demanded by the Church of the couple, that is a very different thing from demanding of the couple, as other cultures do, that the marriage will be devoted to and dedicated to the good of society, the children to be raised out of concern for others and for the good of others. It is no crime not to be married in our society, nor is it wrong for married couples not to have children. In other societies either would be considered dereliction of duty. Marriage is clearly different things to different peoples.

My brush with the institution of marriage was more cerebral than emotional, something rather more common in those days than now when the reverse seems more often to be the case. At Oxford there was a lot of peer pressure to have sexual escapades with the ladies of Somerville or Lady Margaret Hall, which was interestingly different from the greater class consciousness with which boys at Westminster had tended to prefer local serving girls. But there was no suggestion that sex and marriage were in any way linked. Even when a very close friend of mine came and told me that the girl friend he had talked of marrying was pregnant, it was not to ask me to be best man but to borrow money for an abortion. With regard to my own marital prospects a number of social factors were at work, all indicating certain adult values, but restricting any sense of social responsibility to narrow, exclusive, and opposing factions. The various factions in my family discouraged me from consulting them, but familial and territorial pressures led me to make some show of trying.

As far as my current residential territory went, a good hunting county in the south of England, it was a question of demand and supply. The social obligation was to keep the two equal, in other words, not to marry out of the county. That also helped to keep the Hunt in the right hands, a truly social responsibility, to be sure. Since I took my time, the choice was gradually narrowed down to two girls. One was the daughter of a family of famous piano-makers, which warmed me to her, but she was not the least interested in me. The other was the daughter of the Master of the Hunt, and she *was* interested. I disliked hunting intensely and felt rather like a fox at bay with the hounds closing in, much as I had once felt at Westminster; and like a fox I fled.

One of the problems this illustrates is that in our national context the word "society" becomes highly ambiguous. Was my adult duty, my social responsibility as I have defined it, to the county? Or to my Scottish family who made it clear they did not want me to marry a Sassenach? Or to my Irish family who merely expressed the feeling that I really should get married, to make things "look right"? Perhaps today, with more people conscious of the population problem, consideration of marriage does bring in its wake a wider social consciousness, but that is a little late in the day; in any case, the value of marriage to society, and as a marker of adulthood, goes far beyond the number of children you have. Not once in school were we ever taught the social ramifications of marriage; marriage was never even mentioned. This should all be compared with the same marker in India, where the term for those who are married is pointedly "householder."

For me, other lines of social cleavage were revealed by the one relationship that could have led to a real marriage, and that was with an Indian girl from a good Hindu family whose brother was, for a brief while, a good friend of mine at Oxford. We were deeply in love with each other, but she, and by then I too, had a sense of social obligation at the smallest level, that of our individual families; and they were strongly opposed on both racial and religious grounds.

Nonetheless, dismissing our minimal sense of sociality, Kumari and I went through all the preliminary rituals. I escorted her to the Flower Ball in London, where she was considered not quite proper, the reason given being that the then Princesses Elizabeth and Margaret were also attending. Now social considerations at their widest, national extension were impinging. To be a responsible, patriotic adult it was evidently necessary to be a racist. There was much more furor, however, when I brought Kumari into that south country hunting territory and escorted her to the ball given at Arundel Castle for the coming-out of the Duke of Norfolk's daughter. Kumari fled to India and I to Africa. Between us we first established our own economic marker for a joint adulthood, and as soon as I could support her we were to get married. But when with my first job in hand I wrote a formal letter of proposal, it was delayed in the Indian mails and she received it months later, just two weeks after she had finally succumbed and married a Hindu.

In Europe and America, whenever for some reason it becomes known that I am not married, there is neither surprise nor comment and certainly no suggestion that I am not adult. This is not true of other parts of the world we have been discussing. In Africa, particularly, there is surprise and disbelief, and when in addition I have to confess to not having any children that I know of, the disbelief turns into something approaching an accusation of social irresponsibility, and more than once I have been asked if I do not have any feelings about my family and country. Do my parents not want grandchildren, do I not want my country to prosper and multiply? Oh for the social conscience of an Ituri villager or a Hindu sweeper or a Chinese cab driver or a South Sea fisherman. For them, marriage is clearly linked to adulthood and itself is an adult, social way of doing. To ask why it is not so clearly linked in our society is, alas, one of the many questions we can only raise here, since the answer will vary in terms of how each of us defines "our own society." It is much more than simply that we do not need more children, or because other forms of cohabitation are replacing marriage. For me it goes back to the proposition that if the family, whatever form that takes in any particular society, serves as a model for adult society and adult social relationships, then if the latter become the dominant consideration will not the prevalent form of society require and be reflected in a particular form of family? I am not particularly happy when I look at what is happening to the family today, and I am not particularly happy when I look at the fragmentation and emphasis on individuality that is coming to our society. But they are consistent with each other and may be necessary.

Given our ambivalence with respect to the need for adults to be married and the legitimate goals of marriage, and a not inconsiderable ambivalence concerning the need for and goals of national service (not to be confused with a military career), "earning a living" is probably the most reliable marker for adulthood in our society. And, if properly distinguished from merely "having a job" or "making money," adults in all the other societies we have looked at are certainly also expected to earn a living. For them, "earning a living" is not exclusively related to the economic needs of the society; it is any activity that consciously accomplishes a goal beneficial to society. We often dismiss hermits, monastic or otherwise, as parasites; we consider recluses as anti-social. When a youth begins to earn a living, in our usual sense of the words, we congratulate him (and he congratulates himself) for becoming independent. Yet, having achieved that state of adult independence, *how* does he live when he is happily self-supporting? Much of suburban living is very hermitlike; many city dwellers, rich or poor, are recluses living in extraordinary isolation, insulated as well as isolated from effective concern with their neighbors; and rural life can be monastic in more respects than one for those who are independent; but we do not call *them* parasites as long as they are "gainfully employed." Making a living, as distinct from earning it, is indeed compatible with independence and hence with social irresponsibility. Earning a living is not, and here we are talking about earning. That is more of a judgmental term and suggests that values and the opinion of others are important. It implies both cooperation with others and consideration for them; it is "doing" in an adult manner, with a sense of responsibility. In our complex world, unfortunately, the bulk of jobs available neither encourage nor make very possible the kind of constant, intimate social concern that simply has to be manifest in less complex small-scale societies. It is as possible for a politician as it is for a social worker to make rather than earn a living. The focus is more on right performance than on social concern, as management/labor disputes continually demonstrate. Social concern is something too often considered as a matter that should be private, restricted to individual conscience. Even in the kinds of work that could be classified as "intrusive," such as social work, surgery, or education, say, there is a common myth that these services can best be performed by maintaining a personal distance, by not becoming "involved." Objectivity, when carried this far, is the mortal enemy of concern, and objectivity is one of the major values in our workaday life. Yet few of us would claim to be without social concern, and of course that is true; the point that other social systems seem to make is that it is not enough in adulthood to be concerned as an individual, in the privacy of our homes; our whole active life of doing could and should be an act of concern.

The variety of ways of earning a living is so vast in our society that it is obviously impossible to deal here with even a representative selection, so I shall merely try to show how in one adult world, the academic world of which I am a part, social concern as we have seen it manifest in other cultures may not be as unrealistic as might at first sight seem, using those same categories of spiritual, religious, and secular. If those categories seem overly idealistic, inapplicable, or even undesirable in our fast-paced mundane daily lives, all the more reason for sticking to them and forcing ourselves to look even harder to see if qualities that other cultures find essential for the survival of their whole way of life are really so incompatible with ours. We might even discover that those qualities are already to be found in our daily lives, sometimes latent, sometimes more openly manifest.

Before joining the academic way of earning a living I tried, unsuccessfully, a variety of occupations. In all of them one or more of the three approaches—the spiritual, the religious, the secular—was perfectly possible; in none of them was it impossible to combine the work with active social concern. As a result of my experience in India and Africa I was finally dabbling in ethnomusicology when Evans-Pritchard, at Oxford, suggested that I might as well become a social anthropologist. That offers an easy way to begin to look at how, in our modern world, we can indeed live ordinary lives with concern, even consciously transforming the secular and individual, if we wish, into that which is sacred and social. After all, the term "social anthropologist" implies at the outset that we are concerned with society. That unfortunately is not necessarily so, and in looking at the academic world, and specifically that of social scientists, I was at the outset amazed at the lengths to which the scholars I met went to avoid having anything to do with the real world around them. Subsequently, however, there has been a change of attitude, and it is now becoming almost respectable to show concern for society in and through our work.

Anthropology allows for a variety of ways of earning a living; through research and writing, in museum work, and of course by teaching. At all levels we find the controversial ivory tower.

The ivory-tower approach suggests that by just being scholarly we are doing enough. It is rather the same kind of reasoning that we applied to the spiritual recluse in India, and scholarship, of course, is a form of power. However, since scholarship is rational rather than spiritual, I see less chance of it emanating and radiating very effectively from any ivory tower without some further action being taken; and if we are to act at all, by writing our reports or by teaching or by attending conferences, would it not be better to do so without social concern? But even in research there are those who claim that pure science should prevail, uncontaminated by contact with social issues. It is argued that if we allow ourselves to be drawn into the everyday problems of society, our personal opinions and beliefs will come to interfere with our work. That illustrates very nicely one consequence of never having become fully integrated human beings in our adolescence, of never having learned the art of reason in our youth. It is also one of the best arguments I know for social irresponsibility.

But the ivory-tower approach does have, or *can* have validity in the context of a spiritual approach to the anthropologist's way of doing. The very term implies it, suggesting as it does some remote, infinitely valuable and desirable ideal, attainable only by a few. The image, and the ideal of absolute perfection that goes with it, serves a useful function in an academic world that is often less than perfect. Even in teaching it has its place; the reclusive scholar whose ivory tower is his book-lined study performs a service just by having such an impressive study, testifying to his dedication to the quest for truth. But the quest has to be there if the students (or the colleagues) are to feel it. We all recognize a library full of unread books when we see one. The reclusive teacher is often criticized for his inaccessibility to students; he appears on time for his lectures, which he delivers in a masterful way, and then disappears back to his study, where he can be reached, if at all, only by a few select and dedicated students. If such a teacher meets any of his other students while crossing the campus, say, he may greet them in a friendly enough way, but he will not profane his art by discussing academic matters with them unless they are among his elect disciples. It is very much the principle on which the great Hindu teachers work. The weekly lecture is comparable to the *darshan;* what is said matters rather less than the inspiration the presence of perfection provides, an incentive for students to discover for themselves. The ivory-tower approach, in fact, fails in its obligation to society only when it becomes, as for so many it does, exclusive and introverted, as well as seclusive.

The "religious" approach, as an example of which we looked at the Tibetan monastery, is also easy to see at play in the academic world, whether it be in field research, working in a museum, or teaching at some school or university. In some field experiences, but by no means all, I have felt that I am living and working in a monastery, for some cultures manage to make the world around them a kind of sacred temple. This was particularly so when working with the Mbuti, for whom the forest is indeed a sacred place, every bit as much as the monastery is for the Tibetans. And the Mbuti, again like the Tibetans, live life with a lusty zeal and active concern for each other that constantly transform their individual actions into actions replete with social significance and concern.

The mechanisms are all there for making the religious approach to academia just as possible and valid as it is for Tibetans and Mbuti; many indeed earn their living that way, but not all are conscious of the potential that lies at their feet. The very buildings in which we work are often ritually referred to as "temples of learning"; all formal education used to be in the hands of the clergy, and to this day, museums, universities, and libraries frequently imitate ecclesiastical architecture, encouraging if not demanding silence, slow motion, modesty of dress, and other symbols of respect for the sacred peculiar to our culture. The very immensity of some museums and lecture halls make the visitor feel small and insignificant, which is a beginning. At least some museum exhibition design work displays the same flair for theatricality as does many a church and temple, making the same appeal to the unconscious sense of otherness as does ritual; only then, having firmly established the realm of the sacred, is the rational content added that, by a secular exclusivity of approach, makes other exhibits so empty and uninspiring, however technically informative. We all expect a museum exhibition to be more than a textbook, and perhaps it is only because the sacred is so unfashionable that many of us would balk at saying that we wanted to be inspired.

But just as good exhibit work should inspire as well as inform, so should good teaching. We use symbols of the sacred, as well as worldly symbols of the secular, and by transforming knowledge into wisdom we transform the secular into the sacred; if we are lucky we inspire, at least once in a while. And many of us bring our own personal symbols of the sacred into our daily academic world, such as in our manner of dress or speech, often consciously different from dress and speech we use in secular contexts; and such as the pictures we may have in our studies, often strangely unrelated to our specialty, or the music that serves as a background to help us concentrate on our work in the privacy of our studies. Occasionally,

we bring our personal sense of the sacred even more overtly
into our daily working life, not to relieve any drudgery, but by
sharing it with others, to work the magic of transformation
by refusing to isolate one part of our lives from another. The
chairman of the anthropology department at the museum
where I worked in New York was a sort of Bostonian Tibetan,
a great scientist who was not afraid to be guided by his intuition, or by his inner feelings, if you prefer. He was not only
amply endowed with Spirit, he was also an amateur musician,
as was one of the archaeologists, from Cambridge University.
I had a small harpsichord in my office, and after lunch Harry
would bring in his cello and Shirley her violin, and between
us we would massacre Telemann, Bach, or Vivaldi. Among
other things this broke down that dangerous barrier that often
divides our work life from the rest of our life; it allowed us to
be whole beings in whatever we were doing, and it related us
to each other in a way that added to rather than subtracted
from our mere academic relationship. We did not exactly
draw any audiences, though we did begin to attract additional
participants; but it was our equivalent of swinging the prayer
wheel, and for us it brought the sacred and social into what
otherwise might have been a very sterile, secular ivory tower.
Probably everyone in that department had his own way of
achieving the same ends, his own version of the prayer wheel,
and it infected the work of both research and exhibition.

The museum was also rather like a Tibetan monastery in
that, although it was in many ways highly elitist, it changed
with the times and became more and more involved with the
needs of the public through its exhibits, its publications, its
representation on radio and television, and its public lectures.
In this way it was to some extent intrusive as well as inclusive
and seclusive; it offered possibilities for social concern to be
manifest by all three approaches. The more such museums become consciously and actively concerned with the needs of the
communities of which they are (or should be) a part, the more
they will resemble the Tibetan monastery in function, and
the richer their contribution to society. There is no need for
them to be intrusive, to take the more secular approach and
actively engage in the business of bringing about social

change. It is enough for them to be what they are, temples of learning, accessible to all who wish to come. But teaching is another matter.

The secular approach, as we saw it manifest in southern India at Sri Aurobindo *ashram*, is more appropriate to the university context, however much the ivory-tower approach may seem to predominate. Whether we like it or not, consciously or unconsciously, we are molding minds and characters if we truly teach the art of reason. To be content with filling heads with knowledge is to turn a university into a factory. But if we assume that universities are trying to do more than turn their students into walking lexicons, then we have to ask what that something else is. The traditional graduation speech seems to indicate that we are consciously preparing students to go out into the world equipped to be of service to the community, to earn rather than merely make a living. The reality belies this as often as not.

The lack of genuine educational interest in and involvement with the task of socialization, of encouraging youth to be actively occupied with the good of society at large, is witnessed by the fact that in the field of anthropology the "applied anthropologist" and the "humanistic anthropologist" are still regarded by many as second-class citizens, implying that only second-class intellects would bother to concern themselves with social issues. That in turn implies that contemporary social issues, real life problems, are themselves of secondary importance. The result has been an aloofness of the academic world that has discouraged many a government, local or central, from making use of all the talent at its disposal.

In prison work, both by teaching there and by doing research in the problematic area of stress, security, and rehabilitation, I discovered what the reputation that academia has built for itself does to the researcher who genuinely wants to contribute to external problems. Inmates, guards, officers, wardens, and heads of state departments of corrections were all skeptical, if not downright suspicious, although the research was not costing any of them a cent and was conducted according to whatever guidelines they wished to impose. And the more "educated," i.e., equipped with university degrees, was the official, the more resistance I got, with a few significant

exceptions. One warden, who claimed to have no such education, and who described himself as a typical "southern
cracker," gave me an appointment and told me at the outset
that he was going to leave in a half hour and probably less,
since he doubted that anything I could say would be of use
to him or his work. He cited his experience with other academic researchers who came armed with theories which they
wanted to try out without any firsthand detailed experience
of the facts (and feelings) of prison life. We spent several
hours together on that one occasion, largely because when he
asked what *my* theory was, I could tell him that I had none.
That is the way that good applied anthropology often goes
about its work, unlike some other social sciences that have
their own techniques suited to their own goals. And this same
warden discovered that the anthropologist who considers himself a humanist rather than a scientist does not necessarily
come laden with the burden of having to do good, to relieve
the oppressed; he merely sees a problem, a human problem,
and perhaps sees it in very theoretical, structural terms, yet is
concerned with it and wants to work with it because it *is* a
human problem, affecting the very quality of life as we all
live it. But to get that kind of cooperation, as I did in two
southern states, is not easy, because of the aloofness and often
dogmatic arrogance that in the minds of many are characteristic of the academic world.

The significance of this experience goes beyond its significance for the academic world. I think it points to the need for
all of us, whatever we are doing, to do it with the whole of our
being and not just as an intellectual exercise or just to accomplish some physical or mechanical goal, or to create merely
the right sounds at the right moments. Bach put it well when
he said something to the effect that anyone can hit the right
notes at the right moment, the trick is in hitting them with
the right feeling. A mechanic does much the same thing when
in that timeworn phrase he "takes pride in his work." Actually
the phrase would be more apt if it referred to the way that good
mechanics, like good craftsmen in any walk of life, put pride
into their work, doing with their whole being, with concern
for others with whom, through their work, they are in contact. This is exactly what the Ndaka fisherman does in the

Ituri Forest when he sets about making a canoe with which to earn his living. The forest, after all, belongs to all, and the forest itself is power and endowed with Spirit. So with rituals that we readily dismiss as superstition he shows his recognition of his dependence upon and obligation toward others even before he begins to fell the tree of his choice. He may even bring the matter up at one morning palm wine session, letting others know of his intent, giving them a chance to object. That is social concern, unobtrusive. He will make his own ritual propitiation of the forest spirit for taking the tree, ensuring that it will be replaced, and also ensuring that his usage of the tree, as a canoe, will be blessed and not cursed. That is both belief and faith at work. He will even consecrate his tools. And although the canoe is not intended to be a thing of beauty, he will add some tiny touch of his own, most likely invisible to others, that will come from his heart. That is an integrated adult at work.

As in other ways of "doing" in our society, being a museum curator or researcher or teacher does not readily offer much opportunity to "do" fully, and the system often works to persuade us not to do so but rather to fall into the mold that is the overall structure of isolated compartments and which is consistent with what is expected of us as individuals. But the opportunity is there, as we have seen, however unconscious the system may be of it. So it is with other jobs, regardless of their nature. Those who think that they cannot beat the system are wrong, just as they are wrong when they think the only way they can change the system is through economic coercion, political edict, or the persuasiveness of theory. We are all agents of change, simply by being ourselves, and the greater our effect will be upon society when we take the trouble to be more conscious of who and what we are, all that we are, so that we can be ourselves more fully. I do not mean that we have to be directly intrusive, or go around prayer wheel in hand, let alone attempt sainthood. The example of other societies shows that all we have to do is to allow Spirit (social consciousness if you will) to manifest itself in our whole integrated being, in our doing; on its own it will then do all the intruding that is necessary.

If we need assurance that this is so, we should look around

us; at home, at play, at work. We have all met many adults
in our lives who, without seeming to try, have shown us what
a rich thing adulthood can be. We have also met many who
have shown us what an empty thing it can be, sometimes by
trying too hard to be other than what they are. We have also
met all too many who neither try nor succeed, those who are
frankly and openly concerned only with their own immediate
welfare and who make concessions to the demands of society
only so far as they have to under penalty of law, or because
it profits them as individuals to do so. This form of nonsocial
survival does not fit into any of our categories of adult (social)
behavior; it is an entirely new phenomenon without parallel
in the small-scale societies studied by anthropologists. The
assurance we would all like to find may be found by looking
at our neighbors with different eyes, trying to fit them into
our three approaches to adulthood—the spiritual, the religious,
the secular. If we do this, then we may well find that some
of those considered to be very ordinary people are, in fact,
extraordinary. They are likely to be far from perfect, yet
with all their imperfections they are people who have discovered for themselves the art of doing and are making the
world, not just their own lives, all the richer. The following
examples of the three approaches to adulthood are drawn
from some of the ordinary people whom I came to know when
living in New York City.

Robert found the secular way. He was a very ordinary
young man, going prematurely bald, certainly nothing inspir-
ing to look at. He worked as a clerk for a major airline and
talked about it without pride but as though it were *his* airline.
He was anything but a recluse, and he certainly was not
religious, but he could become almost ecstatic when talking
about his work because it involved him in the lives of others.
Most of his coworkers laughed at him for his enthusiasm, and
yet those that I met agreed that he certainly made the office a
fun place to work in. That in itself is typical of the secular
way of doing, but Robert was not content to "be," he wanted
to "do," by helping others enjoy life as much as he did. He
had learned to love from his family, and the poverty of that
family had taught him the value of dependence and interdependence, rather than independence. He was constantly

giving things away, and thereby unwittingly creating a network of friends on whom he could rely and also were bound to him with a strange sense of obligation. Robert belonged to the world, and the world to him.

He lived alone, or with whomever he was allowing to use his two-room apartment at the time; but then he was seldom at home. What he considered his real home was a derelict building on the East Side of Manhattan, a building he had taken over with some others fired with the same enthusiasm and the same rather dangerous faith in goodness. They cleaned up the inside of the building and made it safe by coopting friends with the necessary skills and by getting the materials they needed from other derelict buildings. By the time the police came to evict them, they found a flourishing little community run by these young adults for the express purpose of getting neighborhood adolescents and youths off the streets. At first they did this by getting a pool table and offering other equally harmless attractions. They encouraged kids to make some pocket money, without stealing it, by collecting empty bottles unthinkingly thrown away and in other similar ways. Then, with whatever money they could scrounge, they bought a few books and started helping their youthful patrons with homework. They were at this stage when the police called, and as a result they were given a temporary reprieve until they could find some way of satisfying such legal necessities as conforming to the building and sanitation codes and, of course, paying rent. They not only did this, they also persuaded at least one large corporation to donate educational equipment. Without losing any of their youthful zest for life, which was what attracted the youth from the streets, they now set about a more formal educational program and secured loans from museums for educational exhibits. Robert and his friends were not "religious" in any accepted meaning of the word; no particular religious form of worship was practiced at the project; nor were Robert and his friends saints in any shape or form. Their way of doing, of manifesting social concern, was thoroughly secular, they merely "helped." But they were all adults who, in whatever they were doing, enriched all those they came in contact with, and they were not content to sit back and let the world come to them for enrichment. And this was only one of many such projects that quite accidentally crossed my path in Harlem at this time. They were less exotic and spectacular than the "secular" *ashram* communities I had known in India, but they were all equally fired by the same intense faith that the world could be a better place.

As an example of equally ordinary people who adopted the "religious" approach to adulthood, I think of Arthur and Eileen. They were not religious in the conventional sense; indeed, it was only when they asked me to become godfather to their youngest child that they found it necessary to get married. It is ironic that having from the outset established their home as a thriving (but noncelibate) monastic community, it only began to fall apart after their union was blessed by the Church. Some might say that was because getting married was one of the few things they did without conviction; to both of them it seemed quite unnecessary. Jamaican immigrants, they lived in Brooklyn; Arthur worked in the service department of a garage specializing in imported luxury cars. Their social horizons were effectively limited, in terms of what they could do in a foreign country, by their economic status and their education. But to them that did not matter because their world was the family, and what makes their approach to adult life similar to the "religious" approach of the Tibetan monastic community, and some Hindu *ashram* communities, was that their "family" was not restricted to kin. Family, for them, was a model they had learned from their own families in childhood, a model for an adult way of living in which all were welcome to their home at any time of the day or night. The out-of-work were housed and fed, but it was not forced on them; nor were any restrictions placed on their behavior; and no payment or service was demanded or expected in return. Arthur and Eileen lived according to their ideals and convictions as to social, or family, responsibility. But the ideals they held and cherished were not shared by all those who crowded their home; their *ashram* had no discipline, and the symbols, though they were there, were mostly too subtle and invisible to be effective. They themselves were filled with Spirit, but the receptacles around them were not receptive, and the effects of the quite extraordinary generosity of spirit that emanated from this couple were mostly temporary and minimal.

They came close to success because they interacted so fully and completely with all who came into their home, holding nothing back. They had learned the art of integration. If there had been more discipline, or if their symbols had been plainer, they might have won through and helped transform others. For a time, at least, their adult way of living created a viable community, but its sanctity was fragile. The Tibetan prayer wheel, empty though it is, has the sacred *mantras* embossed all around it; it takes conscious manipulation to make it spin, so it is an overt reminder of the sacred both to the spinner and to all those who see him spin. Here, in the home of Arthur and Eileen, the symbols were both hidden and passive; the open, unlocked door, the overcrowded refrigerator, the table always covered with plates and knives and forks and spoons waiting to be used, the discreetly hidden cots and floor mattresses, the fact that every sofa was a convertible bed; these were all covert, passive symbols and as such were not very effective in furthering the religious task of transformation. This, together with the lack of discipline, resulted in Arthur and Eileen's open home attracting more and more parasites. And like some *ashrams* I have known that similarly lacked discipline, they were destroyed. Their Spirit power was enough to activate them but not others. They seemed afraid to let it grow and give new life and power to their ideals. It was something they themselves did not understand—they were unconscious of their own goodness.

Eventually Arthur lost his job, the "relatives" systematically consumed all that was left of their little material wealth, the children, barely in their teens, fell victim to the local drug pushers. Husband and wife separated, and ultimately the children too went their separate ways via the reformatory. Yet, for a time, as an example of the "religious" way of doing, their life *was* a success story in which a whole community was created and united in the adult, social ideals of one, simple, unmarried couple and their home. And for those of us who knew them and recognized what was at work, it is still a success story, for we were touched if not transformed, by that simple goodness that touched any who crossed their threshold.

When I look for someone I knew in New York at the same time that I knew Robert, Arthur, and Eileen, but someone who represents the spiritual approach, a most unlikely candidate presents herself. I try hard to push her away, but she is irresistible. I try to replace her with someone more suitable, of more saintly mien; a priest perhaps, or a great scholar, or a musician. I can think of several in each category, but Mary brushes them all aside and demands that she be heard. So I give you Mary.

Most of my friends and acquaintances dismissed Mary as a rather inefficient, troublesome housekeeper, not worth a second thought. At best she was plain, more often she looked downright ugly. Always she was beautiful. Middle-aged, overweight, dressed in whatever came out of the closet first, she had a cleft palate and was frequently irascible. It was difficult to understand all that she said, but her tone left no doubt as to what she meant. Mary was a recluse and lived in a damp, dark, dirty basement under a large brownstone on Manhattan's West Side. The odors that permeated the house were one of her means of communication with the outside world, as were the various sounds that traveled up the waterpipes through each apartment. Mary would frequently ask if we had smelled what she had been having for dinner, and she could command the attention of all by rapping smartly on the appropriate pipe, then shouting at it as though it were a microphone. She claimed she could hear every word we spoke merely by putting her ear to the pipes.

Mary was a power who made herself felt, but even when angry she could not conceal her unbounded joy in life, whatever life did to her. One Christmas she made one of her rare sorties from her basement hermitage and went to visit a sister just across the river in New Jersey. Her sister was a kind of secular variation of herself, but without the same unbridled joy in all that happened. So what happened seemed fitting. A few days later Mary came back, brimming over with her own brand of the Christmas spirit. With a happiness bordering on ecstasy, she told me how she had seen her sister run over and gobbled up by a large machine that was removing snow from the streets. She lovingly elaborated on every detail of the grisly affair, sounds and all. Her cleft palate made it all the more vivid. It was a magnificent and powerful moment in her life, and that is how she wanted to share it. Whether it was true or not was quite beside the point; it was impossible not to feel happy with her and for her. I never did see her sister again.

Mary seldom went out, however. She remained for most of each night and day with her eyes glued to the television set; no more than two feet apart, they stared at each other and they talked to each other. With her lived her son, still in his adolescence at thirty years old; he spent much of his time playing ball with himself in the backyard. She took in a sick old man who had been nearly blinded by an accident with lye, and when the two of them tired of television they chased each other around the huge bed in their front room with shrieks of joy and mirth. This they clearly communicated to the tenants via the water pipes, and Mary's language at such times was positively Chaucerian; it was more than plain what she was after. It was not very spiritual.

She lived in a fantasy world and suffered, if that is the right word, from that strange medical condition sometimes known as confabulation. She could start with a fact from external reality, such as a knock she heard at somebody's door, and from that fact she would construct a logical sequence of events that had the makings of a first-class thriller. If I were given to plagiarism or had half her skill, I could probably make a fortune by publishing those stories. But one of her finest confabulations is that she herself is about to do that, and one of my fondest hopes is that someday she will.

But for all her profanity Mary was endowed with Spirit, and for all her confabulation and lack of education and poverty it was Spirit that made her a true adult. She did not set out to change the world, or even to do good. She did not make an open community of her home, nor did she try to teach or transform by her example. When her concern for others did surface, it often appeared to be the concern of a prying busybody. But no, she was activated by Spirit pure and simple, and daily, not annually, like Sri Aurobindo, she gave her *darshan* at the gateway to *her* private and sacred world. She stood there at the sidewalk, leaning over that wrought iron gate like a huge lump of jelly, and she just beamed with good-will and radiated kindness. She was the joy of my life and of the lives of many others, even though we were sometimes the victims of her anger or suffered as a result of her confabulations, such as when the police called to investigate an act of violence that had never taken place, or failed to respond to a genuine call for help just because they thought it was another of Mary's little stories. Once the police came and wanted to know what I had done with a door that was reported to have been battered down; but Mary came to my rescue and continued confabulating, describing exactly how she had put it back and patched up the paintwork and plaster and all. Another time when my door *was* off its hinges and the apartment ransacked, the police did not come. A dead body in the dumbwaiter was one of Mary's best efforts, and of course she had a perfectly rational explanation as to why it was never found.

With all her physical, mental, educational, and economic limitations, Mary was an adult. She was genuinely concerned about all with whom she came in contact. Looking after her son and the old man she took in, and by dispensing inedible food to anyone she thought might like it, she used her economic capacity to its fullest. Even her confabulations were evidence of her all-pervading social concern. She *had* to integrate everything that happened, however trivial, into a single, important, social whole, and fantasy was her way of doing it. Her emotional capacity was boundless. Even her anger was rooted in social concern, however irrational or unjustified it often seemed to be. Her invincible joy in life was what she radiated daily with her whole powerful hulk as she stood at her gate; and like a *sannyasi* greeting the rising sun with the sacred *gayatri mantra*, Mary gave her morning blessing to the street and all things upon it.

Perhaps it is not so strange, after all, that Mary should have intruded so deeply in my consciousness that she was really the only possible example for me to give of the spiritual approach to doing.

Mary was Power, and Mary was Woman.

PART FIVE

OLD AGE

THE ART OF BEING

FOR ALL TOO MANY old people in the Western world the persistent reference to the "golden years" of old age has become a cruel hoax, a lie, a promise that can never possibly be fulfilled. The should-have-been-golden years are discovered instead to be a frightening anteroom to extinction, a time of loneliness and suffering, to be postponed as long as possible. Compulsory retirement for many means little more than compulsory unemployment, bringing with it not only financial stress, but far more significantly, a certain social stigma associated with inutility, incompetence, and dependence, all the more bitter and frustrating because it is compelled, unwanted, and totally unnecessary. Even when old age is accompanied by infirmity or incapacity, the old have a wealth to give, and could continue to give until the very day of their death, as they do in other societies.

Just as each of the other four stages of life—childhood, adolescence, youth, and adulthood—has its own special potential, its own contribution to make, so does old age. Far from being useless and unproductive, the old in every society are a vital source of richness and strength. Their way of contributing to the general good is often so subtle as to be almost invisible, but it is nonetheless real and powerful. Certainly in other cultures, particularly those with a firm belief in an after or other life, the old are accorded a position of often enormous respect and honor and are exploited for the social good until they die, when they continue to be exploited as "ancestors." While alive their contribution may be economic, for certain very practical skills come with old age. In some societies the political role of the old is formalized, their long years of experience being called on to help in the resolution of otherwise intractable disputes; having so little to gain or lose, the old make admirable arbitrators. In a more general social role the old are vitally important as educators, and we throw away this invaluable resource every time we employ a baby-sitter only a few years older than the baby being sat; but then in our society we do not seem to place much value on education, even in our school system, so our young are deprived of the wonders that can so easily be passed on to them by that special, intimate exchange that is perhaps only possible between the very young and the very old. And so also the old are deprived of yet another role. But most of all they are ignored, in our society, for the very thing that makes them so immensely powerful in other societies: their proximity to death. That is perhaps what we most need to explore, this association in other cultures of the old with that vast source of power, Spirit power, that lies beyond death. It provides a whole new perspective on old age.

The Mbuti say that what happens to you in old age is like what happened to Nzoki. Just how old Nzoki was is uncertain, it rather depends on who is telling the story. But all agree that what happened to him explains much of what it means to be old.

Nzoki was a hunter, an adult. But he grew tired of hunting and increasingly stayed behind in the forest camp when others went off with nets and bows and arrows and spear. Nzoki would just sit in the camp and whittle away at a piece of wood, making nothing in particular, just whatever happened to the piece of wood as he whittled was fine with him; that was what he wanted. He wanted the wood to be something else.

Then he took to wandering off into the forest alone, a sure sign of old age. The villagers would have said he was a witch. And in the forest you could see him sitting beside a river or a stream, staring at his reflection. And as he stared, he whittled away at a piece of wood and let it be whatever it wanted to be.

One day, the story goes, he slowly touched his feet to the water, one after the other, and whittling away, he waded out into the river, letting his reflection, his other self, come up through his body and disappear into the world he was leaving behind. He whittled and whittled, and he was still whittling when finally he disappeared beneath the surface, never to be seen again. But if you ever have a piece of wood and want it nicely whittled, just go to that spot, at the edge of the Lelo River, and throw it into the water. Nzoki is there, and he will whittle it for you and give it back to you made into just whatever it wanted to be.

It is because the Mbuti expect so little, and so much, from their old people, that for them old age is truly a time of golden years, years filled with Spirit, increasingly golden as they become filled more and more with the life force of another life, until they become something else.

In old age the problem of recognizing and living to our full potential is less than in adulthood, for in adulthood "doing" is so easily and wrongly seen as involving primarily either our mind *or* our body *or* our heart *or* our soul, and it is during adulthood that all these parts of us are most alive at one and the same time, sometimes at war with each other if they have not been integrated. Many of the problems that we face in old age in our society arise from the overemphasis of adulthood on an active, productive life that stresses the economic aspect of our doing to the detriment of other equally important adult activities and responsibilities. We implement only a small part of our potential, our eyes firmly fixed on the present, steadfastly ignoring the proximity of old age. This in turn tends to lessen our sense of responsibility for actions that will influence others long after we have gone; not just the actions of national policy-makers, for they tend to look a little further into the future, but the actions in our daily life, what we say and do to others. No such act is inconsequential. And that *individuals* should be concerned about the future, as many are, is not enough in a social system; it should be written into the system itself.

By abrogating to itself all the power and the glory, our own concept of adulthood denies the satisfaction and recognition of responsibility that should be felt, as they are in other systems, at every stage of life. It is worth remembering that for the Mbuti, adulthood is recognized to be a time of *akami*, of disputation and conflict, and that they take care *not* to give adults the responsibility for government, but confine their primary, active responsibility to the area of economic activity. This is consistent with the fact that in the traditional Indian system, with the Hindu emphasis on the sacred throughout all stages of life, the second stage, the adult stage of *grhastha* is considered as little more than a profane interlude, important but less sacred by far than the stages that precede and follow it. In both systems adulthood is not given a lesser role, however; it is simply a different role that is complementary to the others, equally necessary and directly related to the qualities and abilities uniquely inherent in that age level. In such societies the transition from adulthood to old age is not seen as a lessening of activity; there is still "much to be done," much that needs doing, and much that the old can do better than any others. In both those societies, as vastly different as they are in their context as in their social structure, old age is not seen as an end to life, but as a source of continuity, linking the future with the past, death with life. This more positive attitude to old age does not demand any belief in afterlife or in God; it depends simply upon the recognition of the vital role that old people have to play in the ongoing life of society.

Old age in every society brings with it an increase in physical and mental defects, a general weakening of the powers of both body and mind; but the heart and the soul are more alive than ever, with that much more experience to feed upon. So the contribution of old age to society, and its manner of fulfilling itself, lies in the art of being. It need not be a time for retreat, though our association of old age with "retirement" seems to imply this. The rite of passage by which employers frequently effect the transition for their employees, with the presentation of some material token of appreciation for years of material service, is a way of saying a final farewell. It signals that the individual should now cease from doing, or earning a living, and implies quite clearly that he has no further contribution to make other than stay out of the way. There is a good deal of resentment when old people remain active, earning (or making) a living beyond retirement age, particularly if they are successful. It is considered unfair competition, in a world where competition is the norm and much of it is far from fair. It is expected that men and women who "retire" will retire from more than their job. It is frequently assumed that they will retire from social responsibility, domestic, economic, and political. To an apparently increasing extent it is also assumed that their retirement supposes the cessation of any responsibility that their family or employer might have felt toward them in the past; they are now on their own. With the high value our society places on independence and individualism this should be a blessing, but I doubt that it is intended as such. The symbolism of the traditional gold watch is all too plain: you should have made your money by now, and your time has run out. The watch will merely tick off the hours that remain between the end of adulthood and death.

If we stick with the notion of old age being a time of retirement, however, but examine the concept of retirement in light of how other societies view it, we begin to find other possibilities. For instance, in the African and Indian societies on which we have touched, the retirement expected of the aged does indeed also suppose that they retire from active participation in subsistence activities. But this is generally seen to be partly because they are no longer physically fitted to fill that economic role, or because there are others better fitted for that work, but more importantly because there are other things that need to be done and which only the old can do. They are, that is, expected to continue to earn their keep and contribute to the overall social good. They are relieved of one set of responsibilities so that they can fulfill another, equally vital role. We shall try to isolate some of these roles that bear comparison with our own society, and right away three come to mind, although we will each need to search for apt comparisons within our own sphere. I think of wise men, witches, and saints; all, note, closely associated with Spirit, just as the old person is getting closer and closer to the source of Spirit. For those who still have difficulty with that word, any of the following will do as well: Power, Society, Life, the Unknown; but ultimately we each have to find our own word.

In discussing adulthood I used three categories of approach to "doing" that at first seemed inapplicable to, if not incompatible with, our own way of life; spiritual, religious, and secular ways of "doing." Yet when we looked at the process behind the words, the cultural distance seemed to diminish. So here, when discussing old age, while we might well find better words, the terms wise men, witches, and saints that were so applicable in other contexts will serve us well, their very oddity prodding us to look and see if there is not, yet again, greater similarity than dissimilarity. Since in our world we are generally uncomfortable with the imagery conjured up by these three categories, it is best first to look for points of comparison in the actual process of transition from adulthood to old age. As stated, in other societies old people are expected to retire from what we would call gainful employment, as in our own society. They are also expected to retire from active doing in the sense of raising a family, but though the nature of their authority over their family (and society) is altered, if anything its extent is enlarged, as we shall see. Further, they are very definitely expected to retire from action (some would say from interference) in a future that is not theirs. Ideas based on a long life and a wealth of experience may or may not be valuable, but the decision as to whether or not such ideas should be implemented in action should be left to others, and preferably to youthful others, to whom the future belongs. And although in one way the authority of the elders expands, in another way their social horizons are expected to contract, almost as though the life cycle were going into reverse. From conscious involvement with society at large, which should be the responsibility of youth and adulthood, in some societies the aged may be expected to disinvolve themselves from that wider society by reinvolving themselves progressively (or regressively) with clan, lineage, back to the nuclear family, and finally, back or beyond to whatever lies the other side of life or death. Above all, it is a time for the aged to accept from the children to whom they have given so much, preserving the continuity for all time. Which supposes that it is a time for those children to give, rather than to ignore.

In all the societies we have discussed, the aged may be considered as repositories of the sacred, the holy, as in the last stage of life, *sannyasi*, for the Hindu. They may not have reached perfection, but by their very dedication to the sacred they radiate it from their being. That is probably as close to being saints as any of us are likely to get, if we get that far. Such elders do not have to preach, they just have to be. Even those we may consider as frauds, who merely take advantage of the saffron robes as an easy way to win respect or reap economic profit, serve a useful function, for their robe, if not their life, is a reminder to all of the ideal they betray. As with wise men, while a saint interacts with all in society, he may be seen as making a special contribution to one or another age level, and the age level that needs the saint more than any is adolescence.

As for witches, the term "witch" is used not to confuse, the concept being so alien to us, but because as understood in other parts of the world, particularly in Africa, it offers an important role to those of us ill-fitted to be either of the other two kinds of old people. As I use the term it refers to the concept of vital force that is prevalent throughout Africa. In many areas it is believed that this force, which is all-pervasive, can sometimes be trapped or extracted. Even a stone or rock may be possessed of such force, and certainly plants and animals; humans probably have the greatest store of it in the material world. The "other" world is the greatest repository of all. Thus a human wishing to add to his power may take possession of certain objects believed to be capable of communicating their force to the owner or wearer; physical contact is sometimes required, contagion being the principle at work, hence charms worn on the body. Sometimes the force has to be extracted through spells, incantations, or manipulation, and this may require the services of a specialist.

A witch, then, is someone who is merely possessed of more than the normal allotment of this vital force. A witch may have inherited it, or may have acquired it consciously through charms, manipulations, or spells, or may have come by it simply by having lived longer than anyone else and so have been in more contact with the many volatile substances that are thought to emanate from such a force, whether we seek it or not. The old are, then, in a sense natural witches, and in Africa, as in India, they may also serve as reminders of the sacred and, depending upon the manner of their behavior or the accidents that befall them, be considered as holy in themselves. That would imply that their excess of power is working for the social good, and then they might fall better into our category of saints. But as witches it is rather as if their power is *not* under control and may thus manifest itself either for the good or the harm of society. And since such old witches are not in control and are seen as merely suffering from an inevitable excess of power, they are not held accountable even if harm results; hence the lack of penalties. We do not punish someone for being sick, though we may hold him accountable if he does not take the necessary precautions and thus allows his sickness to spread and harm others. So if a person is thought to be deliberately using his or her power for personal profit, or for some malevolent antisocial purpose, then they would be classified as something we generally translate as sorcerers, and this is highly culpable. The blame lies not in the act itself, but in the *intent* to do harm.

Any who display excess power, physical or mental, may be considered as witches. The norm is for adults to be equal, so even a farmer who is consistently more successful than his neighbors is suspected of manipulating excessive vital force for his personal gain. In this way the belief in witchcraft exerts a strong pressure on adults to refrain from manifesting any superiority. This is consistent with the absence of the high level of competitiveness that is so encouraged, practiced, and honored in our society. In other cultures cooperation rather than competition is the ideal, though once more this is not to be taken as a value judgment. But in such societies it is the old who make the best candidates for witches because, as noted, of their proximity to death and hence power. Their utility to society goes far beyond simply being a symbol of power, however; they also serve a vital political purpose, for any accusation of witchcraft is in effect a means of making public some hidden or latent social malaise, or some very specific confrontation or dispute. The "witch" serves as a convenient scapegoat enabling the dispute to be resolved without the disruptive effects of attributing guilt exclusively to one party or the other. Since the witch is by definition not in control of his power he is not culpable, he merely absorbs the responsibility for whatever happened. Rather than being punished, he is subjected usually to a ritual cleansing, and the ritual also generally involves a rite of restitution, restoring harmony to society. The real culprits are indirectly coerced into settling their score by the contributions they are expected to make to the ritual, effecting such material restitution as may be necessary in the case of theft or damage, for instance. I have met "witches" who, knowing very well that they are being used in this way, and that the "penalty" will be of no serious consequence to them, quite enjoy the notoriety and the opportunity to voice opinions of their own as to the way the world is going.

An accusation of witchcraft provides the elderly with an opportunity for publicly voicing their criticism of youth and adulthood in such a way that it may be accepted or rejected, as appropriate, without loss of face by those so criticized. Where old age is associated with witchcraft in this way, it also provides a considerable measure of additional social security for the elderly, whether accused of witchcraft or not, because their proximity to power makes them all potential witches. Since nobody wishes to offend a witch, in case he turns into a malevolent sorcerer, the elderly are treated with extra respect and consideration.

Some examples of the three roles filled by the aged will more easily show how wise men, saints, and witches do their work. We can then, each for ourselves, the more easily find counterparts who live all around us, quietly working the magic of old age wherever they are. And since witches are fresh in mind, let us start with one I knew well, and who both looked and played the part. Abazinga was a Bira from the east bank of the Epulu River, but he and his brother had been ostracized by their village, the Ndaka fishermen said, and had moved over to settle among them. His brother was a blacksmith, which in this part of the Ituri Forest, as in many other parts of Africa, is a profession associated with supernatural power. Although blacksmiths are feared for this power, they are also welcomed because of the importance of their craft. Partly because they are often outsiders, and partly because of their association with the supernatural, blacksmiths generally live at the very edge of the village, slightly apart. However, Abazinga's brother set up his forge in the middle of the village so that nobody could avoid passing by, as they would have preferred, while Abazinga and his wife established their compound on the far side of the Nepussi, the forest stream that runs into the Epulu River and where most of the villagers went to bathe and to wash their clothes. It was also where children loved to play in the little waterfalls and leap from overhanging branches into its clear pools. If a villager is not a witch, or a blacksmith, he has no reason to hide himself from the others, the villagers said of Abazinga. Such isolation happens only if someone has an excess of power that needs to be either conserved or protected.

The evidence that Abazinga was a witch was of two kinds, neither of which had anything to do with any aggressive, hostile action on the part of Abazinga or any open manifestation of his alleged supernatural power. On the one hand he had access to such power through his brother, the smith, while on the other he was demonstrably nonsocial, having as little to do with the other villagers as possible, living in isolation. The question that inevitably arose was, How could he and his wife survive alone, on the far side of the Nepussi, as though they were independent? To be independent implies both nonsociality and an excess of power.

When Abazinga's wife died the accusations became open. Death of a spouse, unless it is unduly premature, is one of the markers of old age in this part of the world. It generally happens when the physical capacity of the couple to take an active part in economic life has already begun to wane, and it heralds the approaching death, and increase in supernatural or Spirit power of the survivor.

All old people are thus subject to the accusation of witchcraft, the unconscious manifestation of that power, but Abazinga seemed headed toward an accusation of sorcery, for once his wife died, instead of becoming more social by invoking kinship and becoming more economically dependent upon others, he became even more isolated, and more independent than ever. He used to go off into the forest on his own for days at a time, which is something no normal villager dares to do, since they believe that no mortal could long survive without powerful supernatural protection.

When Abazinga returned from these solitary trips he brought with him all manner of foods and medicinal herbs eagerly sought by other villagers, but which they could obtain only through the Mbuti. Yet Abazinga kept himself as isolated from the Mbuti as he was from the villagers, so it was obvious that his supernatural power extended even to the forest. His fields prospered, yet he did not seem to work unduly hard at tending them; and if he went out to fish, he was never out on the river for more than an hour before he returned with his traps and nets full. If he traded this surfeit it was with distant villages, never his own, except on rare occasions. So he was unusually successful as well as solitary, another criterion of witchcraft and another major social consideration in a society that places such a high value on equality.

Other traits helped convince the village that Abazinga was a witch and possibly a sorcerer. While his house was not within sight of the Nepussi, let alone the village of Epulu, surrounded as it was by dense forest, his banana plantation and a grove of Mabondo palms (from which the wine is made) came to a hilly point just above where people liked to bathe and children liked to play. And when they came to bathe or play they would look up and there was Abazinga, staring at them, watching, alone and silent. Eye contact is another way of exerting power, projecting something into another person or drawing it out of them, particularly if it is a long, unblinking stare. Abazinga never blinked; his little eyes were always open and expressionless, even when his mouth curved into what might otherwise have been quite a pleasant smile. His small head drew attention to his ears which were pointed directly at you when you faced him, listening, just as his eyes were watching and probing. His nose was flatter than most, more like that of an Mbuti, so that the nostrils were clearly visible, their apertures sniffing at you. His small, wiry body was like that of a spider, all arms and legs waiting to reach out and grab you in a lethal embrace. He was a witch all right, this all said. And as if to convince everyone further, after his wife died Abazinga began to dress in a strange way, the way, in fact, that many old people do. He wore two shirts instead of one, and two or three loincloths (which actually he removed and used as sacks on his gathering expeditions, hooked onto a stick and carried over his shoulder).

By such criteria we can probably recognize more than one witch in our own neighborhood. But what do witches, particularly old witches, *do?* The point is, of course, that like Abazinga they don't do anything, they just *are;* and by being they play a useful role in society, contribute to its ongoing life, and themselves reap certain benefits that, for them, make old age well worth living. However, in the lesser sense of "doing" Abazinga was by no means inactive. He farmed and fished and gathered in the forest, but since he did not share either the activity or the produce in any way with his village, it was not the social doing of adulthood, it was just private enterprise. This is a perfectly legitimate activity for old people in the scheme of things we have outlined and as recognized by the villagers. His *social* contribution was simply in allowing himself to be considered a witch. It worked this way.

A child would slip when jumping into the Nepussi and bruise or cut himself. At the moment of jumping he had seen Abazinga watching with his beady, unblinking eyes. Actually, when Abazinga sat on that hilly point of land, he was usually a little drunk from drinking too much of his own palm wine and it is doubtful that he saw anything very much. But *he* was seen, and his "evil eye" was held responsible for the injury. Or someone rashly taking a short cut through his plantation, or *shamba,* found a snake blocking his path. Abazinga was nowhere to be seen. The snake looked at the trespasser with beady eyes; obviously it was Abazinga. The forest is full of snakes and they all have beady eyes, but as far as the villagers were concerned, they were all potential Abazingas, associated with injury and death.

So gradually any injury or death, or sickness, or even mishaps such as crop failure began to be laid at Abazinga's door. He was not accused of willfully doing harm, which would have been an accusation of *uchawi,* or sorcery; he was merely accused of being a *mulozi,* a nasty old witch who had too much power and did not control it as any socially conscious witch would do. When accused, Abazinga denied that he was a witch and demanded if any reason could be shown as to *why* he should have injured this person or caused those crops to fail. Since he was so socially isolated it was difficult to find any such reasons. When the discussion got heated, Abazinga, who was really quite a wise old man, as well as being a witch, fulfilled this other role of the aged by telling the villagers in no uncertain terms just what he thought of them, and as is the way with elderly recluses, he knew everything that was going on in the village. How could they expect anything but calamity and misfortune when they let women sneak food into the initiation camp for their sons? When menstruating women slept with their husbands? When men went out fishing without making an offering to the river spirits? Abazinga once cited the fact that a ritual doctor had drunk palm wine (with its symbolism of sexual potency) *by himself*. At this the villagers immediately accused him of doing the same thing, and Abazinga simply countered, "But I am old." The old are allowed all sorts of freedoms denied the adult, and it was an effective answer. One of their greatest freedoms—and functions—is the right to criticize others, particularly adults.

So, although Abazinga was accused and feared and mistrusted, he was never harmed; he was respected. People kept their distance from him, which is exactly what he wanted; he was perfectly capable of looking after himself. Many old people are that way. And when I saw him again years later, when he was really old and looked more like a witch than ever, and when his brother Baziani was dead and the old smithy gone, if Abazinga needed anything that he could not get or do for himself, somehow it would get done; and usually without his asking. The more daring children and youths would fell a tree for him or pull in a fishtrap or reroof his tumbledown old house. Sometimes he even talked with them and gave them some nuts or honey he had gathered on the solitary trips he still made to the forest. He was becoming more of a wise man than a witch and had little to do with the adults, who by now had found other scapegoats. Then one day Abazinga walked off into the forest and never came back. You see, I was told, he *was* a witch after all, because someone (nobody was quite sure who) had seen him walk into a forest river until it covered him, and he never came out; he became a water spirit. "That is the stuff witchcraft is made of," we think; but we are wrong; that kind of belief in spirits is quite incidental. What is important is the happy old age that Abazinga lived, contributing to society simply by being himself and letting society use him, however unconsciously, for its own advantage.

If witches can become more comprehensible when related in this way to society and its needs, so can saints. At first the thought of sainthood as providing a viable role for the run-of-the-mill old person seems rather remote, but when we look more closely this is not so. The word itself is unfamiliar to us in the normal social context of everyday life, but I do not want to modify it into the bland description with which we so often dismiss an old person, hiding or ignoring his real qualities by saying he or she is "such a *good* person." Saints are much more than that, but neither are they necessarily gods incarnate. However, I do use the term deliberately here, because of its sacred connotations and because of the identity that to me is inescapable, of that which is sacred or touched by Spirit, and that which is social, touched by wholeness. A saint in this sense is a person who brings wholeness into our lives, who touches us with Spirit. And although an elderly saint (or saintly elder) affects to some extent all those with whom he comes in contact, just as witches make their major impact on society at the level of adulthood, so saints make their major contribution at the level of adolescence, the time of transformation. If ever we need the golden touch of Spirit it is then. We already have it within us, as adolescents; we have already sensed it, and the glorious power of creativity that so suddenly comes upon us at adolescence makes us a fit receptacle for the fullness of Spirit that will show us the extent of our creative power and give us the inner urge to control it and use it wisely and well for the good of all. It is the breath of Spirit that fills our bodies as good clean air fills our lungs and makes us want to fill them still fuller until they burst with joy; it is the sight and sound of Spirit that raises our level of consciousness, our awareness of ourselves and of others and of the whole world around us, to an ecstasy that makes the mere fact of our new-found sexual potency, in isolation, a puny thing; not unclean or unwholesome, just puny. So saints, those who manifest their being in old age by a manifestation of Spirit, are most needed by our adolescents. Once again we can see how in other societies this potential is recognized and utilized for the benefit of all.

Some saints may be recluses, even in an intrusive world. As intrusive as Sri Aurobindo's *ashram* was, Sri Aurobindo himself was very much of a recluse; in the middle of the city of Pondicherry he was seen, even by his disciples, on only one day every year. So, in much more dramatic style, was the saint I came across high in the Himalayas, a recluse. I found him in a cave where the perpetual ice melts and mingles with steaming water as it gushes from hot springs, to make the beginnings of a great river. He was the very epitome of sainthood as we like to think of it, but that does him little justice. His splendid isolation, the frugality of his living, the spotless cleanliness of himself and his small rocky cavern with its bedding of branches and leaves were all incidental to me in his presence. I have to recollect those things now from a distance. Only two things struck me at the time other than the presence; one was that he was attended by an acolyte and the other was that the acolyte was strangely invisible, although I can clearly recollect his appearance. He was somewhere in his middle or late teens, clad like the saint in a flimsy saffron robe; he had long black hair freshly washed, glistening, tied in a bun at the back of his head. He had a deep, thick beard. The saint himself was at first just a shadowy figure perched high on a mound of pine branches in a dark corner to the right of the cave's entrance. I was utterly exhausted by the long climb and by the height, though it was merely a little over twelve thousand feet; and I was still shaken by my folly in having attempted such a climb at my age and with my terror of heights. I did not want to think about the fact that I had to retrace those steps and cross those cliff-face ledges all over again. I certainly had not come for instant enlightenment and was not looking for wisdom; I had come all this way (I thought) for some photographs that in the end I never took, except as an afterthought when it was no longer really necessary. I was just glad to find the cave and the hot springs, though a little sorry not to have them to myself. But the shadowy saint greeted me with no surprise by motioning me to sit down on the rocky floor. To the left, part of the cavern was curtained off by a piece of cloth, perhaps just hung there to dry, for outside it would have frozen. Inside, because of the hot springs that had their source beneath the cave, the floor and walls were comfortably warm to touch. I heard some sounds from behind the curtain and could smell food cooking; then, although the saint gave no instructions that I heard, the acolyte appeared and put a leaf piled high with food cooked in one of the hot springs on the ground in front of me. I saw him clearly for a moment. But then the saint said something to him, not to me, and the moment the saint spoke the acolyte disappeared from my vision; and so it was for the next few hours. It is only from a distance in time and space that I can keep a continuous image of that acolyte in my mind, and that is not because my vision was blurred or my health impaired by the strenuous climb, or because the acolyte was an illusion, but simply because the saint was so powerful that he commanded every sense I had and filled his mountain home with his being, so that there was no room for any other being. Yet he was a small man, with nothing impressive about his appearance at all except possibly his eyes, which, like Abazinga's, never blinked and, like Sri Aurobindo's, never let go once they caught you. Perhaps Abazinga, as well as being a witch and a wise man, was also something of a saint.

When the saint spoke it was softly but swiftly and with an urgency, as though he too might vanish before he could finish what he was saying. And it was whenever he spoke or whenever, in silence, his eyes caught mine, that the acolyte disappeared; even when I was looking at him. Only once did the saint move from his corner of the cave. The acolyte was serving me some more food, and I asked him for some cold water to drink. Then, the first time I had spoken to him directly, he disappeared and in his place was the saint, stooping over and pouring me some ice-cold water from a bowl that had stood behind a little butter-lamp-lit shrine. He smiled, as if apologetic for the confusion he had caused me, and went back to his corner. That was the last time I saw the acolyte, though yet another helping of food appeared on my plate, until I left. Then the acolyte appeared again, and in a rather matter-of-fact way asked for my home address.

There is no suggestion of or need for any explanation in terms of divine revelation or psychic powers or ecstatic experience, though it is just as pointless to deny the possibility of such things as it is to insist upon them. It is enough for me, here, to focus on the issue of power. Nor does it matter for the sake of our present discussion whether the power was inherent in the being of the saint or whether it was something that I conjured out of my exhaustion, fear of heights, or susceptibility to suggestion. All that matters is that it happened, and that under other circumstances far less exotic people do sometimes feel that others have a power they do not fully understand, a power that affects their sensations and experience. I cannot help but be interested, in retrospect, in that moment when the saint poured me the water, whereas it had been the acolyte who was crouched in front of me. The dimensions of the cave offered little opportunity for a quick-change act, and my recollection of that moment is as clear and unequivocal in every detail as my recollection of those horrid overhanging ledges I had to cross.

The experience, which was real no matter how much one might question the empirical reality, suggests that in some way the acolyte and the saint were interchangeable. To this I will only add that it is in keeping with the *guru/chela* (teacher/student) tradition for the latter to be encouraged to find himself, to discover his full identity, in the being of the former; the ideal is to uncover the reality of unity by dispelling the illusion of duality. This relationship, and the conscious effort to dispel the duality, is all the more powerful when there is only one teacher and one student, as distinct from the *gurukula*, where there may be several teachers and a number of students. Above all, in this tradition, it is felt to be essential for those who in childhood or early adolescence have consecrated their entire lives to the spiritual quest to place themselves directly and entirely in the hands of one spiritual teacher who can, it is believed, teach the adolescent how to transform his growing sexual energy into pure spiritual energy. This teenage acolyte who kept disappearing in front of me had been the *chela* of the saint since, I was told, he was nine years old. Their aspirations had become one; their lives had become one; it does not seem unduly strange that, knowing of this tradition, it appeared to me that at times their bodies became one. It is rather the same as witchcraft; what counts is not whether there really is any such thing as supernatural witchcraft power in itself; the social reality, an utterly incontrovertible and vital part of the social structure, is the fact that such a belief exists.

This mountain saint seems very esoteric, though we might find parallels in our society if we look hard enough. There are such people around us, but we need to know what we are looking for, and the example is given for that purpose alone. The example relating directly as it does to the concept of transformation also serves as a necessary foundation for understanding the full social implication of the following example, which, in contrast, should seem all the more comprehensible to us although it comes from Tibet. It will also be more recognizable to some, for here Spirit and religion are conjoined, and this Tibetan saint was anything but a recluse.

There is a small Tibetan monastery in the green hills about thirty miles from what is now the border between China and India. It does not matter much which nation claims sovereignty, the monastic institution is infinitely more durable. The composition of a Tibetan monastery is complex; although all the residents may be referred to as monks, they are differentiated, as we saw, by the number of vows they have taken. At one end of the scale we might refer to them as lay monks and at the other end as priest monks. The common bond between them all is that they have all taken at least the minimal vows to uphold the doctrine of the Buddha and the discipline enjoined by the monastery, under the charge of the Abbot. The Abbot in charge of this monastery was a jolly old man. Unlike many Tibetans he was neither big nor tall; if anything he was slightly on the plump side, although the only evidence of this that could be seen was the one, round, brown arm that emerged from the folds of his heavy dark ocher robes, and his rosy, rotund cheeks. His head was shaven, as is the custom for all monks, but not meticulously so. Sometimes it was covered by a thin, gray/black stubble, more of a shadow than anything. Plainly the Abbot was not an ascetic, nor was he a stickler for every rule in the book. He had a great sense of humor, and once when we were on our way into the temple for service he stopped in the entrance hall by the huge prayer wheel that stood on the left-hand side. This "prayer wheel" is actually a great vertical cylinder, about eight feet tall, set in wooden bearings. There is a legend that says that if you take the handle of the heavy wood and metal wheel and walk it around three times before entering the temple, all your sins will be forgiven. I was momentarily disconcerted when the Reverend Abbot gathered up his robes in one hand, and having grasped the handle of the huge prayer wheel firmly, rather like a wrestler, he gave it a mighty whirl that sent it tumbling around in its noisy and ponderous fashion. The bell, which sounds for each complete revolution, sounded once, twice, and then as the wheel slowly grumbled to a halt, it gave a third hesitant clang. The Abbot looked at me with delight. "There!" he said. "Do you think I am saved from rebirth?" Knowing the Abbot's sense of humor, but suspecting a trap, as the last sounds of the bell's third strike faded away I replied, ". . . Just!" The Abbot looked cross at my answer and my feeble attempt at humor, a teacher disappointed with a dull student. He said, "Not at all. The wheel went around, I went nowhere."

He abruptly left me and went, rather than led the way, into the temple, raised his hands to his forehead and prostrated himself on the ground in front of the huge image of the Lord Buddha. This particular image had one hand raised to symbolize Gautama's manifestation as a teacher, emphasizing the importance of learning, of the doctrine. Some insist that it is not even teaching, for the Buddha was humble; he preached and he advised, but did not teach, they say. Those who chose to listen had to find the way for themselves. The eyes of the golden image looked down on us from a height of twenty feet. Even standing, I felt small; and then I looked down at the old Abbot, who had gone nowhere, still flat on his face on the ground in front of me; and I felt smaller still.

Like the Buddha, the Abbot did not teach; he barely even advised; he just was. Under his charge were the teachers who ran the school, attended by about forty young boys all looking like diminutive abbots in their dark red robes and shaven heads, with one bare arm apiece. In some ways the Abbot ran the monastery like a good headmaster runs a school; the teachers and older monks were expected to look after themselves, tend to their own well-being and perform their duties to the monastery and to the students. They were as subject to the discipline of the monastery as any student, and the discipline was every bit as rigorous as that of any *gurukula*. The early morning hours, from four to eight, were devoted to worship in the monastery's old temple, lit by hundreds of butter lamps and candles burning singly—placed by individual worshippers in front of some small image or sacred *thanka* (prayer banner) that had special meaning for them—or in great clusters or on multiple candelabras. Who lit these I do not know, as they were always burning brightly when I got there, however early I was. I rather suspect the jolly Abbot, who never seemed to sleep.

We all sat in rows on either side of the central aisle that led to the great statue of Buddha. Like a small replica, the Abbot sat just in front of the image and a little to one side, but he was anything but impassive, which the image was. Nor did he seem particularly spiritual. Far from levitating he was very much earthbound, and the yellow cushion on his high throne bulged beneath his crossed legs. His conical red hat (it was a *nyingmapa* monastery) was usually slightly askew. He was not even regal, that dumpy little old Abbot; but he was every inch a saint because he radiated, like that other saint above the source of the Jumma, apologetically, as if he just could not help himself. For me there was no question as to what he radiated, and the response of others showed that it was the same for them, though for them it was also almost certainly something more as well. He radiated energy and love, not as two distinct things but as one. It surged around the temple, sometimes calming down to a ripple, sometimes becoming a tidal wave that engulfed us all, galvanizing us to greater efforts and filling us with devotion that was in no way localized, not directed at the image and certainly not at the Abbot, not at each other. Like the Abbot, it just was, within us; a flood of energy and love.

Love and energy? I did not choose the words to suit my purpose; they are the only words I can find that come close to conveying the reality of what I saw and felt. It was an energy real enough to keep us novices from falling asleep; it was a love that made us want not to sleep, for it was too precious to miss. The Abbot did not plan it that way; it was simply there, in his being what he was. Nor did the effect depend upon the drama of the age-old ritual in the dark temple; this saint had the same effect on everyone in broad daylight, out in the courtyard, in the kitchens, wherever he was; but most of all on the adolescents. Everyone wanted to be near him and was happy when he came their way; but he just had to appear around a corner for the young boys, if they were not in class, to rush and swamp him, clutching at his robes and tugging at his arms, joining their young energy and love with his old energy and love. Alas I was neither young enough nor old enough to be a part of that, but I will hazard a guess that those adolescents were learning about what true ecstasy can be even before their young bodies had tricked them into settling for something so much less.

Their transformation was beginning. The boys who came to the monastery, at the age of seven, eight, or nine, all knew the facts of life as well as the Abbot did, he did not have to waste his time with that. Nor did he give much wise counsel, except to the youngest boys, still preadolescent children. With them he would sit under a tree, an enormous *ficus religiosa* that filled the center of the courtyard, and there he let the children chatter at him to their heart's content, and he would sometimes tell them stories about *his* childhood. He neither preached at them nor taught them, but he guided them and advised.

Mostly, however, when outside his study and outside the temple, he was with the adolescents and youths; watching them at play, listening to them in class, but always leaving the instruction to the teachers. It does not seem much of a contribution, but he plainly made a special effort to spend as much time as possible with this age level. With those boys he was sometimes surprisingly austere, receiving rather than demanding the deference due to an abbot, but always returning respect. The discipline was always there. And when advice was needed he was ready to give it, in his own way.

Once he took two boys for a long walk up the mountainside

and invited me to come along. "It will be good for you, too," he said, and briskly started up the twisting path. It was early morning, right after the temple worship. The youths chattered, he chattered back, and I could not understand a word of it since I spoke virtually no Tibetan and could converse only in Hindi and English, which few of the boys knew. Every now and then, without slowing for a moment, the Abbot explained what all the chatter was about. It was mostly a botany lesson, it seemed; how we could find different flowers the higher we climbed, and how the higher we went the more beautiful they became, as if making up for their rarity, just like life itself. Then we reached the top. There were no flowers, just a thin but unbroken covering of snow and, in the middle of a hollow, a deep depression. It had snow down to the bottom, to the edge of a perfect circle that was a pool of still water so dark that it seemed as black as the snow was white. There was not a flower in sight, yet an even greater beauty was to be discovered. As you looked into that stark, black stillness, you found yourself looking into a huge void, and were drawn into beauty itself.

We had gone as high as we could, and after a short rest we made our way back, warm in the afternoon sun. The Abbot was still in front, the rest of us straggled along behind. By the time we got to the bottom, before dusk, he was already inside the monastery, about some other business. The two boys, it turned out, had been caught playing with each other's genitals. There was no reprimand, but the Abbot had been told and this was his response. It was far more than a lecture about birds and bees, and the mountain climb was far more than a lesson in the necessity of conserving energy, the mechanical tricks of which the boys had learned in their classes. The Abbot gave them something worth conserving energy for, the wonder for the greater beauty that always lies a few steps higher, denied us if we rest content with the lesser beauty we have found below.

Saints are few and far between, but we do not have to be Tibetans or abbots to be able to give something of ourselves— and we all have something worthwhile to give—to our adolescents; we just have to have lived fully and well and long, and be ready to share the beauty we have found in life with those who are only beginning to discover it. And old people are full of beauty, they just are.

There is no ranking of importance in the order with which we have taken these categories; there is nothing about a wise man that makes him more or less than a saint or a witch. These are just three ways that old people can serve society by being, and there are certainly others. But wise men are more familiar to us, so I have left them to the last. How foolish we are to employ teenagers as baby-sitters, and even more foolish to pay them. The old are made for the job, particularly if we consider its potential as a service to society rather than concern ourselves only with the safety of the children or furniture. Baby-sitting is nothing new, it occurs in every society; only the motivation is different. In many societies it is a major avenue by which old people manifest their quality of being to its fullest and make their contribution to the growth of a new generation. They do not teach in the formal sense, that is neither what the child wants nor what he needs. Old people are repositories of a mine of information and experience that the child can explore, and because the old and the young are so close to each other, in terms of proximity to life and death, they can communicate in ways that perhaps no parents can. That is another of the problems of adulthood; in isolating itself from death it also isolates itself to some extent from life.

Moké was a wise man; a widower, at times something of a recluse given to sitting by himself or wandering off alone, deep into the forest. He was an Mbuti, and as a baby-sitter he was constantly in demand. His voice was as soft as he was gentle, and although he did not radiate the energy of the abbot, he certainly radiated love. There is an almost universal division of labor between parents and grandparents; the parents have to discipline the child, and they can do so much more freely if the grandparents are there to help restore the trust that is temporarily shattered by the fleeting sense of betrayal and hurt that such discipline often brings. Done wisely, this work of restoration in no way undoes the lesson the parents are trying to teach; in the hands of an artist, it actually underscores both the trust and the discipline. Moké was a master of the art.

Mbuti children, we have said, are first given real names,

then they are given nicknames. One little boy's real name was Kaoya, but because he was so chubby he was called Ibambi, the name of a fat, juicy fruit that from time to time falls from the trees with a great thud. When that happened everyone would laugh, because anything that makes a sudden noise in the forest makes people a little nervous; it was as if their laughter or shouts of derision at the clumsy fruit were to drown out its noise, as if it should have known better. When Kaoya protested about his nickname, his friends gave him another in the language of the villagers, "Hanakiri," which means "He who has no brains." Reluctantly, Kaoya settled for Ibambi, and so he was known throughout his childhood.

He was as full of high spirits as any Mbuti child, not much different from the others except in his excess of baby fat. This made him a little clumsy, and when he tripped and fell to the ground his friends all made a hollow plonking sound by clapping one hand under the other armpit and shouted, "Ué oki? Ué oki? Ibambi a suké a dodo'o!"—"Do you hear that? Do you hear that? An Ibambi fruit has fallen!" and they would all rush in circles around Kaoya as if searching for the fallen fruit. He used to take it in fun, more often than not, falling down again with a plonk and rolling on the ground, this way and that, just like a plump *ibambi* fruit rolling downhill, until the other children caught him and all fell on a heap on top of one another.

But Kaoya was not insensitive, and as he grew a little older and a little less plump and the nickname still stuck, it bothered him. All his mothers and fathers then made a point of calling him by his real name, and he began to spend more time with them than with the children in the *bopi*. That was not good, and not what the adults had intended, so they started scolding him. One day his "real" mother in exasperation called him Ibambi and told him to go back to the *bopi* or she would put him in the *elima* house with the girls. Kaoya was about eight at the time, not quite old enough for the *nkumbi*, but old enough to know the difference between boys and girls, and his mother's threat was more than he could stand. He ran to old Moké for comfort and asked if he was really a girl. Moké gravely reached out and felt the boy's breasts, pondered, looking terribly serious, and said, no, not like any girls he knew, anyway! Both dissolved into fits of laughter. I remember that scene well because, like Kaoya, I was often the subject of gentle ridicule, also being clumsy and odd-looking; and catching sight of me Moké pointed to me and said, "Is he a girl?" Kaoya shrieked with laughter and said, "NO!" loudly. Moké countered, "Is he a hunter?" "No!" said Kaoya, a little less loudly. "Is he a child?" "No," again. "Is he a youth?" Kaoya hesitated and slowly said that yes, he thought so. "How do you know?" said Moké. "Does he dance into the *elima* house and dance with the girls like other youths?" Then without waiting for an answer he got up, and taking Kaoya's hand, they walked off into the forest together.

That might have been the end of it, but Kaoya brooded over this strange riddle and decided that as young as he was he was ready for the *nkumbi*, and announced his intention of being initiated at the very next village initiation, which was to be in a couple of years. This caused no great stir, since the *nkumbi* is a village ritual, and unlike the villagers the Mbuti tend to let their children enter whenever they feel like it. Encouraged, but feeling he had not made his point strongly enough, Kaoya decided that he had to place his masculinity beyond all doubt. One afternoon he left his friends in the *bopi* and swaggered into the main camp where the male youths were busily engaged dancing with the *elima* girls. Kaoya went over and joined them. The boys would not have minded, but the girls were going to have nothing to do with a child not well enough endowed to give them even the pretense of satisfaction, so they all surrounded him with their whips. These are the lithe saplings with which they whip the boys of their choice, inviting them to come and sleep with them. But instead of whipping Kaoya, who was now a little scared, they playfully whipped each other as they danced around Kaoya, singing, "*Ka! Ka! Ka, bi na uéué!*"; "Go! Go! Go and dance with yourself!" The word for dance also means play, and it also refers to premarital sex. If what the girls did seems unkind, remember that for the Mbuti the four age groups are perhaps the most important structural device in their lives, and although you progress from childhood to youth when you are ready, which is at puberty, Kaoya was by no means ready; he was threatening the system, breaking the discipline. Kaoya's mother ran into the fray when she saw what was happening, and grabbing the boy she picked him up bodily as mothers usually do only with much smaller children. She carried him back to the family hearth and dumped him on the ground as though he were an infant who had crawled off and got into trouble or had just annoyed someone. She had rescued him from one indignity and saddled him with another. Kaoya burst into floods of tears. He rushed at the fire where a meal was cooking, scattering burning logs and food in all directions; then he picked up a small stick and threw it at his mother and fled to the other end of the camp into the waiting arms of old Moké.

Wise old Moké did not try to explain in words the age structure of Mbuti society, nor did he try to explain, through words, that Kaoya's mother had done what she did because she loved him. Nor did he reassure Kaoya that he would indeed be ready for the *nkumbi* in two years' time (as in two years he was) and that after that he would be the best dancer of all and dance with the loveliest of the girls. He ignored Kaoya's tears, grabbed both his hands and started dancing with him, himself. As he danced he sang, repeating over and over again:

"Ba bi na kali, zu bi ekadi!"

It was a catchy little jingle, playing on the similar sound of the two last words:

> "THEY [the boys] are dancing with girls,
>   WE are dancing as one!"

It was irresistible, and soon Kaoya was joining in with him, and together they tried all sorts of variations of sound, as Mbuti love to do when singing. They played with the word *kali*, making "girls" sound quite ridiculous as they mispronounced it with gusto. But the word *ekadi* they always sang with care and love, correctly. It was a nice first lesson in the ecstasy of unity. It went on. Here are some of the other jingles they invented between them, making fun of the boys and the girls.

> *Na bambongu ba també,*
>   *Na balendu zu pandé.*
> Like elephants they crash,
>   Like antelopes we leap!

Na balozi wakami,
Zu luphu ekimi!
Like witches [their] noise,
We sing with joy.

(*Ekimi* is quiet, beloved by all Mbuti; *akami* is noise, feared and shunned.)

When verbal inventiveness ran out, Moké still did not stop dancing. Now he was in his element as a wise man, as himself. The two were one, as old people and children can so easily be. He took the raffia hat off his head and they both danced with that, then with a leaf, a flower, and a fat lump of wood that, of all things, Moké pretended was an Ibambi fruit. He moved each object around with his hands and arms, making it fly or leap or swoop, and Kaoya would have to guess how the thing was dancing, and dancing himself, answer with another jingle. The raffia hat danced like the wind, the leaf like the rain, the flower like water, and the Ibambi just fell to the ground, "Plonk!"

That was Moké's magic at work, the magic of old age. The dance he danced with Kaoya was so much more beautiful than anything the youths were doing that the mothers, who generally keep quite a strict eye on the *elima* activities, began to watch and imitate the dance of oneness, the dance of an old person at one with childhood, and the dance of both with the forest and all its creatures and plants and fruits; the dance of true atonement. Seeing this, Moké suddenly stopped, held Kaoya tightly in his arms and pointed to his mother dancing with the other mothers. "You see? Your mother is dancing! Now, show me . . . *who* is she dancing with?" Kaoya climbed out of Moké's arms and stood unsurely, looking at his mother. She was dancing with another woman who was crouching close to the ground as she danced, as though she were a child. They might well have been making fun of old Moké and young Kaoya, but that was not how Kaoya saw it. He thought for a moment, then turned to Moké with a sly smile, grabbed the old man's hands and they began again, faster and faster:

> *A bi na miki,*
> *A bi na MIMI!*
> She is dancing with a child,
> She is dancing with ME!

That is what I mean by a wise man, and that is what the old who are wise have to give to society, to us all, by just being.

A little over two years later Kaoya entered the *nkumbi.* Once more I was in the field and lived in the initiation camp with him and all the others, and I saw him transformed. I had seen him as a child in the *bopi*, and I had seen the groundwork laid by Moké, who transferred so much of his own wealth of spirit into the child, preparing him for all the good things in life, which should be a dance of oneness from start to finish. Soon after his *nkumbi*, independence came to the Congo, and in its wake came all the bitter fighting between nationalists, rebels, and mercenaries, fighting that tore the forest apart. It was eleven years before I saw Kaoya again. When I arrived I found that Epulu had changed greatly; the old village had disappeared, swallowed by heavy undergrowth. Many of the villagers and some Mbuti, including old Moké, had died. But palm wine was brought and food was cooked, and the day after my arrival there was a great dance to welcome back the old times, though the forest was still not entirely safe from either rebels or mercenaries. The boys of the last *nkumbi* came as one, now strong young men, married and with children of their own. Only Kaoya and one other were not there. Kaoya limped into the camp later; he had not been able to keep up with the others, and he had no wife or children. In the first days of the fighting he had been caught and held captive and had fallen sick. He was about twenty years old now, but he was emaciated and looked smaller, though taller, than he had been when he was a fat *ibambi* fruit. Only a few days later he was dead. But without Moké, and others like him, he would never have lived at all.

Of all these four old men, one witch, two saints, and one wise man, only one had found a one-track way of living his old age; the other three were multitrack elders, as many old people are. The Himalayan holy man, singlemindedly devoted to the quest for truth, had secluded himself from the rest of

the world, as far away as he could and still survive. His contact with others, of any age level, was reduced to a minimum.
Few managed to seek him out, a few more stumbled across
him, but he gave of his being to only one acolyte, at the most
two, at a time, each acolyte staying through adolescence and
youth until he was ready to face adulthood his own way. It
was only with adolescents and youths that this saint's manner
of being worked its art; with those most in need of help and
inspiration during their time of transformation, and in need
of some sense of purpose and direction while they learned
the difficult art of reason: for reason is full of pitfalls, closely
associated with the lesser arts of deceit and prevarication,
fantasy and confabulation, treachery and self-justification.
But to teach even one or two youths well, in isolation, is no
small contribution.

And Abazinga was a witch from the start, almost to the
finish. He was also much of a recluse, but made frequent forays
into the adult world, tweaking it by the ears and making it
burn with a self-criticism it might have avoided had it not
been for the old witch's beady eyes and sharp tongue. Toward
the end, however, Abazinga was something of a wise man too,
and even perhaps something of a saint, for who knows what
he did when he finally left the world for the forest, or why?

Most old people probably follow several tracks at once, being of value simultaneously to people of all ages. Moké was a
wise man with children, a saint to adolescents and youths, and
the adults were scared stiff of him, as much as they loved him.
Moké just had to raise one finger, let a gentle smile spread
across his face, slowly shake his head as he waggled his finger,
and disputatious adults would stop their noise. The Tibetan
Abbot also dealt with people from all stages of life, and from
the fullness of his being had something to give to any who
came his way.

So it is in our world, not just in Africa or Asia. Old people
everywhere share certain characteristics, determined by the
physiological process of aging, that inevitably influence the
nature of their relationship with others who are similarly defined to some extent by *their* physical age. The nature of any
specific culture merely modifies and adapts these general
tendencies to its own needs. In considering old age in our own

culture, perhaps because I myself, in my late fifties, am only tottering on the brink of old age and so can claim no personal experience of its wonders, I find it necessary to spend a little more time looking at the processes. We can all find our own comparisons and parallels with other cultures more easily when we are clearer about some of the things that old age does to all of us, and how these things then link us to others in very special ways.

Old people are close to death, and if we define death as non-existence (in the material world at least), this undeniable characteristic links the oldest and the youngest more directly than any, for the young share this characteristic of proximity to nonexistence and also command, through its power, a certain respect. The very fear of death, be it death of children or of the old, is a power that motivates action. Mortality and vitality are not as far apart as we like to think.

The old, again like children at the other extreme of life, are removed from active participation in the physically, intellectually demanding, wage-earning manifestations of youth and adulthood; but far from being useless they both have other abilities and potential that make them no less productive. The old are effectively beyond child-bearing; at least I find it useful to define them as such, remembering that the Mbuti do not find it significant to differentiate the sexes except at the child-bearing stage of adulthood; and that for them to give birth to children is a social responsibility, not a mere physiological possibility, and is therefore limited according to the needs of society. And I think we could say that for us also the male/female distinction is far less clearly defined in old age than at any other stage of life, except possibly early childhood. It is certainly of much less immediate social significance. Like children, then, in a way they are sexless, beyond sex.

The old seem to go through a great ritual of reversal, reverting to childhood in many ways. The body becomes less efficient than it was in adulthood, the power of reason eventually diminishes to less than it was in youth, the sexual potential retreats to what it was the far side of adolescence. But only in the physiological sense is this "deterioration," for in a strange way this is also progress and fulfillment, both for the

individual and for society. It is in this way that the old recapture an ancient vitality, and by their contact with the
young, revitalize society with their regained capacity for loving and feeling and with their renewed and heightened contact
with Spirit. This enables them to communicate with the as
yet partially formed young in a way that no adult can.

This is not an empty attempt to classify for the sake of classification, nor to impose arbitrary definitions. That could
have been done, as academics are wont to do, in a few pages
of tables, graphs, and charts. The theme of old age is repeated
over and over again, with cultural variations, because that is
how it is in real life. The classification is merely a tool, with
inadequacies, that can help us to understand just what old
people can and do accomplish by being what they are. No
special skill or training is needed; their age is their qualification.

Now perhaps, at last, we can see what potential our own
old people have and how much we lose by retiring them as we
do, relegating them to a premature limbo of predeath and social nonexistence. What a terrible thing retirement can be;
of all the markers in our society we have made it the clearest
and often the most painful. The death of our own parents acts
as a powerful reminder of our own mortality, but does not
necessarily mark our own entry into old age. Institutionaliza-
tion as a result of premature aging can come before the age
of retirement, but that too is not the general pattern. Most of
us, I think, can consider either voluntary or compulsory retirement from active preoccupation with earning a living as
the dominant marker provided by our society; and thus all
too many of the old are denied the wonders of old age. Our
elderly struggle toward death more as crippled adults than
as the new being they really are.

If we retire from an active, monetarily productive life of
doing, into what do we retire? We have seen some of the
choices that others make and their social consequences. What
is the social consequence of retiring, voluntarily or otherwise,
into a home for the aged, be it one strewn with luxury chalets,
golf courses, and gymnasia, or one strewn with beds, chairs,
and sterile recreation rooms in which people wait less com-

fortably to die, as if in an anteroom of a crematorium? Here we must consider the relationship between old people and others, not in the context of age levels, but in the context of family. All too often in these homes they are denied *effective* contact with both, for the very structure of both the luxury retirement homes and the state institutions precludes the possibility of protracted contact with family and friends; visitation may be limited to specific days, even hours. This does not give the old much opportunity for practicing the art of being in relationship to anyone except their aged coresidents and the staff. While the staff of many such institutions find their work rewarding, this is generally taken to mean that they feel pleasure and find satisfaction in the knowledge that they are helping others. However, it might well be that it is also because their lives are being enriched in some of the other ways that we have seen.

But other than the staff, who benefits from this segregation of the old, separating them from the rest of us like lepers? The family may suffer economic loss if they have to pay for the home, or if their prospects of inheritance are diminished by the extent to which their old parents are paying for it themselves; these are serious considerations frequently discussed. The family may, however, derive economic benefit if the expenses are paid by the state or by some retirement or insurance plan. They certainly derive benefit, as many see it, by being freed from the responsibility of looking after their parents and thus being at greater liberty to pursue their own lives unfettered. Some who feel uneasy at the sense of liberation they feel as they pack their parents off to a home (as their parents once packed them off to school—another reversal) try to justify it by saying they are not qualified to look after them. That is a debatable issue. But rather than make any moral judgment about the resentment so many feel and express when their aged parents become, as they see it, a "liability," and since we have, I hope, established how wrong they are in this by seeing what an *asset* old people can be, we should simply recognize that this attitude is thoroughly consistent with a society that places such high value on individualism and independence rather than on cooperation and interdependence. And we must not discount the emotional benefits felt by many of those left behind when the old have thus been dismissed from their lives, if not their thoughts; this too is consistent with our refusal to accept aging and death as a natural and even productive, beneficial part of life. All too often we fight to the end as though death can and should be averted, if not avoided.

But what benefits do the segregated elders themselves derive from the system? Again, there is a consistency that alerts us to the fact that we are not discussing just individual behavior but a social system. We value and practice segregation rather than integration at all sorts of levels in our society; we are well used to segregation according to sex, color, religion, age, class, caste, economic status, political inclination or affiliation, personal interests, hobbies and tastes, diet, and in heaven knows how many other ways. Thus many old people accept the segregation of elders as a natural part of the scheme of things, and like the rest of us, fail to realize what a loss this is to them and to society at large. Many are all too happy to be rid of children who have not learned to be adults, in our sense of the word, and whom they know regard them as a burden; though I know some who, while feeling this happiness, also feel a deep hurt and regret that it has to be so, that the system has ordained that it be so. Having given us everything, life itself, at the very end of *their* lives we demand that they give us still more, our freedom from the opportunity to reciprocate and give something in return. A weekly visit with a bunch of flowers and an occasional phone call is not much of a return for the investment they have made.

However, although the placing of people in old persons' homes is not yet in itself a social institution, the ritual of retirement is; it comes to most of us whether we are self-employed and merely announce that we are "retired," or whether we are employed and have a more formal ritual provided by our employers and are retired rather in the manner that we "retire" an old car that has given us long and faithful service, effectively consigning it to a scrap heap after keeping it around for a while for its sentimental value. For many it is a traumatic, terrifying, and even destructive institution. Those who dream only of all the things they are going to "do" fail to find the state of grace that lies in just being. And the more they try to do, the more they find that they cannot do; the longer and harder they try, the more the recognition of their ultimate failure is impressed upon them. Their golf handicap increases; they win fewer and fewer games of chess; their fingers are less nimble on the keyboard; increasingly they forget to water their prize-winning flowers; their eyesight fails them and makes it difficult and painful to read those un-read books. They compete with themselves as well as with others and with life itself to the bitter end. It *is* a bitter end, for society; for even if an old lady dies of a heart attack as she finally holes out in one, that is not for society quite the same thing as if old Moké had died from exhaustion when dancing to help transform Ibambi into Kaoya, or if the old Abbot had collapsed at the top of the mountain. Nor would there be as much significance in the dying thought that, in such an event, Moké and the Abbot might have shared with the old golfer: "I did it . . . once again, I did it."

Many old people know all this when they retire, but they ignore it and try to make the best of a lesser reality. We give them little other option. Those who do not ignore it and try in old age to find a new way of contributing to society are faced with the reality that they have been crippled, or at least hobbled. They recognize that for economic and other reasons the system has demanded that they give over their doing into the hands of someone younger, even if less quali-fied; but then they find they have also been prohibited from continuing to contribute by being what they are. I have not once in my life met a person at the age of retirement who has not believed that he is still a person of value. The more an adult is convinced of his worth at retirement, the harder it is for him to navigate the transition into an old age that we have made into a world of doing nothing. Its patent emptiness and irrelevance to anyone but their isolated selves often leads to rapid physical or mental deterioration and premature death, or even to suicide. The stereotyped suicide notes that say, "Nobody wants me" and "I am of no use to anyone any-more" are not necessarily penned by individuals in a moment of self-pity; they may well be simple, sober assessments of an agonizing and protracted reality to which, for a socially conscious human being in our individualistic society, only one answer may seem logical. It does not pay to be too socially conscious.

Luckily for us there are plenty of others, with better sense I would like to think, who are perhaps blessed with greater abilities and have a wider and more comprehensive sense of sociality, and who thus make the transition into old age more fruitfully. Some of the hurt and regret may still be there, but there is also the recognition that they still have a contribution to make and the means to make it by just being themselves; neither trying for more nor settling for anything less. For them life is a constant reiteration of "I did it!" but in the different sense of having done something yet once again to enrich the lives of others, rather than in the sense of having repeated some feat of their youth or having made a satisfactory imitation of being adult.

How lucky those of us are who have had saints and wise people in our young lives. I would still have been a very empty vessel had it not been for the Great-uncle Willies and Freds and the rare wild old organist like Arthur Poyser. There were quite a number of witches in my life too and, properly, they all cast a spell on my adult life by nagging at me and tempting me to accuse them of being responsible for all the things that were really my fault. University deans make admirable adult witches in relationship with their faculties. Conductors for orchestras perhaps, and sheriffs and magistrates for rural communities sometimes. But the older they are, the more effective they are. Old people who live alone and mind their own business, the business of being, and who do very well in the process, silently suggest that others, less successful, would do well to mind *their* business of doing. Other witches are more active and compel us to dance with them, not in covens at night, but in public and in broad daylight.

The biggest witch in my adult life, without question, was my mother. For her, old age began in earnest when my father died and she came to live with me. She often used to provoke me long before that, but provocation became a full-time occupation after my father's death, and not just with me. Any adult was her prey, and she had an uncanny knack of knowing what was in someone's mind just by squinting at them.

Just like Abazinga, I would catch her in the act of looking at me. I would be going through the main gate and something would make me look around, and there she would be in the window of the gate house, peering through the curtains, squinting. Or I would be working in the garden, having left her doing the same in hers, and all of a sudden there she was, leaning on her stick, watching. If I ignored her she just stayed put; immobile, eyes glinting through her spectacles, radiating Irish power, making me wonder what on earth I had done wrong now. That made it easy to blame her when nothing I planted that day ever showed any signs of growing. But if I made a move to go and greet her and find out what she wanted, by the time I had straightened my back she was gone.

She was a witch all right, and many is the time that I cursed her as I hit my thumb with a hammer or swerved into a ditch as she suddenly appeared from nowhere, spectacles ablaze. "What do you want?" I would ask, testily. "Nothing, dear!" she would answer, and that made me more angry and accusatory than ever because it was true: she did not want anything. Like other thoroughly good, old people, she just was; but like witches in particular, she was everywhere.

As much as I would try to blame her when things went wrong, the net result was that in trying to find good solid grounds for the accusation I discovered where the real cause lay. It is sad that it is only in retrospect that I know all this. She would have enjoyed it if I had called her a witch instead of all those other things I called her. But she was as imperturbable as she was unreformable, though her Irish temper used to make me think I could perturb her. It is also sad that it is only in retrospect that I realize what an extraordinary mother/woman she was; I would like to have thanked her.

She was a witch to the last. On one of her periodic emigrations from England to the United States, where we lived in exciting proximity to each other, she decided to die. She had tried everything else and had made a couple of test runs at dying, so to speak; I know two hospitals that dreaded her visitations because she could put on such a convincing show of dying. But now she felt she was ready for the real thing. Of course nobody believed her, except for one or two other old witches in the quiet rural neighborhood. I was having a particularly enjoyable time at the University of West Virginia just then, and of course blamed my mother for a nagging impulse that would creep up on me and make me undertake that wretched drive back to the Chesapeake Bay. I made it more frequently than I would have done because I just had to see what the old witch was up to now, what other of my friendships had she subverted in my absence, what neighbors or county officials had she alienated by squinting at them, what new (and always expensive) changes had she ordered made on the property, or whether she had just burned it down as she tried to do on more than one occasion. At midterm recess I felt an urge to hurry home to see what she was up to. While there I gave in to her latest whim and myself plowed up the whole of the lawn that had just been planted at her request. For once things seemed to be working out well; she surveyed the muddy mess and expressed satisfaction. "Just wait until spring!" she said.

I should have known better. I had a foreboding. She was not one to wait for anything; it would have been more like her to have it turfed the next day. Also, she seemed strangely relaxed and content, which made me nervous. Then, as the ten days drew to a close, she retreated as usual into her witchy self and I would find her crouched over a horrid half-cooked egg or a piece of dry toast, staring at me with the look that said, "You want to get back to your friends, don't you! You want to leave your mother all alone and dying!" But if she saw I was reading her mind, or what I took to be her mind, the squint would widen into an innocent smile and she would offer me yet another cup of tea and say how glad she was that I enjoyed my work.

The morning I went to say I was leaving she was really doing it properly. She was still in bed and remained unmoved as I sacrificed a few minutes of good West Virginia time to half-cook her awful egg for her. The moment I said, cheerfully enough, "Well, I'll be seeing you in a couple of weeks I suppose," my mother just rolled over, turned her back to me, and said quite firmly, "No, I don't think so, dear." Of course it was just her old "You'll be sorry someday" trick, and after half a century I was inured to it.

Three days later I was back again, and my mother was on

a slab in the local mortuary, looking slightly cross as though I had done something wrong yet again. The mortician had put her glasses on, and suspecting a squint I hurriedly took them off. All her diamond rings had prudently been removed, but her wedding ring remained. Not knowing quite what to do at this difficult encounter, but feeling I had to do something, I took the ring off her finger. She seemed a little less cross. But then I did not know what to do with the ring, so for safe-keeping I put it on my own finger. As I did that I was sure that her face settled into a final smile of triumph. Not a trace of a squint was left; she had cast her last spell, the spell of motherhood. From that day onward I have been unable to get the ring off; it is stuck firmly on the little finger of my left hand, and every morning it squints at me. Some say I cannot get it off because my hand has grown fat, but I know otherwise. My mother was a witch. But now that I understand, I wonder how many more witches there are, like her, just asking to be allowed to *be*, waiting to be allowed to give all they have so that their death will be a rich fulfillment rather than an empty loss for them and for others.

PART SIX

THE ART OF LIVING

In SOUTHERN AFRICA the Bushmen tell a wonderful story. I first heard it from Laurence van der Post, and since then have heard several variations among other African peoples. Always it refers to life, and the art of living, as a quest.

A Bushman child, drinking from a clear waterhole, saw in the shimmering surface the reflection of a beautiful bird. It was the most beautiful thing he had ever seen. But looking upward, he knew that the bird had already gone. The boy decided he had to follow and find it, so off he set. He sought it throughout his adolescence and throughout his youth. In other stories the quest becomes in turn mystical then rational, associated by the storytellers with the place of both faith and belief in their societies. The quest is always associated with social concern. Far from being criticized for abandoning his adult role as a hunter, it is recognized by his fellows that the young man is contributing effectively to society by pushing both his faith and his belief, as he sees them, and as shared by his fellows, to their maximum. He is a symbol of consecration to beauty and goodness.

The quest continues throughout adulthood, and the hunter, who has become a hunter after truth, is always one step behind his quarry. Village after village tells him it has just left, heading northward. In his old age the hunter reaches the lower slopes of Mount Kilimanjaro and is told that the bird has been seen high up on the snowy summit. With the last of his strength the old man, whose quest began with the vision of a child, climbs laboriously up the mountainside. Nowhere does he see any trace of the great bird he has devoted his life to finding.

Finally he reaches the top and he knows that his quest is over, for up there in the equatorial snow and ice all his strength is gone and there is no bird, nothing but emptiness. He lies down to wait for the end, recalling the vision of his childhood, content with a life well spent, for he had been lucky enough to find beauty once, and in his heart he had never lost it. As he closed his eyes for the last time on an empty sky, he called on the name of his mother, who had given him such a wonderful and joyous life. And as he stretched out his arms in a final gesture, his open hands upturned, down from the sky came a solitary feather and settled in one hand. The hand closed slowly, then held it as tightly in death as the vision of beauty had been held during life.

That, the Bushmen say, was a life well lived, and the story is a lasting joy to all.

There is so much potential for beauty and goodness at every stage of life, in any culture; so much potential for living life (and enjoying it) better by living it for others as well as for ourselves; how is it that so many of us find so much of life to be unsatisfactory, somehow not quite what it should have been, filled with little disappointments? And, indeed, there are all too many for whom life holds little satisfaction of any kind, for whom it is one long, uphill battle. If what has gone before suggests that even for those generally counted as fortunate or successful there is more to life than they are getting out of it, and if this is so for us as a society, then we should do some rethinking.

To start with, it should be apparent that the very obvious differences between the diversity of cultures we have touched on are only skin-deep. We may have many different ways of doing things, but for all of us the *process* of living, of being born, growing old, and dying, is much the same. At each age, in whatever society we live, our body offers us certain possibilities and denies others. The way we go about responding to those possibilities depends more on what our concept of society really is than on our cultural or national affiliations, let alone the color of our skin. We have examined all five stages of life from one single viewpoint, the anthropological view of society as a network of interrelating human relationships and social institutions. The psychologist will claim the right to examine the same data from the point of view of the individual; and anyone has the right to change the classifications for his or her own ends. Different approaches are valid and necessary, but if it comes to priorities I go along with the Ituri villager who says that society comes first and that the laws of society, those sometimes aggravating restrictions on individual freedom, are not only essential for survival, but are the very food that enables us to grow and live full, rich, and happy lives, dealing effectively with the setbacks as they come.

The major difference between African tribal life, or the life of the orthodox Hindu, and our own way of life, is not in the vast differences between how we do things, but rather in the much more subtle and vital difference in our concepts of both self and society. There is no question of the one being right and the other wrong. Just as we have the right to choose one life style over another, to prefer the American way of life to that of the French or English or Chinese or whatever, so we have the right to choose our own ideal of what "society" should mean and be. But as vital as that issue is, it is given far too little thought. We take it for granted that we are social creatures, that we are socially conscious, yet few can clearly make a significant distinction between society and community, and fewer still can agree on what is meant by the two terms. And if we cannot be clear about what is meant by the word "society," then we have no way in the world of being clear about what we mean by sociality. "Social concern" together with "social rights and obligations" become meaningless phrases that we each interpret according to our individual tastes, needs, or necessities.

In looking at the way we and others do and do not manifest social concern at various stages of life, two things should have become clear. One of them is that anyone who wants to understand the social process, whether he is an anthropologist or a miner or a business executive, does not have to go to some exotic land to gather data. He does not even have to go beyond himself and his own experience. We all have our own mine of data about human behavior and human relationships, social and otherwise. By looking at our personal experience of life critically, trying to understand *why* things happened, what external, systematic social forces were at work, and *what* any given action or situation achieved beyond its narrow, immediate context, how far the ripples made by our own life extended into the lives of other people, we expand our knowledge both of ourselves and the immediate world we live in, our immediate society. Comparison with the social process elsewhere is a highly important tool, but too often we ignore the wealth of information that lies in our own experience. However, we have to go beyond our personal experience and our personal feelings and attitudes, and try to discover the system that to some extent governs our emotional life just as much as it governs our daily actions.

As well as eschewing personal experience at this stage, as we try to come to know our widest self, our social self, we will also have to go beyond reference to specific alternative ways of doing things, such as those we have been looking at in Africa and India. Those examples, successfully or not, were intended to show alternative social systems at work, how other societies handle the business of living together, facing conflict and resolving it, ordering interpersonal and intergroup relationships into a comprehensible system that achieves the maximum advantages for the society as a whole while allowing the maximum possible freedom for each individual to develop his own way and make his own unique contribution to society.

Treading lightly, then, let us start by contrasting the two major forms of society that we have looked at: our own Western, industrialized, highly complex national society and the small-scale tribal societies of the Ituri Forest, which represent, for our purposes, all the thousands of others that we frequently classify as "primitive" societies. We can ignore the red herring that leads to endless debate about the relative merits of civilization as against the primitive way of life. The more important difference between the two ways, each of which is an appropriate response to its own specific context, is revealed in the term "small-scale societies," by which many anthropologists avoid the insult implied by the word "primitive" and other words like it, such as "tribal," however useful such words might be if properly understood. Obviously, the "primitive," "tribal" society is generally much smaller, both in population and territory, than most modern nations, but by no means always. Sometimes these societies form confederations, nations, and even empires that number millions of individuals and cover vast territories. The essential factor concerning us here, however, is the quality of life in the small-scale society as compared with that found in the large-scale society.

When a population that perceives itself as a distinct unit, let us say "society" for the moment, consists of only a few thousand people, it is plainly possible for any one individual to know and interact with a majority of others in his society. In some cases an individual may be able to trace kinship connections to every single other individual. At the very least, since most of these societies are divided into relatively small village units, or small nomadic or transhumant bands or lineages of hunters or herders, kinship is likely to bind you to almost everyone within that smallest unit as well as to quite a few individuals in neighboring units. The affinal relationship that is created by marriage links you to a whole other kinship network, equally concentrated in another village perhaps, and with its own further affinal network in still more villages. Your wife's brother married a girl from a village you have never been to, and although you have never even met your wife's brother, let alone his second cousin's niece's maternal great-uncle, as "kin" you will be able to enter the village of any one of these people and, in such a society, have instant access to a set of specified rights and privileges. You will also immediately be saddled with specified responsibilities, for that is what reciprocity is all about, and reciprocity is the basis of sociality.

So in small-scale societies, the careful tracing of both consanguineal ("blood") relationships and affinal (marital) connections is most often a major part, even the basis, of the overall social structure. The "laws" of such a society are embodied in the mutual responsibilities that are mandatory for the various degrees and categories of kinship. The network can be stretched even further by the "classificatory" system in which even nonkin are incorporated by being given a fictitious relationship: in fact, with the Mbuti, we saw an example of a society that utilizes fictive kinship rather than actual kinship to define its network of obligations and responsibilities. Plainly, in our huge and much more mobile society such a system could not work, though we see the same identical process at work in many a rural village or urban ghetto. There the important thing to note is that whereas the small-scale society institutionalizes it, we do not; with us it may in certain contexts be convenient and useful to invoke kinship, but it is not mandatory or embodied in the law. Nor is there even any generally accepted body of public opinion governing our attitudes to such exploitation of kinship.

That last point is crucial to our understanding of different concepts of family, because as individuals, in making comparisons with other ways of dealing with the life cycle, many of us will say that we care for our children as much as the Mbuti, that we as individuals tried hard to encourage our adolescent offspring to look beyond the physical pleasures of sex and cultivate a sense of social responsibility; and certainly many of us will say that our religious belief, our sense of morality, not the armed policeman or threat of imprisonment or execution, is what governs our behavior and persuades us to lead orderly, social lives. That can all be true, and it can be true for the majority of the population, but in looking at the social process and the social structure, just as we are not concerned any longer with individual experience, so we are not concerned with a collection of individual experiences, however quantitatively impressive, *unless they are determined or systematically encouraged and sanctioned by society*, which for the large-scale societies with legal systems means by law or governmental policy. That does not discount the importance of "customary behavior," it merely sets it apart from the rest of the social system.

We can easily see that in a society where kinship is central to the structure and ordering of daily human relationships, the family structure is an essential core of the wider social structure, permeating all aspects of economic, political, and religious life. Given the minimal use of kinship in determining our daily interaction, there should be no cause for surprise that our own family structure seems, by comparison, to be so limited; nor should there be any cause for surprise that our family responsibilities and obligations are equally limited and that once our children reach the age of discretion (and what an ambiguous term *that* is!), they are no longer under any legal obligation toward their parents nor are their parents under any further legal obligation to them. Regardless of what our individual religious belief or morality tells us, there should be no cause for surprise at the number of old people effectively abandoned by their children. There is absolutely nothing in the system that says that it *should* be otherwise, let alone ordain that it *must* be otherwise. Family, in our social system, has come to play a minimal structural role.

One other major characteristic differentiates the small from the large-scale society. Anthropologists sometimes get into trouble by referring to the one as simple and the other as complex, and this conceals the fact that whereas an industrial nation does, undoubtedly, have a much more complex economic and political *system* (again as defined clearly by the constitution and the law), our kinship system is infinitely *less* complex, and indeed, it is questionable as to whether we have a kinship *system* at all. The most we have is the law that pertains to marriage and cohabitation and parental responsibilities for minors. But complexity, heightened by heterogeneity, is undoubtedly more a characteristic of the large-scale society. Plainly, in a highly industrialized society specialization is necessary, and this in turn demands a different kind of educational system that leads to segregation, not only of one type of laborer (or adult) from another, but also segregates those who are learning different specialized skills. It is all part of the systematic fragmentation and isolation that is built into our society as a structural necessity. Yet we strive hard to achieve an overall national unity, to bring together these divergent elements in our population. Our political system does this through local, state, and national elections, something in which we are all expected to participate, though it is important again to note that nonparticipation is not penalized. You cannot lose your citizenship by ignoring this primary responsibility to the nation and your fellow citizens. In some societies this would be considered a criminal offense. In small-scale societies it would be more likely to be considered a sacrilege. And that brings us to the other area of social organization in which the small-scale society is infinitely more complex than our own, the area of religious belief and practice.

Instantly we think of our cherished doctrine (which *is* an integral part of our system, written into the Constitution) of freedom of religious belief, accompanied by our (again systematic) separation of Church and State. We place enormous importance on this freedom, and quite rightly so, since yet again it is, in a sense, required by our context, in this case a context of an immigrant population of highly diverse national, ethnic, and religious origins. It may be necessary, given our particular concept of "religion," which consistently enough is also fragmentary and focuses on the diversity of belief systems and even of doctrinal interpretations within any one system, rather than focusing on the fact that all are unified by the common phenomenon of faith. But by comparison with the social system of the small-scale society, we can see that because of this structural necessity, if that is really what it is, we are denied a powerful force toward the very unity that our otherwise fragmented society so desperately needs. Religious "freedom" may be a major structural weakness rather than some kind of moral strength, which is how we tend to regard it.

I think it is a fair generalization to say that in their social system and structure, small-scale societies give as much prominence to religion as they do to political, economic, and domestic life. Each religious system, in such societies, has its doctrine in which people more or less believe, just as we more or less believe in ours; for instance, in Christianity individuals and sects may differ as to whether heaven is really in the sky or whether angels have wings, but by and large Christians believe in the divinity of Christ; the one is the less and the other the more. Each religious system in small-scale societies also involves a body of ethical behavior, sanctioned by the doctrine, which provides a powerful incentive to social behavior. We saw, for example, how the Mbuti belief in man's original sin, the killing of an animal, is eventually translated into prescribed action that is both an ecological and sociological necessity in their context and makes of them, as hunters, some of the best game conservationists in the world, as well as the truest of egalitarians. They do not all see it that way themselves, but that is how the system works. In appraising the social rather than individual importance of our system of belief, we would have to trace similar functional social implications.

Each religious system also embodies a certain form of ritual behavior, some of it individual and some of it corporate; from our viewpoint our attention should primarily be on the corporate rituals, those that bring different individuals together in one common action. Going to church may not in itself be a ritual, but the form of the service is, and all group participation in religious ritual is a form of communion between participants just as much as it is, or may be, of communion with Spirit. One of the major differences here between the two forms of society is that whereas we tend to confine such corporate rituals to one day of each week, augmented by certain holy days and occasions of social importance for which ritual is prescribed (such as the various stages of the life cycle from birth through marriage to death), the small-scale society tends rather to disperse ritual behavior, even corporate ritual behavior, throughout the week or year. Rather than consecrate a specific day or date, it consecrates a greater number of occasions. We may celebrate birth, death, and marriage by ritual behavior that brings even distant kin together, one of its important social functions. The small-scale society adds puberty to the list and then goes on to add sickness and conflict (which is considered a form of social sickness), various stages of the economic cycle (we celebrate harvest), the formation of economic or political bonds between groups or individuals who represent groups (we do *not* celebrate mergers by religious ritual); and in many other ways, through *obligatory* ritual performance, they relate their daily life in all spheres to their system of religious belief. On top of this the individual ritual practice in such systems still further adds to the pervasiveness of the belief system *which is essentially communal rather than individual.*

The difference we drew between witchcraft and sorcery illustrates this point. Just as any individual is culpable if he uses his Spirit force (or ritual that can attract Spirit force) against the best interests of society, so is he culpable if he makes use of ritual for his individual profit, for that is at the very least not with the good of society in mind, and *may* be detrimental to society. It is a shadowy area, but those who make excessive use of private ritual practice are often suspect of being antisocial and subject to a measure of ostracism. So plainly, in these small-scale societies, the systems of belief and practice are consciously directed toward the social good rather than individual salvation. That is a rather different orientation from our own, where religious belief and practice *can* be used for the good of society, and sometimes are, especially in times of crisis, but where that is not written into the system.

It seems that we *can* do a lot of things, social things, that the small-scale society does, but we do not ordain that they be done. We don't like to be *ordered* to do things. Once again we demand that the argument take into account our value of individual freedom. Well, for one thing this is not an argument, it is merely an examination of the facts, and for another we are deliberately focusing on society, not on the individual. Nonetheless, by all means consider the issue of individual freedom, for whereas that concept is very definitely not written into the constitution of the small-scale society, but exists there just as much as it does here, it *is* written into our Constitution and body of law. Yet to say we have individual freedom is an absolute nonsense and we all know it, and I doubt that any rational person *could* want it in any absolute sense, even if such a thing were possible. In fact, as individuals, we are hedged and bound by far more restrictions, and most of them couched in terms that are far more specific and thus more restrictive than in any small-scale society. There are restrictions on our domestic life, on our economic life and on our political life, and failure to observe those restrictions may be met by the full force of the law with all its prescribed penalties. In sharp contrast, however, in religious belief and practice we *are* free, within a few but very generous bounds, to worship as we please. Only the gross excess of a Jonestown or a Manson bring about censure or proscription. In the small-scale society it is almost the reverse, for the system prescribes general patterns of behavior in domestic, economic, and political life, under the guiding principle that all such behavior shall be social, and orders that social ritual shall be frequent, public, corporate, and largely obligatory. But it rigorously proscribes any ritual or religious practice that is *not* social. It allows little freedom of religious behavior or practice, and here is the crux of the matter, virtually no freedom of belief.

It seems at first glance that it should be the other way around, for if religious belief and practice are the powerfully integrative, socially unifying forces that anthropological studies indicate them to be, then surely we need them far more than the small-scale society, since so much of our system is necessarily disintegrative. They have kinship working to draw them together; at their technological level cooperation is as much a necessity in their economic life as individual enterprise has come to be in ours; politically the concept of family as well as other forces operate again to help bind them together, linking families into lineages into clans into tribes into nations. Everything seems to combine to pull their society together. But here we are at the point where we have to deal with the term "society" itself, for it seems that we are not talking about the same kind of animal at all. And in a way we are not; but we *are* talking about the same process at work. The small-scale society is perhaps most different from ours in that it tends to be a community of believers rather than an association of nationals, or citizens. They are bound, ultimately, by a common and sacred belief system; we are bound, primarily, by a body of secular law.

It is obvious that size and homogeneity are governing factors here; there is no implication that our "society" could be or should be a community of believers, though the possibility bears examination. But examining the social process as revealed in the life cycle, we have seen how it is that this community of belief makes order without law possible in the small-scale society. It is reasonable to suggest then that the lack of any such community of belief may be in part responsible for the fact that we find it increasingly difficult to maintain order through law. In the absence of a community of belief we *see* ourselves as different from our neighbors, even from kin, for our innermost beliefs define us most clearly to ourselves and just as clearly differentiate us from others wherever differentiation of belief arises. In the small-scale society it does not arise.

Community of belief is without doubt a highly integrative force, and all the more so when that essentially rational belief is supported by faith. But without the common body of belief, faith in itself has no binding force, for it is something that has its source in the individual. It is in connection with faith that the individual must be taken most into account when considering the otherwise impersonal social system. Whereas belief, as I am using the word throughout, is essentially rational, and therefore subject to question, disputation, and interpretation, to all the forces that threaten the integrative power of any belief system if tolerated, faith is essentially internal, perhaps emotional. Experience may show you that your faith is wrong, reason never can. It is in some ways akin to what some people call intuition, a nonrational conviction that something is so, even though nothing in our conscious experience can give any explanation as to why it should be so. What we so often dismiss as magic in the religious practices of other societies, because there is no demonstrable causal connection, is frequently an exercise of faith; and the absence of demonstrable causal connection is the heart of such ritual and practice. The prominence of ritual behavior in small-scale societies allows for the frequent expression of individual faith; it encourages it to grow, and it is this individual faculty for faith that gives to religious belief, in such societies, its overwhelming social power. Religion, then, can perhaps now be defined as the conjunction of faith and belief, pervading every aspect of daily life, making the secular and the sacred one and the same thing.

"Community of belief" is clear and unambivalent enough, but if we use that as our definition of society then we have to say that the United States is not a society. That might be a healthy start, for the United States is a nation, and there is no need to call it a society. Is it a union of societies? Is each state a society? I think, looking at the structure, the state is no more a society than the nation. Is a village a society, or is a ghetto a society; a town or a city? Now we seem to be getting closer; we are more given to talking about villages as communities, so the word "society" seems to imply something a bit larger and more complex, but less large and less complex than the nation. Be it a nation or a village, to deserve the appellation of "society" its members must be bound to each other in a network of reciprocal obligations, felt and observed in daily interaction just as they are in a community, if to a lesser degree.

This definition of society is obviously a narrow one, but it serves our purpose well and removes the ambivalence otherwise attached to the word and which renders it next to meaningless. Just as "community" implies a community of belief, so now we can take "society" to mean an association, generally territorially distinct, of communities; an association that manifests its unity as a corporate unit in opposition to other such units. Outwardly it can be recognized mainly by the material symbols of life style, behavior; but what makes it a society is that this community of behavior rests on a community of belief. The difference between community and society is largely one of both size and complexity. The success of both and the joys of living in either depend not on external conformity of behavior or life style, but on a deep sense of community that overrides material differences and has its source of power in the perceived necessity for interdependence, so that the affective identity becomes an effective identity.

If we define "society" as an association of communities, in this sense, then no more than a community can a society rely on necessity alone to bind its members together, and since the necessity is less visible in terms of personal interaction in the larger unit, it is all the more essential to inculcate the habit of mutual interdependence, the habit of sharing and caring in a manner that is both consistent and effective in daily life. Each stage of the life cycle seems to be devoted to this end in small-scale societies, consciously and overtly; life itself is seen as a constant process of socialization, and binding the various stages of life together, just as it binds individuals into communities and communities into societies, is the integrative force of religious belief and practice.

Why is that not so, or so much so, in Western cultures? We certainly have to recognize that the belief that binds all Americans together is certainly not religious. It is primarily political and secondarily economic; as Americans we are concerned with our territorial integrity and our economy-based life style. Since we have created a secular state, formally separating Church and State, then perhaps rather than compromise our definition of society we have to distinguish large- and small-scale societies as being secular states or religious (or sacred) societies. Given all that we have seen of the enormous power of an integrated system of religious belief and practice, and since the religious society has everything that the secular state has (identity of economic and political aspiration) plus more (spiritual and religious identity of faith, belief and values), I cannot for the life of me see that we can deny that a religious society is structurally a much sounder, stronger, more durable, more effective social unit than a secular state.

The process of socialization that takes place throughout the life cycle now has added significance, a significance that has been implicit throughout by the comparisons we have been making. It is only through such a process, intensively implemented, that the modern nation can in any way regain the vitality of the religious society and deserve to be called such. By denying in our educational system a proper place for the development of a community of belief that must rest on a concept of Spirit if it is to be religious belief, we are denying the possibility of the most powerful form of sociality, and we are denying our national state access to a major source of strength and unity. In taking a final look at the process of socialization, which is the process by which we become whatever we are, an educational process, let us then keep in mind the concept of Spirit. To keep it in mind is all we can attempt to do, for to attempt any definition would be to limit it, and Spirit is without limits. Just as we are what the system makes us to a large extent, so Spirit is what we make it to be. It is a wonderful cycle, because if we *do* make something of Spirit, then that in turn gives us the power to make of ourselves more than we have been made. It is our greatest source of individual freedom within the necessary confines of social behavior. It seems to me entirely possible that given a different educational, socializing system, the role of religion itself might be transformed and become sacred instead of secular, that formal religion instead of being a mere secular adjunct to political power might become an integral part of a much greater power that is both secular and sacred.

At childhood, the time of becoming, what would we lose by insisting that the child be allowed to develop its emotional life fully while its small body gains physical strength and potential? What would we lose if we restored to the home and the family not just the authority but the responsibility for instilling a confidence in human reciprocity, in the simple but effective manner of the Mbuti? None of the techniques, ritual, symbolic, and otherwise, employed by the African and Asian systems we have looked at are denied to us by the material constraints of our different context. There are plenty of working mothers who wish that it were otherwise, that they could spend more time with their children, giving and getting all that the mother/child relationship offers, perhaps only once in any individual's lifetime, certainly only once for all male children. There are plenty of working mothers who wish that the role of motherhood and the responsibility of homemaking were honored and respected as other than the task of reproduction and the chore of housekeeping. What is required there is a change of values; just as we have devalued Spirit, we have devalued the home and the mother and have denied both the possibility of manifesting their full potential. No wonder that women are in revolt. But there are also mothers who like it the way it is, who do *not* want the responsibility of looking after the child or of making the houes into a home, because that is what our system has made of them; we have given them other values, and neither their reason nor their experience suggests that it could or should be otherwise. We have a system that will perpetuate itself unless the basic values are changed, and the place to start that change is in childhood. If we start there, then eventually the cycle will complete itself and we might end up as the Mbuti begin, by finding an ecstasy in the act of creation that will then result in mothers wanting nothing more than to fulfill their whole being, a major part of which they will see as in fulfilling the utterly unique relationship, denied even to fathers, that the mother has with each child. The house will again become a home, and motherhood will become more than a physiological or economic enterprise. What would our children lose?

And at adolescence, what have we to lose by *consciously* aiming at nothing short of transformation? There should be no equivocation here, no playing with words to make it sound less strange, less "out of this world." We have banished it from our world, and either we bring it back or we do not. We have seen transformation at work elsewhere; it works in a wide variety of belief systems. It does not depend upon an individual belief in gods or spirits, in heaven and hell; it depends on whether or not we choose to work toward a society in which people *want* not only to cooperate with each other rather than compete with each other (either of which is an art we begin to learn in childhood), but also want a world in which each individual is a fully integrated whole, using his whole being in all that he does. The mind, body, heart, and soul, or Spirit, should function simultaneously, not sequentially. Unless we bring them together at adolescence, if we allow them to develop as separate entities, then one or more parts of ourselves may all too easily become atrophied. If brought together, however, there is no such possibility, for they feed on each other and revitalize each other. We have seen how adolescence offers us a unique opportunity for effecting this transformation, just as childbirth and motherhood offer to society a unique opportunity for giving the child an experience of trust and mutuality and responsibility that he will *want* to maintain throughout his life. If at adolescence we strengthen and reinforce, or perhaps re-enforce, the social traits already learned in interpersonal relationships, and show the adolescent the value of interrelating his various powers and potentials, what do we lose? If the boy or girl is shown that the pleasurable feelings of sexual expression can be heightened by conjunction with the pleasurable feelings of mutual trust and responsibility, have we done that child, or society, any harm? If those adolescents then find a new joy in the sexual act, a joy that derives from their already developed sense of having a social as well as an individual identity, under what kind of code can that be defined as immoral? Far from weakening the institution of marriage it can only strengthen it. We have seen that the very joy and responsibility felt are themselves, in fact, integral parts of the structure and closely associate cohabitation with marital responsibility. What then do we lose by effecting this kind of transformation from a partial being into an integrated being?

In youth we devote much energy to filling heads with knowledge. There is nothing wrong with that unless we exclude the art of reason. Do we lose anything by systematically teaching youth the art of manifesting that knowledge in social responsibility; by encouraging youth to relate their entire world of experience to the experience they will already have had of themselves as social beings, instead of limiting and confining them to the realm of individual achievement? If we can teach them to think in terms of individual achievement, as we do in the school system through the curricula, by means of games, sports, and other activities that we encourage at this time of life, can we not equally systematically and effectively teach them to think in terms of social achievement and social responsibility? There can be little loss there. It does not negate the value of competitiveness in our national society, it merely places it in context.

With that accomplished, adult doing would of its own become social doing; individual activity, while still fully satisfying the demands we all feel for individual expression and satisfaction, would also become social activity, and we would see it as such, recognizing the social implications of what we are doing even when consciously setting out to achieve individual goals. I fail to see what is lost there.

And in old age, I refuse any longer to take the negative approach and ask what is there to be lost, because in a sense there is nothing to be lost. We have so abused old age that there is nothing there, as far as society is concerned, except an economic burden. There was even a suggestion made in England, not too many years ago, that at a certain age people should be put to death. As I remember, the proposal did not gain much support, perhaps because too many politicians were verging on old age themselves. But it is not unthinkable. We put people to death for a strange variety of reasons, and in considering old age, with its proximity to death, it is necessary to look at that issue. All societies claim to value life, yet increasingly, as they acquire the structure of the modern state, they find it necessary to take life from some while allowing it to others. In our own nation there is the ongoing and seemingly everlasting debate as to whether we should execute murderers, and what allowances should be made for motivation, insanity, and other extenuating circumstances, if any. In Iran, adultery and homosexuality are met with summary execution. In Malaysia, possession of a lethal weapon carries the death penalty, at the moment enforced almost weekly. In Singapore, which someone has aptly described as being like a primary school where you are not allowed to run in the corridors, this past week, as I write, one young boy was sentenced to death for shooting his girl friend's mother in the arm. She bled a bit and cried a lot, but the boy is now awaiting execution. And a while back they executed another youth for running over and killing a pedestrian *while exceeding the speed limit,* the latter consideration evidently being of critical legal importance.

If we are to be consistent in penalizing those who threaten life, then why not execute the old? They are nonproductive, and in a world of diminishing resources they are threatening the life and survival of others. And do we not, in a sense, condemn them to death anyway, by expelling them from the world of the active, productive living the way we do? In our strictly secular system we would lose nothing, there is nothing left to be lost; but what a gain there would be if, by following the other stages of life through with more positive attention to the process of socialization, we created a world in which we needed the old and demanded of them that they continue producing and giving and contributing right to the very last glorious moment of life. Sociality rests on a belief in the continuity of life, which gives us the incentive to be as responsible for the effects our actions will have on tomorrow as for what they achieve today. It is the old who can be the symbol of that continuity and who can, in very practical ways that we have seen, bring that continuity about. Far from being a signal of our own approaching death, old age should be the symbol of the continuation of life. Under a true social system what seems to be the end in other systems becomes a beginning.

Supposing we shift our emphasis—and that may be all that is required if it is done systematically—and through application of these ideas throughout each stage of life concentrate on inculcating the spirit of cooperation rather than that of competition; the spirit of integration and incorporation rather than the mechanics of fragmentation and isolation; and on shifting the driving force from legality to a belief system that made of morality a rewarding experience rather than a penance; then much would be accomplished that so many of us want accomplished. If we can judge by the experience of the small-scale societies, and there is no reason why that experience should not be valid on a larger scale, we would again have a human society instead of a mechanical state. There would be opportunity for a much higher level of individual satisfaction with life; conflict and violence would be reduced because alternative social means that would negate the currently felt need for self-help would be readily accessible; and in any case there would be a greater degree of equality and a greater sense of security in the social system, both inherent in the whole concept of living together rather than in isolation. It all depends on whether we want a society or are content with a state. And whereas we know that social systems endure through time, the modern state system, accompanied by the myth of individual liberty, has not yet had an opportunity for showing any longevity; if anything, it shows the opposite tendency to instability and transience.

Presupposing any change from one emphasis to another, or one way of life to another, is the will to make the change. For this in turn to be effective, it must come from the individual recognition of how much greater would personal fulfillment be in a truly social system. Out of that recognition only can such a change take place, out of the consciousness of social self only can a true society emerge. It cannot be imposed. All that is holding us back is our own ignorance of the potential that is being lost by the present system, and that is why it is so essential, by looking at others, to know ourselves and our full potential better than we do. We are like the piglets who like it that way and have quite forgotten the ecstasy of divinity. Like them, for us the human cycle has become bogged down in the muddy business of survival rather than being a soaring flight of rich fulfillment.

Outstanding Paperback Books from the Touchstone Library